Wiley Global Finance is a market-leading provider of over 400 annual books, mobile applications, elearning products, workflow training tools, newsletters and web-sites for both professionals and consumers in institutional finance, trading, corporate accounting, exam preparation, investing, and performance management.

www.wileyglobalfinance.com

The Aftershock Investor

The Aftershock Investor

A CRASH COURSE IN STAYING AFLOAT IN A SINKING ECONOMY

David Wiedemer, PhD

Robert A. Wiedemer

Cindy S. Spitzer

WILEY

John Wiley & Sons, Inc.

Important Disclaimers: This book reflects the personal opinions, viewpoints, and
analyses of the authors. Nothing in this book constitutes specific investment advice
or any specific recommendation for any specific individual with respect to a particular country, sector, industry, security, or portfolio of securities. All information
is impersonal and not tailored to the circumstances or investment needs of any
specific person.

Limit of Liability/Disclaimer of Warranty: While the publisher and author have
used their best efforts in preparing this book, they make no representations or
warranties with respect to the accuracy or completeness of the contents of this
book and specifically disclaim any implied warranties of merchantability or fitness
for a particular purpose. No warranty may be created or extended by sales repre-
sentatives or written sales materials. The advice and strategies contained herein
may not be suitable for your situation. You should consult with a professional
where appropriate. Neither the publisher nor author shall be liable for any loss of
profit or any other commercial damages, including but not limited to special, inci-
dental, consequential, or other damages.

Cartoons used with permission of Cartoon Stock, www.CartoonStock.com and
Cartoon Bank.

For general information on our other products and services or for technical support, please contact our Customer Care Department within the United States at
(800) 762-2974, outside the United States at (317) 572-3993 or fax (317) 572-4002.

Wiley also publishes its books in a variety of electronic formats. Some content that
appears in print may not be available in electronic books. For more information
about Wiley products, visit our web site at www.wiley.com.

978-1-118-07354-4 (cloth); 978-1-118-22248-5 (ebk); 978-1-118-26109-5 (ebk);
978-1-118-23338-2 (ebk)

Printed in the United States of America
10 9 8 7 6 5 4 3 2 1

Contents

Part III: Your Aftershock Game Plan

Acknowledgments

The authors thank John Silbersack of Trident Media Group and David Pugh, Laura Walsh, and Joan O'Neil from John Wiley & Sons for their relentless support of this book. We would also like to thank Stephen Mack and Jeff Garigliano for their help in writing this book. We thank Jim Fazone, Jay Harrison, and Nancy McSally for their work on the graphics, Michael Lebowitz for his help on the data, and Beth Ganser for her help in proofreading. We also want to acknowledge Christine Peglar's and Jennifer Schoenefeldt's help in keeping us organized.

David Wiedemer

I thank my co-authors, Bob and Cindy, for being indispensable in the writing of this book. Without them this book would not have been published and, even if written, would have been inaccessible for most audiences. I also thank Dr. Rod Stevenson for his long-term support of the foundational work that is the basis for this book. Dr. Jeff Williamson and Dr. Lee Hansen also provided me with important support in my academic career. And I am especially grateful to my wife, Betsy, and son, Benson, for their ongoing support in what has been an often arduous and trying process.

Robert Wiedemer

I, along with my brother, want to dedicate this book to our mother, who died late last year. She inspired us to think creatively and see the joy in learning and teaching. We also dedicate this to our father, the original author in the family. We also want to thank our brother, Jim, for his lifelong support of the ideas behind this book. Chris Ruddy and Aaron De Hoog have been enormous supporters of *Aftershock*. It's been great to have such support. I also want to thank early supporters Stan Goldstein, Tim Selby, Sam Stovall, and

Phil Gross. I also want to thank Dan Cohen and Michael Calkin for their support of this book. I am most grateful to Weldon Rackley, who helped my father to become an author and who did the same for me. A very heartfelt thanks goes to John R. Douglas for his very special role in making our books a reality.

Of course, my gratitude goes to Dave Wiedemer and Cindy Spitzer for being, quite clearly, the best collaborators you could ever have. It was truly a great team effort. Most of all, I thank my wife, Serap, and children, Seline and John, without whose love and support this book, and a really great life, would not be possible.

Cindy Spitzer

Thank you, David and Bob Wiedemer, once again for the honor of collaborating with you on our fourth book. It is always an exciting experience, and I look forward to many more.

For their endless patience and support, my deep appreciation and love go to my husband, Philip Terbush, our children Chelsea, Anya, and Zachary, and my dear friend Cindi Callanan.

I am also filled with a lifetime of gratitude for two wonderful teachers: Christine Gronkowski (SUNY Purchase College) and two-time Pulitzer Prize winner Jon Franklin (UMCP College of Journalism), who each in their own ways moved me along a path exceptional.

My appreciation also goes to Beth Goldstein and Christie Chroniger for their ongoing help with all things great and small.

Introduction

We wrote our first book, *America's Bubble Economy*, back in 2004 and finished it in 2005, long before the housing bubble was visible to many people. We asked our publisher, John Wiley & Sons, to hold the book as long as they could because we were concerned that nobody would buy it. Few people believed there was a housing bubble at that time, much less a whole bubble economy. They wouldn't hold it any longer than fall 2006, and so it was published.

With that book and *Aftershock*, we have built up a good track record of predicting much of what has happened since then, certainly better than most analysts. Almost no economists or analysts wrote an entire book about such issues at the time, although many have written books since. But many of those books are more historical than predictive. It's still scary to predict the future. It's much easier to review the past.

We have been criticized by some as being one-trick ponies—that we made one good prediction and that's it. Certainly, there have been cases of this in the past, such as Elaine Garzarelli, the market analyst who famously predicted the 1987 stock market crash. But we're not trying to predict a crash. What we are trying to do is predict a far larger change in the entire economy. Yes, an earlier real estate crash and stock market crash was part of that, but there is much more to what's going on in the U.S. economy and world economy. Anyone who reads our books will see that.

Some people may say we were right about one prediction, but in fact, it was a range of related predictions, many of which we predicted will not occur for years more. We'll have to wait to see if those come true. But even if we got only one prediction right, that's better than many people who get far more attention for their predictions than we do, such as Ben Bernanke. He predicted, after the Bear Stearns collapse in June 2008 and just four months before the biggest financial crisis in our history, that all was fine with our financial system. Well, it's better to be right once than never. At least it should give us more credibility.

But our forecasts are not meant to cheerlead or paint a rosy picture, and we know that leads many people to giving us less credibility, for obvious reasons. They would rather listen to a more bullish outlook, such as Mr. Bernanke's, especially on the stock market. As one of our good friends on Wall Street said, "Nobody likes a bear, especially when they're right!"

We're not trying to be a bear or a bull, we're just trying to help people better understand the economy. As another friend on Wall Street said, "What you're really doing is teaching people." And that's exactly what we want to do. Some people have said we are arrogant, but we try not to be arrogant. Of course, maybe in the act of teaching something very new that others aren't teaching, there is a certain inherent arrogance.

The best teachers have a passion for what they teach. And when you have a passion, you try to make strong points of great substance that will stick with the people you are teaching. If we have overreached in some of our chapters and appeared arrogant, we apologize. We try to keep the book as nonarrogant and easy to read and enjoyable as possible, while still getting our message across. In fact, we think that is critical to good writing and good teaching.

We don't try to attack anyone personally. If we do make a reference to someone personally, it is to make a larger point about the economy or the way people look at the economy, not to personally put anyone down.

We try to be as fair as possible because we need to be as believable as possible. That is absolutely critical to teaching anything new.

In this book we hope to expand on what we have taught in the past, and we hope more people will benefit. The greatest joy of writing a book is that someone benefits from it—whether that's because they are entertained, or live a more financially secure life, or simply have a better understanding of the way our society works. It's all about feeling that you are somehow better off after reading the book than before. We wrote this latest book, *The Aftershock Investor*, in response to our readers' demands for more details about how to put the ideas in *Aftershock* into action. The old ways of investing based on Conventional Wisdom are becoming increasingly ineffective and even dangerous. For those lucky enough to see what is coming, we need a new investing approach. Rather than passively waiting for things to get better, we need to actively manage our investment portfolios, based on the correct macroeconomic view of the current and future economy. For that, we now offer you *The Aftershock Investor*.

PART I

AFTERSHOCK

CHAPTER 1

Bubblequake and Aftershock—A Quick Review of How We Got Here and What's Next

WHY READ THIS BOOK? BECAUSE WE WERE RIGHT, NOW YOU CAN BE RIGHT, TOO

We are not Ben Bernanke, chairman of the Federal Reserve. We are not economic Nobel Prize winners, like Paul Krugman. We don't run huge investment firms, such as Goldman Sachs or Merrill Lynch. *But they were all wrong, and we were right.* That is why this book is worth reading. We don't have a crystal ball—no one does. But we do have something even more reliable over the long term: the *correct* macroeconomic view of what is occurring and what's coming next. Once you have this correct Big Picture, too, you can be just as right as we have been. With this book, you and your family and associates will likely have a better chance than most to cover your assets, protect yourself, and perhaps even find profits in the coming Aftershock.

The purpose of this book is to move you closer to that with every page.

Please note: If you have not yet read any of our previous books, the rest of this chapter will serve as your quick executive summary. **If you have already read *Aftershock*, Second Edition, you could just skip ahead to Chapter 2**, which offers a brief update since our 2011 book. However, you may want to stay with us here just for the quick review. If nothing else, it will help you hold up your end of the discussion with some people who may still be in the dark about what is really happening.

You Are Not Asleep with the Sheep

Back in 2006, when the U.S. economy was still looking pretty good, our first book, *America's Bubble Economy*, accurately predicted the future popping of the real estate bubble, the fall of the stock market bubble, the decline of the private debt and consumer spending bubbles, and the widespread pain all this was about to inflict on our vulnerable, multibubble economy. Of these bubbles, we said the real estate bubble would be the first to go, kicking off the fall of stocks and the decline of private debt and consumer spending— exactly what occurred in the financial crisis of 2008. We also predicted the eventual bursting of the dollar bubble and the massive government debt bubble, which are both still to come.

Other bearish analysts have also predicted some of our current economic troubles, but very few did so as early as 2006. Even those who did see parts of this mess coming are still failing to connect all of the dots. They don't fully understand what's happened so far, and they can't tell us what will happen next. *America's Bubble Economy* was the only book to *both* warn about the current economic problems here and around the world, and also to go way out on a limb by predicting in substantial detail what would occur, why it would occur, and when. Not too many authors have been willing to go that far out on a limb, mostly because they can't. They don't yet see the whole story, and they don't dare take a chance on making inaccurate predictions that may come back to haunt them later. We went out on a limb and it turned out to be rock solid.

Of course, back in 2006, our prescient predictions were largely ignored.

Then our next two books, *Aftershock* (2009) and *Aftershock, Second Edition* (2011), further fine-tuned our forecasts, explaining in more detail how massive stimulus spending by the federal government and massive money printing by the Federal Reserve would temporarily boost the falling multibubble economy, particularly the stock market, but would only kick the can down the road and later make our bubble economy crash even harder.

This time, with the memory of the 2008 financial crisis still painfully fresh, more people began to take notice. In 2009, *Aftershock* was named one of *SmartMoney*'s Best Books. And in 2011, within weeks of publication in August, *Aftershock*, Second Edition, became a *New York Times* business bestseller, a *Wall Street Journal* business bestseller, and the number one Amazon personal finance book and number one Amazon economics book. Since then, the book has been translated into Japanese, Chinese, Polish, and Korean, and recently became a Korean bestseller. The book was made even more accessible in the form of an audio book, beautifully read by Christopher Kipiniak, which was nominated for an Audie Award. By the end of 2011, *Aftershock*, Second Edition, was named by *The Economist* magazine as Amazon's third bestselling personal finance book, not just in the United States but in the world.

What a difference a crash makes! Some people are clearly starting to wake up.

But despite all the kudos and recognition our books have gotten, our basic macroeconomic message is still falling mostly on deaf ears— or, more accurately, on *denying minds*. Most people simply do not want to wake up and fully face the truth of what is really happening. Even the bear-oriented analysts are missing the bigger picture. This is not merely a bearish "down cycle" that will eventually be followed by a bullish "up cycle." *This economy is evolving.* We are not going back to how it was before. We are going forward to something new.

For a fuller explanation of our macroeconomic views, we encourage you to take a look at *Aftershock*, Second Edition. For your convenience, we are also summarizing the key ideas of that book in this first chapter, before we tell you how you can potentially protect and grow assets in this dangerous and evolving economy.

But before we get to that, we would like to take a moment to congratulate you—the person who is reading these words right now—not just for opening this book, but more importantly for *opening your mind*, if not to our entire macroeconomic point of view, at least to the *possibility* that something is not quite right with this so-called "recovery." Perhaps we are headed not back to the prosperity of the past but forward, toward something entirely new, highly dangerous, and potentially profitable. You are part of an elite, early group of people with their eyes open and their lights on. You may not know everything about what is occurring or exactly what to do about it, but you, dear reader, are not asleep with the sheep!

"Tell me the fairytale about the economy."

Bubblequake! First a Rising Bubble Economy, Now a Falling Bubble Economy

The first thing you need to know about our current and future economic problems is that they didn't start yesterday. It all started decades ago with a combination of declining productivity growth beginning in the 1970s, coupled with a growing propensity to run big government deficits beginning in the 1980s.

Please understand that, in and of itself, running big deficits is not necessarily a bad thing. In fact, there are times when borrowing big money is really quite smart. For example, you might borrow a large sum of money to start a profitable business or to go to medical school, which among other benefits can increase your real wealth in the future. But this big government borrowing was not the equivalent of starting a profitable business or going to medical school, and it did not lead to increasing the nation's *real* wealth in the future. Instead, we just borrowed money to buy things we wanted without having to raise taxes—the equivalent of being able to go shopping with a credit card without having to get a better-paying job.

Now, to be fair, the $1 trillion federal debt in 1982 really wasn't that much compared to today's nearly $16 trillion federal debt, but the relatively small annual federal budget deficits in the 1980s were significant because they were the early beginnings of the big federal borrowing and big deficit spending that would come later.

Of course, at the time, no one was too worried about the beginnings of big federal borrowing and deficit spending in the 1980s. In fact, the U.S. economy grew nicely over the next couple of decades, with a 260 percent increase in U.S. gross domestic product (GDP) from 1980 to 2000. And asset values, such as stocks, bonds, and real estate grew even faster.

However, there was a hidden driver behind much of this rapidly rising abundance: *bubbles!*

What Is a Bubble?

This should be a relatively easy question to answer, but, believe it or not, there is no academically accepted definition of a financial or economic bubble. For our purposes, we define a bubble as an asset value that temporarily rises and eventually falls, primarily due to changing investor psychology rather than due to underlying, fundamental economic drivers that are sustainable over time.

Before it is a bubble, an asset value may first begin to rise because of real fundamental economic drivers, such as when population growth pushes up the demand for housing and therefore the price. But at some point, the impact of the underlying fundamental driver has a diminishing effect and hopeful investor psychology takes over, pushing the asset value temporarily higher, creating a bubble.

In the course of history, asset bubbles have varied greatly in their causes, duration, height, and crash impact, but one thing has remained absolutely constant about all bubbles of every type and size: *they all eventually pop.* By definition, if it is a bubble, what goes up must come down. That is the economic reality that no bubble can escape. *Gravity happens.* It's only a matter of time.

Because bubbles go up primarily due to investor psychology rather than due to fundamental economic drivers, all it takes for a bubble to fall is a significant enough change in investor psychology. What makes investor psychology change significantly? Investor psychology changes when enough people figure out that they have bought into a bubble, leading to a sell-off and a bubble pop. If it weren't really a bubble, the deep sell-off wouldn't last. Nonbubble asset values can certainly drop, but the underlying fundamental economic drivers would still be in place and eventually investors would soon return to buy back the asset, stopping its fall. Only bubbles pop; nonbubbles may fall but eventually recover.

Is it possible to stop a bubble from falling or to reinflate it once it falls? The short answer is no. You cannot indefinitely prevent a popping bubble from popping, nor can you push it back up and keep it up once it fully pops.

However, the longer, more nuanced answer is yes and no. While we can't permanently prevent a bubble from popping, we can *delay* it from falling and even push it back up a bit with a lot of resources and artificial stimulus. As we will see later in this chapter, that is only temporary and often leads to a much bigger bubble crash down the road.

Why doesn't artificial stimulus work to *permanently* reinflate a bubble? Because, generally speaking, you cannot fool the same people twice, and even when you can fool the same people twice, you cannot fool them for as long. For example, if you were among the investors who lost money when the Internet bubble popped, how willing have you been since then to buy stock in technology companies that show no profits? Investors do generally learn and move on.

However, with massive amounts of artificial stimulus (like massive money printing by the Federal Reserve), it is possible for a falling bubble to defy gravity and temporarily rise again. But because of the enormous costs, massive stimulus cannot continue forever. Eventually, the stimulus has to stop and gravity wins. So, for various reasons, including artificial stimulus, a popping bubble may not go down in a straight line. Instead, it may pause in its descent or even lift up for a while, but in the end *down* is its destiny.

How to Spot a Bubble

How can we know if an asset value is rising primarily due to positive investor psychology (speculation leading to a bubble), rather than due to underlying, fundamental economic drivers that are sustainable over time (real growth)?

While it is not always easy, it is possible to analyze and identify a not-yet-popped bubble if you are willing to stay rational and objective, and not get caught up in wishful thinking. It is human nature to want to believe in a rising bubble, especially when it is a bubble that you profit from or depend on. The only way to see a bubble that has not yet fully popped is to make a firm commitment to clear-eyed logic. *You cannot stay asleep with the sheep.*

As we pointed out in our earlier books, there are two important truths about bubbles.

Bubbles Are a Lot Easier to See *After* They Pop
and
The Hardest Bubble to See Is the One You're In

Throughout the ages, asset bubbles have always been largely invisible right up until the end. For example, no one could see the Dutch tulip bubble before it popped in 1637. Virtually no one saw through the appealing South Seas stock bubble until it burst in 1720. Investors were not the least bit worried about the great Florida land boom in the 1920s until the property values crashed back to earth, just as few people concerned themselves about the intoxicating stock market boom of the 1920s until it evaporated into the crash of 1929 and the Great Depression. And more recently, precious few investors and analysts recognized the irrational exuberance of the Internet stock bubble in time to get out before it popped in 2000.

Looking back, these examples of past bubble booms and busts seem so obvious now, don't they? Of course, it makes no logical sense to overpay for tulips, buy swamp land in Florida, or invest in dot-com companies with no profits, but at the time, all these seemed perfectly plausible, even desirable to investors. Regardless of the time, place, or type of asset in question, all bubbles share this common feature: positive investor psychology pushes the bubble up, and negative investor psychology pushes the bubble down.

Here is the typical bubble-up, then bubble-down pattern:

- An asset value begins to rise due to some underlying, real economic drivers that begin to boost demand and therefore the price.
- As the asset value begins to rise, investor psychology begins to rise as well, leading to some investor speculation about the future value of the asset.

- Investors become even more interested in owning the rising asset, pushing up the price.
- More and more investors take notice and want to buy in before the asset price rises even further.
- As the bubble approaches its peak, some investors become anxious about future growth and sustainability, which leads some investors to increase their profit taking (selling the asset).
- Other investors take notice and become anxious or at least do not feel as positive about owning the asset, also deciding to sell.
- The asset price no longer rises and begins to decline.
- Positive investor psychology is increasingly replaced with neutral or negative investor psychology, sparking a larger sell-off.
- A critical level of negative investor psychology is reached, a mass exit begins, and the bubble pops.
- Most people cannot exit quickly enough and much of their assets go to Money Heaven.

After the fact, it all seems so terribly obvious, doesn't it? However, this pattern is anything but easy to recognize *before* a bubble pops. Not-yet-popped bubbles are amazingly difficult to see. Why? Because we don't want to see them! We want the big run-up in prices to be real and sustainable, not a bubble. It takes a firm commitment to logic to see a bubble before it pops.

Now let's take a clear-eyed look at our current bubbles, the ones that have been working together to help push up the U.S. economy over many years, and more recently have started to deflate and lean heavily on each other, helping to push down the falling U.S. economy as they pop.

America's Bubble Economy

The U.S. economy has been such a strong and prosperous powerhouse for so long, it's difficult to imagine anything else. Our goal is not to convince you of anything you wouldn't conclude for yourself, if you had the right facts. Most people don't get the right facts because most financial analysis today is based on preconceived ideas about a hoped-for positive outcome. People want analysis that says the economy will improve in the future, not get worse. So they look for ways to create that analysis, drawing on outdated and incorrect ideas, such as repeating "market cycles," to support their case. Such is human nature. We all naturally prefer a future that is better than the past, and luckily for many Americans, that is what we have enjoyed for many years.

Up until a few decades ago, we grew our rising economic prosperity the old-fashioned way: by increasing real productivity. We laid railroad track from coast to coast that led to an explosion of trade. We invented cars and airplanes that changed how we lived and did business, and that impacted economies around the world. It wasn't all perfect, but rising productivity growth worked like Miracle-Gro on the rising U.S. economy.

Then something changed. Instead of rising productivity growth, real productivity growth began to slow down in the 1970s. In addition to declining productivity growth (and perhaps in some ways because of it), we also began to borrow massive amounts of money. Please do not waste precious time assigning political blame. Over the years, presidents and congressional leaders from both parties participated in this orgy of borrowing and deficit spending. Love or hate what we spent the money on, the fact is we have been borrowing and spending a whole lot of OPM (other people's money) since the early 1980s.

And please don't just blame the politicians. All this public borrowing and spending by governments was accompanied by plenty of private borrowing and spending by businesses and consumers. Plus, there were plenty of investments in what would eventually become asset bubbles, all combining to give us what we call America's Bubble Economy (spurring us to publish a book by that name in 2006).

To quickly review, we identified six colinked, economy-boosting bubbles that together helped boost the rising multibubble economy in the 1980s and 1990s. Since 2006 (with the popping of the real estate bubble), these bubbles have been deflating and falling, each putting increasing downward pressure on the others. These are . . .

The Real Estate Bubble

Now that it is partially popped, the real estate bubble is easy to see. As shown in Figure 1.1, from 2000 to 2006, home prices grew almost 100 percent.

If nothing else, looking at Figure 1.2 on inflation-adjusted housing prices since 1890, created by Yale economist Robert Shiller,

Income Up 2%   Housing Prices Up 80%

Figure 1.1   Income Growth versus Housing Price Growth 2001–2006

Contrary to what some experts say, the earlier rapid growth of housing prices was not driven by rising wage and salary income. In fact, from 2001 to 2006, housing price growth far exceeded income growth.

Source: Bureau of Labor Statistics and the S&P/Case-Shiller Home Price Index.

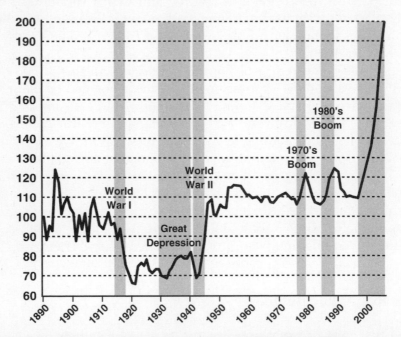

Figure 1.2   Price of Homes Adjusted for Inflation Since 1890

Contrary to popular belief, housing prices do not ordinarily rise rapidly. In fact, until recently, inflation-adjusted home prices haven't increased that significantly, but then they just exploded after 2001 (1890 index equals 100).

Source: Irrational Exuberance, Second Edition, 2006, by Robert J. Shiller.

should make anyone suspicious that there was a very big real estate bubble in the making. Note that home prices barely rose on an inflation-adjusted basis until the 1980s and then just exploded in 2001.

According to the Case-Shiller Home Price Index, while the inflation-adjusted wages and salaries of the people buying the homes went up only 2 percent for the same period (according to the Bureau of Labor Statistics), home prices shot up. The rise in home prices so profoundly outpaced the rise of incomes that even our most conservative analysis back in 2005 led us to correctly predict that the vulnerable real estate bubble would be the first to fall. (We have a lot more to say about what's ahead for the housing market in Chapter 6, and it's not what the economic cheerleaders want you to think.)

The Stock Market Bubble

The stock market bubble is one of the easiest, most obvious bubbles to spot, yet so very difficult for most people to see. Stocks can be analyzed in so many different ways. We find the state of the stock market is easier to grasp by looking at Figure 1.3. If this doesn't

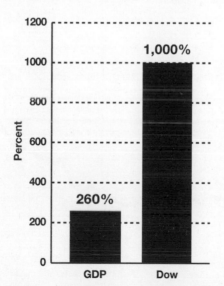

Figure 1.3   GDP up 260 Percent, Dow up More than 1,100 Percent, 1980–2000

The stock market rose almost four times as much as the economy grew from 1980 to 2000. That's a good indicator of a bubble.

Source: Dow Jones and Federal Reserve.

convince you that there was a stock bubble, we don't know what will. From 1980 to 2000, GDP rose a very decent 260 percent. However, the U.S. stock market, as measured by the Dow Jones Industrial Average, leaped up an astounding 1,100 percent!

We call that a stock market bubble! It looks even more out of line when you consider that the population of the United States grew only 25 percent from 1980 to 2000. Given that population growth is one driver of GDP growth, and given that GDP growth is the fundamental driver of corporate earnings growth and therefore stock prices, we would more or less expect to see the Dow rise about as much as GDP, which was about 260 percent. A 1,100 percent rise in the Dow is a giant flag, spelling out the word *B-U-B-B-L-E*.

Shown in a different way in Figure 1.4, the value of financial assets as a percentage of GDP held relatively steady at around 450 percent from 1960 to 1980. But starting in 1981, financial assets as a percentage of GDP rose to *more than 1,000 percent* by 2007, according to the Federal Reserve. We call that prima facie evidence of both a stock market bubble and a real estate bubble.

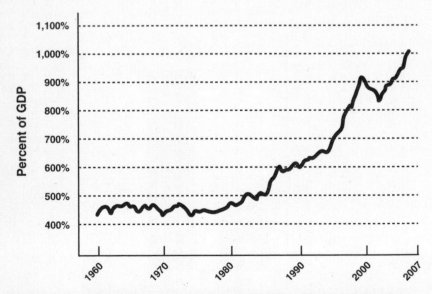

Figure 1.4   Rise of the Financial Assets Bubble: Financial Assets as a Percentage of GDP

The exploding value of financial assets as a percentage of GDP is strong evidence of a financial asset bubble.

Sources: Thomson Datastream and the Federal Reserve.

The Private Debt Bubble

We can simplify the complex private debt bubble by seeing it as essentially a derivative bubble, driven by two other bubbles: (1) the rapidly rising home price bubble; and (2) the rapidly rising stock market bubble, which combined to make for a rapidly growing economy. In both cases, lenders of all forms (not just banks) began to feel very comfortable with the false belief that the risk of a falling economy had been essentially eliminated, and the risk of any type of lending in that environment was minimal. This fantasy was supported for a time by the fact that very few loans went into default. Certainly, at the time we wrote our first book (one year before its publication in 2006) commercial and consumer loan default rates were at historic lows.

The problem was not so much the amount of private debt that made it a bubble, but taking on so much risky debt under the false assumption that nothing would go wrong with the economy. For us, it was easy to see even in 2006 that if the value of housing or stocks were to fall dramatically (as bubbles always eventually do), a tremendous number of loan defaults would occur. We felt the private debt bubble was an obvious derivative bubble that was bound to pop when the real estate and stock market bubbles popped.

The Consumer Discretionary Spending Bubble

Consumer spending accounts for about 70 percent of the U.S. economy. A large portion of consumer spending is discretionary spending, meaning it's optional (how big a portion depends on exactly how you define *discretionary*). Easy bubble-generated money and easy consumer credit made lots of easy discretionary spending possible at every income level. When the real estate stock market, and private debt bubbles began to pop and people started losing their jobs or were increasingly concerned they might, consumers began to reduce their spending, especially unnecessary, discretionary spending.

This is typical in any recession, but this time the effect has been much more profound for two key reasons. First, the private debt bubble allowed consumers to spend like crazy because of huge growth in housing prices and a growing stock market and economy, which gave them more access to credit than ever before, via credit cards and home equity loans. As the bubbles popped, that credit started drying up, and so did the huge consumer spending that was driven by it.

Second, much of our spending on necessities has a high discretionary component, which is relatively easy for us to cut back. We need food, but we don't need Whole Foods. We need to eat, but we don't need to eat at Bennigan's or Steak & Ale (both now bankrupt). We need refrigerators and countertops, but we don't need stainless steel refrigerators and granite countertops. The list of necessities that can have a high discretionary component, complete with elevated prices, goes on and on. And, of course, there is a lot of other discretionary spending, beyond necessities, such as entertainment and vacation travel.

The combined fall of these first four bubbles—housing, stock market, private debt, and consumer spending bubbles—make up what we call the Bubblequake of late 2008 and 2009. Unfortunately, our troubles don't end there. Two more giant bubbles are about to burst in the coming Aftershock.

The Dollar Bubble

Perhaps the hardest reality of all to face, the once mighty greenback has become an unsustainable currency bubble. Due to a rising bubble economy, investors from all over the world were getting huge returns on their dollar-denominated assets. This made the dollar more valuable but also more vulnerable. Why? Because we didn't really have a true booming economy based on real underlying, fundamental economic drivers. We had a rising multibubble economy. Therefore, the value of a currency in a multibubble economy is linked not to real, underlying, fundamental drivers of economic growth (like true productivity gains), but to the rising and falling bubbles. For many years our dollars rose in value because of rising demand for dollars to make investments in our bubbles. More recently, demand for U.S. dollars has remained pretty strong, especially in light of the current European debt crisis. But that strength will wane as the falling bubbles lead to falling demand for dollars, despite all kinds of government efforts to stop it.

The Dollar Bubble and Future Inflation

Making matters worse for the dollar bubble, in our effort to stop the fall of our multibubble economy, the Federal Reserve has been

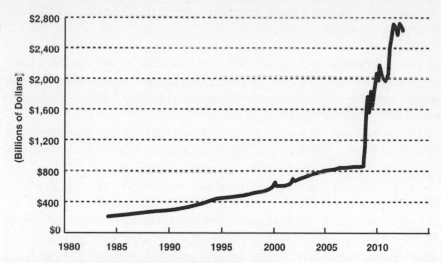

Figure 1.5   Growth of the U.S. Monetary Base

Money printing basically kept pace with economic growth until financial crisis, when it exploded in 2009.

Source: Federal Reserve.

printing massive amounts of new money through their program of quantitative easing (QE). Two rounds of massive money printing (QE1 and QE2) have increased the U.S. money supply from $800 billion in March 2009 to more than $2.4 trillion by July 2011 (see Figure 1.5). This massive amount of money printing will eventually cause significant rising inflation.

Future Inflation Will Cause Rising Interest Rates

In and of itself, rising inflation would not be so bad if the only consequence were rising prices and wages. But rising inflation also eventually causes *rising interest rates* (see *Aftershock*, Second Edition, for more details), and rising interest rates will have a very negative impact on the rest of the bubbles and the economy.

Rising interest rates will certainly be a big downer for the bond market (bond values drop as interest rates rise), as well as the real estate market (housing is not improving much now, even with mortgage rates at record lows).

Higher interest rates also mean consumers will buy less on credit, if they even qualify for credit cards and loans, further depressing consumer spending, on which 70 percent of the U.S. economy depends.

And, of course, rising interest rates will also mean that businesses will borrow less money, buy less inventory, hire fewer workers, and generally expand less. That will negatively impact employment, which will negatively impact consumer spending, reduce company earnings, and lower stock values.

Even without the already falling bubbles, rising interest rates would not be good for a nonbubble economy recovering from a recession. For a falling bubble economy, rising interest rates will be the beginning of the final multibubble pop. While that is still off in the future, when it finally occurs, it will not take long for U.S. stocks, bonds, real estate, and other dollar-denominated assets to drop. Many investors, including many foreign investors who now own an enormous amount of U.S. assets (see Figure 1.6) will not want to hold on to these declining investments. Foreign investors don't have to all run away at once to cause a big downward drop in dollar-denominated assets. Even a significant decline would do the trick. And, of course, domestic investors will not want to stick around either.

With inflation and interest rates rising, and even more money printing likely in the future as the Fed tries to support the falling

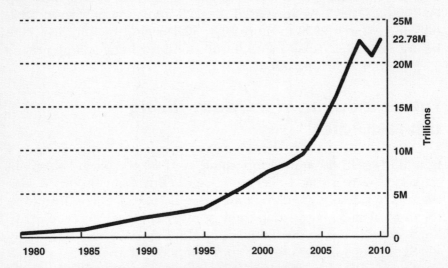

Figure 1.6   Growth of the Foreign-Held U.S. Assets

Part of what fueled our bubble economy in the 1980s and 1990s was massive inflows of capital from foreign investors, which grew from less than a trillion dollars in 1980 to $22.78 trillion in 2010. We remain highly vulnerable to their continued support.

Source: Bureau of Economic Analysis.

bubbles with more quantitative easing, it is only a matter of time before the big dollar bubble pops.

The Government Debt Bubble

Weighing in at more than $8.5 trillion when our 2006 book was published and now (2012) nearing $16 trillion, the whopping U.S. government debt bubble, as shown in Figure 1.7, is currently the biggest, baddest bubble of all. Much of this debt has been funded by foreign investors, primarily from Asia and Europe. But as our multibubble economy continues to fall and the dollar starts to sink, who in the world will be willing—or even able—to lend us more?

From Boom to Bust: The Virtuous Upward Spiral Becomes a Vicious Downward Spiral

On the way up, the six conjoined bubbles described above helped co-create America's booming multibubble economy. In a seemingly virtuous upward spiral, the inflating bubbles helped the United

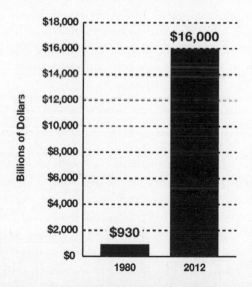

Figure 1.7   Growth of the U.S. Government's Debt

The U.S. government's debt is massive and growing rapidly. With no plan and little ability to pay it off, the debt is quickly becoming the world's largest toxic asset.

Source: Federal Reserve.

States maintain its status as the biggest economy the world has ever known, even in the past few decades, when declines in real productivity growth could have slowed our expanding economic growth. Instead, these bubbles helped us ignore slowing productivity growth, boost our prosperity, disregard some fundamental problems, and keep the party going.

Not only did the U.S. economy continue to grow and remain strong, but the rest of the world benefited as well. Money we paid for rapidly increasing imports boosted the economies of developing countries like China and India. First World economies benefited from America's Bubble Economy, as well. Because of our rising bubbles, developed economies, such as Japan and Europe, were able to sell us lots of their cars and other high-end exports, which helped their home economies prosper. The growing world economy created a rising demand for energy, pushing up oil prices, which made some Russian billionaires, among others, very happy. Growing demand for minerals, like iron, oil, and copper, pumped money into every resource-producing country. For example, China's and India's expanding appetite for steel boosted iron ore exports from Australia, lifting their economy. All combined, America's rising bubble economy helped boom the world's rising bubble economy.

Now, as our intermingled global party bubbles are beginning to deflate and fall, the virtuous upward spiral has become a vicious downward spiral. Linked together and pushing hard against each other, each time a bubble begins to sag and pop, it puts tremendous downward pressure on the rest.

First the Bubblequake, Next the Aftershock

As we said earlier, the first four of the six bubbles—real estate stock, private debt, and discretionary spending—have begun to pop, creating the beginning of what we call the Bubblequake. In response, the federal government and the Federal Reserve have been pumping up the remaining two bubbles—the dollar and government debt bubbles—with massive money printing and massive deficit spending since early 2009 in a dramatic attempt to stop the falling bubbles and to boost the overall economy. This massive stimulus spending and especially the massive money printing have been helping *in the short term* to temporarily boost the stock market and keep the overall bubble economy from sagging further.

But this massive stimulus cannot continue forever, and in the longer term, the bubbles will continue to fall. Not only will the massive stimulus eventually have to end, it will actually make our bubbles crash even harder when they finally do pop. Continued use of massive stimulus is like using a powerful short-term drug that will later become a toxic poison. The stimulus itself will later make the future crash all the worse.

It is important to understand that the Bubblequake problems we are now facing are due to much more than merely a popped real estate bubble. If all we had was a burst real estate bubble, it would not have created so much financial pain here and around the globe. In addition to the real estate bubble, the private debt bubble and the stock market bubble also began to fall. These Bubblequake problems are not going to be permanently resolved anytime soon, not even with the temporary boost from massive stimulus spending and massive money printing. Rather than a real economic recovery, the combination of sagging bubbles and the future poisonous consequences of the massive stimulus will put increasing downward pressure on our entire bubble-based economy.

Once our last two bubbles—the dollar and government debt bubbles—finally burst, we will enter the next phase, what we have dubbed the Aftershock, in which all our asset bubbles will burst and the U.S. economy will fall dramatically.

It's Not Just America's Bubble Economy—The World Has a Bubble Economy, Too

When America's bubble economy fully pops, so will the world's bubble economy. Why? Because all these bubbles are *linked together*. On their way up, each supported and fueled the others; and on the way down, each falling bubble will put increasingly downward pressure on the rest.

For example, the real estate boom in the United States created a consumer spending orgy here that helped fuel China's rapid economic growth and boomed China's own real estate bubble. To keep up with growing demand for their exports, China in turn has been buying more natural resources from other regions, such as South America. But when our real estate bubble began to pop and U.S. consumer spending dropped a bit, China's growth also began to cool down over the past few years, although it is still growing, just at a slower rate. In the coming Aftershock, when U.S. consumers will buy much less than they do today, China's bubble economy will take a deep hit, which will then spill over to South America, Australia, and other places that currently supply China's commodities demand.

Meanwhile, back in the United States, stocks, bonds, real estate, consumer spending, and government spending will be down, inflation and interest rates will be up, and the bubble economy will be over. In the coming Aftershock, the global multibubble crash will kick off a deep, long-term downturn here and around the globe.

Please understand that we are not intrinsically pessimistic or doom-and-gloomy by nature. We are not driven by any particular political agenda, left, right, or sideways. We are not fanatical gold bugs (although we think gold will do quite well). And we are not paranoid survivalists who think you should run out and build a fallout shelter filled with two years' worth of food. We are just calling it as we see it, based on facts and rational analysis, and we would like to help you see it, too, while there's still time to protect your assets and prepare.

All Dogs Go to Heaven, and So Will a Whole Lot of Money!

People often ask where the massive amount of investment capital in stocks, bonds, and real estate will go in the future. The answer is Money Heaven. Most investment money will go to Money Heaven in the future because most people won't pull their money out of falling stocks, real estate, and bonds soon enough. Anyone who doesn't move money out early won't be able to move it out at all. That's because other people will have moved their money out of those investments earlier, most importantly, and there will be little demand for those investments afterwards. Hence, the values of most people's investments will decline dramatically.

At that point most people will realize they should have moved their money out, but it will be too late. Their portfolios will have been automatically rebalanced for them, heavily weighted toward Money Heaven. For the money managers and financial advisers who will preside over this reweighting of investors' portfolios into Money Heaven, it's going to feel a lot less like Money Heaven and a lot more like Money Hell.

Why Don't We Have the Aftershock Right Now? Temporary "Airbags" Are Supporting the Partially Popped Bubbles

Question: We have four falling bubbles but they are not yet fully popped. What is keeping these bubbles partially inflated?

Answer: The pumping up of the final two bubbles!

The easiest way to understand the economy right now is to look at it as a set of deflating bubbles (stock, real estate private credit, and consumer spending) whose fall is being cushioned by the rapid inflation of the two final bubbles: the dollar bubble and the government debt bubble. By rapidly pumping up these two bubbles, the government is temporarily postponing the fall of America's multibubble economy. Because they are cushioning and supporting the other bursting bubbles, we like to think of these last two yet-to-pop bubbles as America's airbags—they are preventing a dangerous crash for a while, but eventually they, too, will fall. When these final airbags overinflate and burst, the rest of our bubble economy will burst, bringing on the global Aftershock. But, these airbags aren't going to pop immediately and that's why we don't have the Aftershock right now.

Airbag #1: Massive Government Borrowing

Massive government borrowing (the government debt bubble) is boosting the economy. In fact, most of the growth in the economy since the financial crisis has been directly related to the massive 500 percent increase in federal government borrowing since 2007. And let's not forget that the U.S. deficit wasn't exactly tiny in 2007, when it was already weighing in at $170 billion. Now our deficit is nearing *$1.2 trillion.* That is a big fat government debt bubble becoming a truly colossal government debt bubble.

Naturally, with the country awash in so much deficit spending, the not-yet-popped government debt bubble is acting like a still-inflated, protective airbag, keeping the other bubbles from fully falling. Surely, had we not borrowed and spent all that extra money, the U.S. economy would be in far worse shape today. The problem is, airbags eventually pop, too. By pumping up this protective airbag so gigantically, it will only make the future crash all the bigger.

Airbag #2: Massive Money Printing

Massive money printing (the dollar bubble) by the Federal Reserve, mostly in the form of quantitative easing or QE, has also been acting as an airbag, keeping the U.S. and world economies protected from the popping bubbles. Massive money printing has worked like Viagra to reinvigorate the stock market bubble whenever it shows signs of deflating. This temporary lift to the stock market also indirectly boosts the rest of the consumer-based economy. Stock investors spend more when their portfolios are up, and studies show that even people who own no stocks spend more when the stock market is doing well. So massive money printing has been doing its temporary airbag job, first with QE1 and QE2 (2009–2011), and next with more money printing ahead.

But the Airbags Only Postpone the Inevitable

The trouble with pumping up America's airbags (the dollar bubble and government debt bubble) is that it is just a short-term fix. And worse than being just a short-term fix, it is a short-term fix that comes at an incredibly high long-term price. We're not just kicking the can down the road—we're just piling up sticks of dynamite in the can that will cause an even more massive explosion when we can kick the can down the road no further.

Rising Future Inflation Is Key

When the airbags fail, all the bubbles will pop. What will cause the airbags to fail? *Rising future inflation.* In a terribly ironic twist, the very things we are doing to support the economy (by printing money and borrowing money) will lead to what eventually pops these airbags and causes the rest of the bubbles to fall even harder. (For more details, please see *Aftershock*, Second Edition.)

Right now, we can keep on borrowing (pumping up airbag #1, the government debt bubble) as long as we can keep on printing money (pumping up airbag #2, the dollar bubble). Massive money printing keeps interest rates low so we can keep borrowing. We will keep printing money to fund our borrowing for as long as we can print money *without creating inflation.* As long as inflation remains low, as it is today, America's airbags can continue to keep America's Bubble Economy from fully popping. Rising future inflation (and the rising interest rates it will cause) can be avoided for a while longer, but rising inflation cannot be avoided forever. We simply cannot increase the money supply threefold, with even more money printing to come, and not eventually get some very significant inflation.

Rising inflation will force interest rates higher, whether the Fed likes it or not. The Fed can't control interest rates once we have significant inflation. Printing money can solve many of our ills short term, but one ill it can never solve is inflation. That inflation will push up interest rates, and rising interest rates will devastate the stock, bond, and real estate markets, and all the bubbles will fall.

Inflation is key. When rising inflation and rising interest rates force the airbags to fail (i.e., when we can do no more money printing and borrowing), all the bubbles will fall. Until then, the airbags will hold off the coming Aftershock right up until they no longer work.

Why Don't Most Conventional Investors See This Coming?

The reasons for the current widespread bubble blindness by conventional investors are many. They include:

- A deep faith in "the myth of the natural growth rate" that is supposed to guarantee us continued economic growth no matter what. (The myth of the natural growth rate is described in detail in Chapter 3.)
- Denial: Human psychology makes it difficult to think rationally in the face of things we don't want to be true. (Investor psychology is also addressed in Chapter 3.)
- What we call "The Hamptons Effect": Conventional investors and analysts desperately need the current status quo (from which they greatly benefit) to continue; otherwise, they will lose everything: their jobs, wealth, homes (in the Hamptons, for example, for wealthy New York investors), social status, and so on. These people will fight to the end to keep what they have, even if that means complete bubble blindness. If you are counting on blind people to guide you, we suggest you keep your expectations low.

What's a Savvy Aftershock Investor to Do?

The deadly combination of declining productivity and the multi-bubble economy is giving us massive debt, massive money printing, future rising inflation and interest rates, falling assets bubbles, and an increasingly dangerous investment environment. Conventional wisdom on investing, such as the buy-and-hold value investing practiced by Warren Buffett, for example, will not hold up well under these worsening conditions. Instead of conventional wisdom, we need a new kind of Aftershock wisdom (see Chapter 3) for a new way of investing (see Chapters 4 to 11) that will guide you to and through the coming Aftershock. Ignore this new Aftershock wisdom at your peril.

The key to Aftershock wisdom for successful investing is to ignore the economic cheerleaders and stay focused on what really matters: *inflation*. Rising future inflation and future rising interest rates pose the biggest threat to the future health of your portfolio. Not too many people are worried about inflation and interest rates right now because both are remarkably low and pose no immediate threat. But rising inflation and rising interest rates will strike the final blow to the vulnerable dollar and government debt bubbles, and will send your hard-earned assets to Money Heaven faster than you can log onto your online brokerage account and hit "Sell!"

The rest of this book is entirely focused on helping you protect your wealth, whether it is $200 or $200 million. But there is only so much we can tell you in a book. This is an evolving economy and investment environment, and therefore the actions you take must also evolve over time. Beyond our books, you can keep up with us through our newsletters, or invest with us, and you will see each step we take as the Aftershock approaches. With or without our help, please understand that you must keep up with changing economic conditions in order to correctly manage and protect your assets in this increasingly dangerous investment environment.

Since We Last Spoke . . .

AFTERSHOCK UPDATE: THEY READ OUR PLAYBOOK, THE WORLD IS PRINTING MONEY

Since the most recent update of our outlook on the economy with the release of *Aftershock*, Second Edition, in August 2011, much has happened. The most striking change is that the stock market has recovered somewhat, up about 10 percent since its low in October 2011 as of this writing in mid-June 2012. In fact, because of that recovery a lot of people have been asking us, "Do you still think there will be an aftershock?" As if all we needed to wipe out the fundamental problems with the bubble economy was a 1,000-point increase in the Dow.

We understand how tempting wishful thinking can be. People naturally hope that the bad dream is over and all is on the upswing. And it is good that people are optimistic. But that outlook simply is not realistic in the longer term. Even in the shorter term, there are big questions looming. Could this be like 2011, which started very optimistically with hopes of "green shoots" (new growth) in the spring, only for those green shoots to wither and turn brown in the summer of 2011, if they really even existed in the first place. Plus, the stock market had external shocks from Europe, Libya, and the Japanese tsunami.

The same could happen in 2012: dreams of green shoots at the start and a browning out as the year goes on, although it is unlikely there will be an exact repeat of the year before. There are certainly many potential external shocks that could further negatively impact the U.S. economy, such as from Iran or Europe or China, which we discuss in more detail later in this chapter. In addition, that economic "recovery" that everyone was hoping for, and even some declared that we already were in, simply has not materialized to much of an extent, if there is one at all.

In fact, the Economic Cycle Research Institute (ECRI), the most accurate forecaster of recessions (having correctly forecasted every recession since they were founded in 1996), still holds strongly to the prediction it made in September 2011 that the United States is heading into a recession. The CEO of ECRI, Lakshman Achuthan, further says that he has enough data since September to say it is no longer just a prediction but almost a certainty, based on the various leading economic indicators he uses. He thinks that such a recession could happen late this summer, although job growth could continue past that point because job growth tends to lag economic growth. Employment is considered a lagging indicator because employers don't tend to hire until growth in demand has been more proven and they don't fire until declining demand has been more proven.

Most important, the fundamental issues we discussed in both *America's Bubble Economy* and *Aftershock* have not changed—far from it. They have only been further confirmed by recent events. In fact, so much so that it almost seems like the Fed and other central banks around the world have been reading our playbook. We said that the final bubble to be pumped up will be the dollar bubble because it's the easiest way for politicians in the United States and around the world to solve the bubble problems temporarily. As we have said before, printing money can solve almost any financial problem—except for one: inflation. Money printing allows governments to borrow more massively, it calms nervous stock and bond markets, and it helps boost general economic activity.

Hence, almost exactly as we had predicted, governments around the world have opened the floodgates of printed money (see Figure 2.1). Discussion of an "exit strategy" for the Fed's pulling back its printed money out of the system, which was quite in vogue only a year ago, has been *completely* forgotten.

The European Central Bank (ECB) has flooded the European economy with more than 1 trillion euros of easy money loans. That has also taken pressure off the U.S. financial markets as well

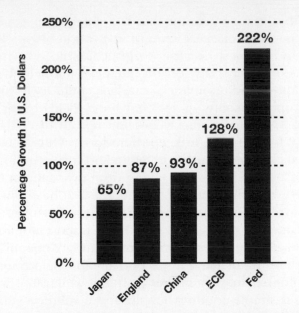

Figure 2.1   Around the World, Central Banks Are Printing Money

In response to the 2008 financial crisis, central banks around the world, not just our Federal Reserve, have responded by printing money. This is a world bubble economy.

Source: Various central banks.

and helped pave the way for the stock market recovery we had in the winter and early spring of 2012.

Not to be left out of the party, the Bank of England keeps adding to its printed money pile with more quantitative easing (QE) most recently a 50-billion-pound round in February.

Meanwhile, China's massive government-controlled banking machine continues to stimulate its economy with money printing, although at a slower rate than when the financial crisis first hit China's economy with a baseball bat. More on China, too, later in this chapter.

Japan has also continued to increase its money supply. They are up about 125 percent since 2007. Japan's exports are falling and the printed money will help drive down the value of the yen, making its exports cheaper. More importantly, the Japanese economy, which recovered smartly after the tsunami, has slowed down again, partly due to slowing European demand for Japanese exports, as well as slowing demand from other Asian countries, in particular China.

All of this money printing has helped boost economies and especially financial markets around the world. Now, it may not appear like a big boost because world economic growth is so slow. But it is working, especially on the financial markets. Without this massive money printing, financial markets could melt down. In the case of Europe, it is easy to see that bond yields on Spanish and Italian debt would have quickly spiraled up out of control without massive ECB intervention to keep them lower. Out-of-control interest rates in such large countries as Spain and Italy would rattle financial markets around the world, taking the European, United States, and Japanese economies down with them. So the money printing madness may not look like it's helping because European, U.S., and Japanese economic growth is so slow, but it is most certainly helping keep the financial markets from deteriorating dramatically, which would have a severe negative impact on all of those economies.

But, of course, massive money printing, while supportive in the short term, is simply another bubble, not a solution. Pumping up the huge dollar bubble with massive money printing is only going to make its crash even bigger and more uncontrollable later. That's because massive money printing eventually causes significant inflation; rising inflation causes rising interest rates; and rising interest rates will pop what is left of the first four partially popped bubbles (stocks, real estate, private debt, and consumer spending) and will fully burst the last two: the dollar and the government debt bubbles.

In the meantime, no one wants you to think about that.

Ignoring the Massive Money Printing (the Dollar Bubble) Is a Key Goal of the Cheerleaders

As with any bubble, the key to its short-term success is *ignoring it*. If you don't ignore the bubble, it is a lot harder to keep it going. So, part of the key to the short-term success of this money-printing madness will be for cheerleading financial analysts and economists to overlook the bubble it is creating. For help in overlooking bubbles it is always good to have some academic support. And, sure enough, as if on command, there is growing support for a new economic theory called New Monetarist Theory.

The group of economists who support this theory think that deficits are good and cannot cause economic problems. Actually, deficits do help governments solve economic problems in the short term. Governments can borrow massive amounts of money and never have to default on their debt because their central banks can always buy their debt with more printed money. But these economists don't just believe this will help in the short term, they see it as an acceptable, even desirable, long-term solution because they don't see any long-term problems with it. They believe that this printed money won't cause inflation because the new money is simply a "balance sheet adjustment" in the economy. Like a magic trick, it doesn't really count and it won't hurt us in any way.

New Monetarist Theory is like Keynesian economics on steroids. And, to a large degree, at least in the short term, it is true. Government borrowing *does* help the economy. And, yes, the Federal Reserve, with printed money, can buy *every single* government bond Congress wants to sell if need be. Hence, there is no possibility of a failed Treasury auction and no possibility of default even if government debt became incredibly massive.

Of course, as we have been pointing out for years, there is a giant flaw in this plan. Using printed money to buy bonds will eventually cause inflation. If it won't cause inflation, then, using the logic of the New Monetarists, the government could simply eliminate all taxes and borrow all the money it needs by selling bonds to the Fed, who will pay them in newly printed money that didn't exist before. No taxes and lots of government spending (funded by printed money) certainly would boost the economy. And if all that printed money doesn't cause inflation, you have created the perfect solution to any economy's ills. It would truly be "Money from Heaven," and it could basically move any economy in the world into hyperdrive.

But, of course, Money from Heaven does not really exist. As we have said before, Money from Heaven is the path to Hell. It is amazing that such a line of economic thought is getting increasingly greater and more serious attention. It is also a reflection of the sad state of the economics profession that this line of thinking represents cutting edge non-mainstream economists. That's a big problem because almost all real change in economic thought over the next few decades will come outside of the mainstream. That this represents current nonmainstream thinking shows how far the field of economics has yet to go.

The fact that the economics profession has failed so miserably is a key part of the reason we are in this current economic mess and, more important, it will be a key part of the reason we will have so much trouble getting out of this mess after the Aftershock hits. Moving economics into a much more sensible direction is so important that we devoted a whole chapter to this issue in *Aftershock*, Second Edition (Chapter 9).

The Fool in the Shower

One issue that is not terribly important in the current economy, which was discussed in great detail in *Aftershock*, Second Edition, is inflation. Hence, we are often asked why past money printing hasn't created inflation. Of course, we point out that we do have higher inflation, but, admittedly, it has not been high enough to increase interest rates, which is the key negative effect of inflation in a bubble economy. And it likely won't be high enough to increase interest rates for at least the rest of 2012. So, why isn't inflation higher? It's due to what are called lag factors. There is always a lag between printing money and inflation. We discussed lag factors in detail in *Aftershock*, Second Edition (Chapter 3).

The easiest way to understand lag factors is the "fool in the shower" analogy used by Nobel Prize–winning monetarist economist Milton Friedman. The fool walks into a shower and turns on the hot water. At first, all he gets is very cold water. So he turns the knob higher to get hot water, and still nothing, so he keeps turning it up. Then, all of a sudden, the hot water hits and scalds him.

That's what happens with inflation and lag factors. We don't get inflation immediately, so we see no harm in "turning up the hot water" by increasing the money supply. All we see are the short-term benefits, and we keep printing more money without getting burnt. In fact, as we have said before, the reason inflation could be very high in the future is not because of the money we have already printed, but, most important, because of the money we will likely print in the future (just like the fool in the shower, who keeps turning up the hot water because he's not burnt yet). More money printing will go from being somewhat discretionary to being more mandatory due to the need for increasing support for financial markets here and abroad. Since we are simply trying to support falling bubbles in housing, stocks, private credit, and consumer spending, there will be a continuing need to print money. Not that the money we have already printed won't create inflation—it will. But the greatest contributor to future inflation will be future money printing.

However, even with massive money printing, a lot can go wrong long before we get high inflation. Printed money helps to solve some of our economic problems short term, but it doesn't work perfectly and it isn't a one-stop cure-all. Governments can print money, but that doesn't mean they have an economic steering wheel, accelerator, and brake that allows them to drive the economy perfectly. Much of the economy is entirely out of their control. So even if we don't have high inflation, we can still have financial crises, falling stock markets, and very sluggish real estate markets.

In all fairness, it is true that if we were really willing to open the money-printing spigot, we probably could solve all our problems short term ($10 trillion would likely do the trick). But few people would support it. And, that tells you that they actually know more than they are saying—they know that printing lots of money will create inflation—otherwise, why not print $10 trillion right now? They know full well the dangers; they are just hoping beyond hope that somehow $2 trillion dollars won't be dangerous and won't cause future inflation.

Potential Triggers That Could Accelerate a Downtrend in the U.S. Economy

There are many possible situations that could accelerate a downturn in the economy. Some are more likely than others and some are less probable but are still possible, depending on unpredictable wildcard events. Potential triggers include:

- Greece
- China
- Iran
- The passage of time

Greece: Between a Rock and a Hard Place

Part of the bullish feeling in the stock market currently is a result of the "resolution" of the Greek crisis. Like the economic "recovery," the Greek "resolution" is likely not for the long term. The Greek economy is still in serious trouble. Only an immediate default has been avoided through the bailout and another round of loans. More important, the spread of the Greek debt crisis to Spain and Italy has been temporarily stopped. As we have said all along, the Greek crisis is really a Spanish and Italian crisis. The European banking system can withstand a Greek default, but it can't weather a Spanish and/or Italian default. So the ECB's move to buy Spanish and Italian bonds with printed money and also to provide over 500 billion euros in loans to European banks in late 2011 (known as a long-term refinancing operation [LTRO]) and another 500 billion euros in March has helped keep the Greek problem from spreading to Italy and Spain in a catastrophic way.

But, fundamentally, the problem remains severe. Greece's economy has continued to spiral down, with unemployment now over 22 percent, up from 7 percent in 2007. There is simply no way it can pay off or pay down its debt. Even optimistic projections show Greece's debt to gross domestic product (GDP) ratio being at 120 percent eight years from now. Needless to say, those optimistic projections are likely to be very optimistic. The real numbers will probably be far worse.

This also shows a fundamental dilemma that many economies face, including the U.S. economy. Government austerity hurts growth. Lots of government borrowing helps economic growth, short term. If that is cut, the economy heads down. Now, if we weren't in a bubble economy, the fundamental long-term drivers of real growth would ultimately help move the economy toward recovery. Argentina defaulted on its debt and, due to strong growth in the world economy, especially in the United States and China, its strong exports helped the Argentine economy to recover to a large degree. But if there are no fundamental drivers of growth and past growth was based on a rising bubble economy that has popped, then austerity simply becomes part of a vicious downward spiral. In the past decade, the Greek economy has been propelled by a rising bubble of debt that financed its spending. Now that debt bubble has popped and there is nothing to replace it to propel their economy. Plus, there is no strong growth in the European economy or the rest of the world to lift it up.

The situation in the United States is similar. Most of the growth from 2000 to 2010 was due to bubbles, not fundamental growth. So, once those bubbles have popped, there aren't any growth drivers left. The lack of fundamental growth is evidenced in the job creation numbers. Between 2000 and 2010, there were *zero* net new jobs created. In fact, we actually lost about 200,000 jobs.

However, unlike Greece, we have the ability to create two more bubbles to help pull us out of trouble temporarily—the government debt and dollar bubbles. To the extent we try to reduce the government debt or dollar bubbles, our growth will fall. Hence, we are between a rock and a hard place, just like Greece. Either we embrace austerity and let the bubbles fall, or we try to pump up more bubbles, which will temporarily keep the other bubbles from popping but make the final pop much worse. We think this is an easy choice for politicians—pump up the bubbles! This is also why there will be more and more discussion about how government debt and money printing isn't so bad, but actually very good. Of course, this is nuts, but when times get tough, people tend to go a bit nuts.

What's the solution? That's easy—don't blow up the bubbles in the first place. Once you have one, there is no easy way out of a bubble, no soft landing. After you have a bubble, the only choices are pop it now or pop it later. Both are painful. One is painful now; the other is even more painful later. These bubbles were a mistake to begin with and, unfortunately, there is no easy way to correct that mistake now. Ultimately, we will have to focus on increasing productivity to grow the economy rather than blowing bubbles. Increasing productivity is not just the best way to grow an economy; it is the *only* way to grow an economy in the long term.

Since Greece doesn't have the ability to pump up two more bubbles, it is facing a vicious downward spiral in its economy. Its unemployment could jump far higher than it is today—maybe even 30 percent within the next 12 to 18 months. Fueled by growing joblessness, businesses will lack confidence to invest and consumers will lack confidence to spend. It's a bad downward spiral that doesn't end quickly. We could have a full-blown Greek economic meltdown.

A Greek default on its debt won't solve the problem either. Much more is hurting the Greek economy than having too much debt. The big problem is the inability to borrow as they did before to pump up the debt-fueled spending bubble that was so critical to their growth. Without a bubble to drive growth, the only option is increasing productivity. And, for Greece, that is likely to be a very slow process.

China: A Short-Term Threat to the Party

China's construction boom is unprecedented in human history. By some estimates, as much as 50 percent of their GDP is now driven by fixed investment, a large part of which is construction. Far from encouraging a more consumer-driven economy rather than export-driven, consumer spending as a percentage of the economy has actually decreased while the construction part of the economy has become absolutely dominant. Even at the height of our housing bubble, construction was only 17 percent of our economy. At its height during Spain's housing bubble it was 23 percent, and in Dubai it approached 30 percent at the peak of its speculative construction boom. China, with 50 percent of its economy driven by construction is truly astronomical and, unlike Spain or Dubai, it is the world's second-largest economy, so 50 percent is a big deal for the rest of the world.

Some people feel this construction bubble is unsustainable, although not surprisingly most people do not see it as unsustainable and think it can go on for many more years. For those who think it will slow down, a lot of the discussion surrounding the fall of this construction boom revolves around whether it will have a soft landing or a hard landing. Massive state-controlled and -directed bank lending, which was fueled in part by printed money, has been the driver for all these construction projects. Hence, many believe that it is well within the government's ability to control the slowdown.

However, there is also the possibility that the Chinese government can't so easily control economic growth, especially if the growth is based on an economically unsustainable driver. In fact, using nonmarket methods, such as forced bank lending, to create construction projects for which there is no market demand could easily make a downturn even harder for the government to control when it begins to go bad—as it inevitably will.

China's growth over the past couple of decades has been driven by the government's opening up the Chinese economy increasingly to market competition and market forces. However, its growth in the past few years has come from just the opposite—government-controlled nonmarket intervention. And, we might add, the only reason they have the financial power to do something so unwise and nonmarket driven as forced bank lending for constructions is the enormous economic gains made from their move toward a more free-market-driven economy.

So, we think the possibility arises for China to endure not just a hard landing, but an economic meltdown due to a collapse in construction compounded by slowing exports. At the very least, it seems highly unlikely that China's government can navigate an exit out of this construction bubble any more carefully than the United States or Spain. Just maintaining their current growth rates means maintaining the unbelievable amount of construction they are currently doing and then doing even more every year, plus not having any downturn in exports—in fact, they need continuous increases in exports. It all sounds highly unlikely and very much like the Japanese export- and construction-fueled economy of the 1970s and 1980s that finally popped in a most spectacular fashion.

Yes, some cheerleaders might be able to tell us why China is so well managed that it can avoid what happened to the United States, Japan, and Spain, but it seems like pure cheerleading at its best. Not only do we not believe China is better managed but that China's non-market economic management—the massive government intervention to circumvent market forces—is actually going to result in a far bigger collapse than that faced by any of those countries when their construction bubbles popped. The best comparison is Japan, since, like China, it was fueled by massive export growth as well as massive internal construction-related growth. The Japanese story ended in great turmoil, even though it was a much more advanced and capably managed economy than China when its bubbles popped.

For the world's bubble economy, a meltdown by China would have unusually harsh consequences. That is part of the reason so many people are cheerleaders for China's construction bubble, even though they wouldn't normally support such extreme nonmarket intervention in the economy in their own country. China is not only the second biggest economy in the world; it is providing almost all of the growth in the world since the financial crisis. So it is having an outsized impact on the United States and world economy. It is almost important psychologically to the financial markets, giving them some real teeth behind the belief that high economic growth will continue, just not driven by the United States anymore. If it pops, it will be a big disappointment, especially if the hard landing becomes a meltdown.

Like so much about China and the economy in general, it is hard to know exactly when such a meltdown could occur because it is so dependent on government actions (Chinese government) and psychology. But it is likely we will see a more pronounced slowdown than we are already seeing in the second half of this year, and 2013 will be the first real chance for a meltdown to occur. Like our own government, the Chinese government will fight this with money printing, but they have been doing this for some time and, at some point, it simply won't work. China is already a huge economy, and maintaining its high growth rates will become increasingly difficult under any circumstances. And when that growth stops, it won't go gently into the night, but rather will likely go from dream straight to nightmare.

Iran: Our Next Black Swan?

On almost everyone's list of potential "black swan" events this year is Iran. We think it is unlikely that the current administration would support bombing Iran's nuclear facilities in an election year. However, the possibility of an Israeli strike on Iran looms as a real possibility. The reason is that many in the Israeli military and government believe that there is only a limited period of time left to attack those facilities before it is too late. They certainly have said little to dampen discussion of an attack. Given their past successes, they may feel they can pull off a repeat performance.

If such an attack is made, it's not that relevant to investors whether it is successful or not. Any attack would upset Iran and they will attack back. Any such attacks will naturally drive up the price of oil. Even the threat of such attacks has already driven up the price of oil. Higher oil prices could be just the economic shock the world *doesn't* need given the fragile state of many of the world's economies, especially Europe and Japan.

Jim Chanos—A Realistic View of China

There are a few voices out there saying that China's problems are far greater than most economists and financial analysts realize, most notably hedge fund manager Jim Chanos of Kynikos Fund, which is why we give him an ABE Award for Intellectual Courage (ABE stands for the name of our first book, *America's Bubble Economy*).

Jim Chanos is the founder and president of Kynikos Associates, a hedge fund with a particular focus on short selling. While the practice of short selling has been somewhat controversial, especially in recent years, one value of companies like Kynikos is that they can point out critical flaws in the market long before most people see them. For example, back in 2000, Kynikos took short positions in a huge energy company, one that *Fortune* had consistently labeled America's most innovative company. Within the next 14 months, the stock had lost 99 percent of its value and the company ended up in bankruptcy. You've probably heard of Enron.

Chanos admits that he's not a "macro guy." His focus is intensive fundamental research and analysis to find stocks that are overvalued. But that hasn't stopped him from seeing some big picture problems, too, and in recent years he has pinpointed a major bubble in the world economy: the Chinese construction bubble.

Chanos noticed several years ago that property development in China was reaching unsustainable proportions. If the average Chinese couple makes a combined $8,000 or so a year, how can they afford condominiums that can easily cost up to $150,000? It didn't add up. Much of this growth was driven by bad loans pushed by the government. In fact, Chanos found that many new apartment buildings stay empty and are flipped from speculator to speculator on the greater fool theory.

As Chanos explains it, China starts with, 'We are going to grow 9 percent next year. Now how do we get there?'" Because so much of China's GDP growth comes from construction, the government needs to push new property development in order to keep the growth going. If construction slows, the whole Chinese economy slows and that will hurt China's suppliers in Australia, Canada, Germany, and elsewhere (many of which are shorted by Kynikos).

Chanos's insights aren't especially popular in a financial community that's counting on China to lead the global economic recovery. He has been publicly berated by some, though the attacks against him tend to be very short on data. While he may not be a macro guy, and doesn't agree with us on everything, he deserves big kudos for ignoring the cheerleaders and letting the facts speak for themselves.

One question is just how long the oil price shock will last. If the United States is able to control any attacks on oil supplies militarily, the impact will be lessened. But if it spirals out of control, then all bets are off. The Libyan uprising had far less impact on oil supplies than an Iran war likely would, and it still had significant long-term impacts last year. Iran could be bigger, with much depending on exactly what happens. No doubt, all financial markets will take a short term hit if there is an attack on Iran. Stocks will be hit. There will likely be a flight to safety that will help bonds and the dollar. Gold will also likely benefit. If there are no other problems in the world economy, there may be a relatively quick recovery. But, if combined with other problems in Europe or a slowdown in the U.S. "recovery," its effects will be multiplied and longer lasting. It's certainly the Black Swan du jour and one to keep an eye on.

The Passage of Time

While we tend to focus on possible future dangers that could kick off the coming Aftershock, the most likely trigger will simply be the passage of time. It would be quite wonderful if we really could print all the money we want forever, without ever having to face a single bad consequence. Think of all the problems we could solve, think of all the fun we could have! But such nonsense is the stuff of childhood dreams. Of course, we cannot print money endlessly without a future cost. And, of course, that cost is going to eventually come.

Even if, by some miracle or magic trick, high future inflation is somehow avoided, what about all these bubbles? In what universe do rising bubbles never fall? Sooner or later, *bubbles always pop.* That is why, regardless of what triggers may or may not occur, regardless of what manipulations may be deployed, even regardless of what marginal economic growth we may be able to somehow produce, *time happens.* The passage of time, alone, will be enough to make the colinked multibubble U.S. and world economies eventually burst.

A Closer Look at the Current U.S. "Recovery"

We sometimes put the word "recovery" in quotation marks because it's not clear just how strong this economic recovery really is. We can easily see the recovery in the stock market, which is enormous.

The Good Doctor

As we have so often said, this is not just America's Bubble Economy; it is the World's Bubble Economy. China is an excellent example of this, which brings us to another issue. Some people say that we are anti-American because we talk about America's Bubble Economy, but we most certainly are not. We try very hard to be *anti-nothing*. We try to be unbiased, although we know that many people say that and are not. But we hope we are. Given our very pointed assertion in *America's Bubble Economy* and *Aftershock* that the United States will absolutely perform the best after the Aftershock because of the inherent flexibility of its economy and the structure of its economy, which encourages growth and innovation, it seems that would indicate that we are not anti–United States. In addition, we also say that China and its nonmarket, heavily government-controlled economy will do the worst (with Japan doing the next worst and Europe doing the best outside of the United States). We further say that it will be so bad that there will ultimately be a popular revolt against the government (a Tiananmen Square that succeeds) that will move the country to a more democratic state.

The point of this example is that we try not to have any bias, although after reading this, some people would say we are too pro–United States. It's hard to please everyone, and we certainly do not try. We try to call it as we see it, just as any good doctor should in diagnosing and treating a patient. We strive to be the best and most unbiased economic doctor in the house. Short term, that may anger some people—investors, economists, and financial media members—and it may please others. Long term, we are absolutely sure it is the best, and only, approach to take if we are to truly understand and solve our economic problems.

But that's to be expected. Since the financial crisis, the stock market has always jumped on any signs of green shoots as an excuse to shoot up. The market is also very careful in the numbers it looks at. It closely watches good numbers and ignores bad numbers. It also doesn't look too closely at those good numbers to see how real or accurate they really are.

A good example of the bad numbers they are ignoring right now are corporate earnings. First quarter earnings have not been that good, and companies are not giving good signs that we should be expecting a big improvement ahead.

Another number they ignore is how much Wall Street insider selling there has been. Insider selling in the first quarter of 2012 was the heaviest first quarter in a decade. Insider selling is not always a good reason to doubt the market, but it sure looks bad when it changes so fast and management decides to sell so much. It seems like they aren't long-term believers in the market.

In addition, stock market volume has been very weak. In a bull market, you would normally like to see big increases on increasing volume, not increases on decreasing volume. That doesn't indicate a lot of conviction. According to Bloomberg, the average monthly trading volume for stocks was down 32 percent since October 2011 (see Figure 2.2). And it's been down almost 50 percent since 2009. Plus, about half of that decreased volume is due to high-frequency trading, not longer-term investors.

But, despite all this, the market has gone up, which in the end is all that most investors care about. Part of the reason it has gone up are the good numbers we have seen, most notably in employment. Up until April, we had 11 months in a row where we created over 100,000 jobs.

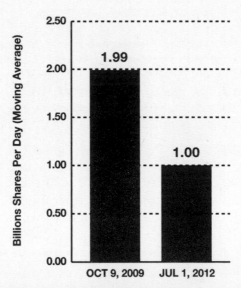

Figure 2.2   Stock Market Volume Is Falling

The stock market has risen from the depths of the financial crisis on greatly falling volume indicating a lack of widespread market support.

Source: Bloomberg.

However, the economy clearly began to slow down in late spring. Job growth fell well below 100,000, and it had been declining every month in 2012. Other indicators were indicating a fairly sharp slowdown. That led to a lot of readjustments in economic outlooks for the year. Because of these bad numbers, in June, Goldman Sachs revised their estimate for GDP growth in 2012 to 1.6 percent from 3 percent in the spring.

We have a good increase in manufacturing since August 2011, but that, too, slowed down in the spring. Future manufacturing growth will likely be crimped by declining European and Chinese demand.

There was a lot of cheerleading going on since August when things were looking bad. No surprise. Remember the big cheers over holiday sales on Black Friday in November 2011? But when the holidays were over, they were actually flat after adjusting for inflation.

Despite the cheerleading over the fake "good" numbers, they carefully ignore one of the most important real numbers: how much we borrow each month. No one even talks about how government borrowing is increasing (see Figure 2.3). Do you ever see it as

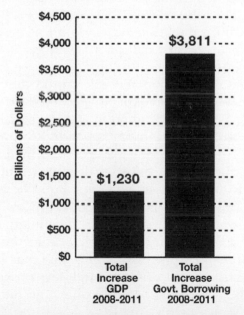

Figure 2.3   Increase in GDP and Government Borrowing, 2008–2011

The "recovery" is being driven by government borrowing and money printing. Increased government borrowing greatly exceeded *all* increased growth in GDP.

Source: U.S. Department of Treasury.

one of the major numbers of the month? Yet it is the most important number of the month by far. Without that money we would
not only be in recession, we'd be in an extremely deep recession
because, without it, the stock, housing, private credit, and consumer spending bubbles would pop. Lack of borrowing would set
off a vicious downward spiral. Yet do you see that often mentioned
on the business TV shows or the major financial print media? No
one mentions how vitally important massive borrowing (made possible by massive money printing) is to our continued "recovery."

The Fed's Next Steps

So what's a Fed to do? The stock market is up. The economy is
doing okay, especially to cheerleaders like the Fed. Europe is no
longer on the doorstep of a financial crisis. There's no real need to
print money right now. Yet they keep talking about it. Maybe they
want to keep assuring the stock market that they stand ready with
the money hose should it be needed. They might be much more
concerned about contagion from Greece, Spain, and Italy than
they are saying. They also may see that this "recovery" is very fragile.
We don't know, but we think another round of money printing is
likely this year or in the first half of 2013. However, it's definitely a
wait-and-see situation.

Another option is that the Fed has found other ways to stimulate the stock market without explicit QE, at least temporarily. The
question of direct Fed intervention in the stock market is always a
tricky one. We brought it up in an appendix to *Aftershock*, Second
Edition. It's still not something discussed in mainstream media,
even though it should be. However, the suspicion of it certainly
goes beyond our doors. In fact, coauthor Bob Wiedemer attended
a lunch of Wall Street analysts and investors in New York in August
2011 and decided to ask the attendees how many thought it was
possible that the Fed was directly intervening in the stock market.
Not that they thought it was happening, just that it was possible.
Surprisingly, almost two thirds of the attendees raised their hands.

Certainly, there are days recently when the market has acted
awfully funny. Most notably August 9, when the Dow was down
300 points in the afternoon and, for no significant apparent reason, reversed course, climbing very rapidly, and closed up 300
points by the end of the day. From that point forward, the market

*"We're still the same, great company we've
always been, only we've ceased to exist."*

continued to climb in a bullish fashion with few retreats through
the end of February.

But whatever the Fed is doing directly or indirectly to support
the market, one thing is clear: They are very worried. How do we
know they are worried? Because never in the history of the United
States have they printed so much money so fast. And, unlike before,
there is absolutely no talk about how to pull that money out of the
system—another sign of their very serious concern about the economy. So, clearly, they are very worried, even though they tell us not
to be. And, actually, we should be very worried, too.

Bottom Line: "Recovery" Is Still Driven by Massive Borrowing and Massive Money Printing

The "recovery" is *still* driven by government borrowing and printing. Take away either one and we would be in a *deep* recession.

Government borrowing has soared since the financial crisis. As an example, in February 2011, the government borrowed more money than in *all* of 2007. As mentioned earlier, we are borrowing about $100 billion *per month*. It's worth mentioning again because it is so important. That equates to borrowing about $1.2 *trillion* per year or about 10 percent of our total GDP. Eliminate that borrowing and you effectively cut our GDP by 10 percent. And that doesn't include the negative effects such a deep recession would have on consumer confidence, investor confidence, and the bubbles.

Even the small reduction in borrowing discussed at the end of 2011 (eliminating the Bush tax cuts, eliminating the unemployment benefits extension, and cutting Medicare reimbursement levels) would have reduced GDP by 1 to 2 percent. Well, GDP growth this year may be only about 1.5 percent. So we owe almost our *entire* growth this year to borrowing the money to avoid those reductions! That's a fragile basis for any economic recovery.

Money printing is playing an important role as well. It has been critical to maintaining our stock market bubble. Without it, the stock market may have never recovered much from the financial crisis or certainly fallen again even if it did recover somewhat. And a falling stock market would have big negative impacts on the economy.

Combined, government borrowing and money printing are not only key to our current "recovery"—they *are* the recovery.

Our Investment Outlook

As of this writing in mid-June 2012, here are our thoughts on:

- Stocks
- Bonds
- Europe
- International equities
- Gold
- Silver and commodities

Stocks

Believe it or not, we actually think 2012 might end up being a decent year for stocks. Stocks will likely be highly volatile, as they were in 2011. However, if stocks fall significantly, the Fed will likely intervene with yet another round of QE. This may be done surreptitiously, or it may go by another name. The Fed will *consider* such actions if the Dow drops below 11,000, and it will very likely *take* action if it falls below 10,000.

This will work to boost the stock market—in the short term, at least. A big round of money printing could even send the Dow toward its all-time high of 14,164. When this happens, we will be much more bullish on stocks in the short term although there's still plenty of long-term risk.

So when will this bubble pop? In the past, stocks have fallen within weeks after the quantitative easing ended. In the future, it may not be so clear cut. The next round of QE may be more open-ended and that will provide more ongoing support for the stock market in the short term. In the longer term, the stock market bubble will still pop, but it's difficult to set a clear expiration date right now. Stay tuned and we will keep you updated as this develops.

In the meantime, high-dividend stocks of stable, conservative, large-cap companies such as electric utilities, Johnson & Johnson, and Procter & Gamble are still worth looking at in a conservative portfolio. There is less potential for short-term growth, but they also carry lower long-term risk.

Bonds

Interest rates on bonds in the United States are about as low as they can go—meaning the potential for capital gains from bonds is pretty slim. However, there could be some small gains to be had in 2012. Financial uncertainty in Europe will likely continue to make Treasurys a relative safe haven. However, if the Fed prints money in another round of QE, that traditionally has been a short-term negative for bonds since investors will be moving out of bonds and into stocks. And remember, even a relatively small increase in interest rates could send bonds downward very quickly.

So we recommend keeping shorter-duration high-quality bonds, such as two-, three-, and five-year Treasurys. In addition, special bonds, such as mortgage-backed bonds and (which stands for Treasurys Inflation-protected Securities), treasury inflation-protected securities (TIPS) are likely to outperform traditional bonds in a QE-type environment. Overall, they should be a good source for total return this year, although not as good as 2011. Exchange-traded funds (ETFs) such as TIP (for TIPS) and MBB (for mortgage-backed bonds) are potentially good ways to invest in those bonds.

Europe

As we predicted, the European Central Bank has turned to printing money (and hence devaluing the currency) in order to buy Italian and Spanish bonds to prevent the Greek financial crisis from spreading throughout Europe and threatening the collapse of the French and German banking systems. While the extent of the money printing is nothing compared to the Fed's QE, it has prevented the European banking system from melting down for the time being.

In 2012 we can expect more of the same. Countries with large debts and weak economies, such as Italy, Spain, and Greece, will continue to run into liquidity problems and threaten to topple the banking system. The ECB, ever reluctant to print money, will nonetheless have no choice but to continue to print money to save the day. Of course, this will lead to more inflation eventually, but in the meantime it will have the intended effect of keeping the European banking system from collapsing. Ultimately, saving the banking system is the primary goal of the ECB.

In summary, we don't expect the Eurozone to collapse this year or the euro to be abandoned. What we do expect is an increasingly reluctant ECB to print increasing amounts of money. No one will like it, but it's the easiest "solution," and politicians usually choose the easiest solution.

One caveat is that the Greek/Spanish/Italian debt situation could deteriorate more rapidly than a reluctant ECB is willing to act. This could cause a lot of panic around world financial markets, but we expect the ECB will be forced to act before it becomes a true Lehman Brothers–type meltdown (but no guarantee!).

International Equities

Although international equity funds have been touted by many brokerage firms over the past couple of years as a way to diversify out of the U.S. stock market, they performed very poorly last year. Indian and Chinese markets were both down over 20 percent. Many European markets were down from 10 to 20 percent. You would have been better off in U.S. markets. Could there be a rebound this year? Sure, especially if the U.S. market rebounds due to some Fed money printing. However, just as we didn't like them before, we still don't think international equities are worth the risk of a longer-term hold. The issues we previously discussed regarding Europe and China will continue to weigh on the entire world economy and also on their stock markets this year. Could there be short-term gains? Of course. But, overall, we would continue to avoid international equities as having too much risk and volatility for the potential gain.

Gold

First, let's be clear that we view gold as a long-term investment. With governments around the world turning to money printing in order to artificially prop up struggling stock markets and banking systems, the fundamentals in our economy are set up perfectly for a long-term rise in gold. When inflation goes up, interest rates follow, which will spell doom for stocks, bonds, and real estate. At that point, gold is the only place to turn for many investors, and it is likely to have explosive growth. According to some estimates, gold comprises only 0.14 percent of investable assets in the world. Less than a quarter percent is not much, so any movement out of stocks or bonds and into gold will have a *big* effect on gold.

Even in the past decade, with very low inflation, gold has been an excellent investment, quintupling in value over that span while the stock market performed poorly—the S&P 500 was flat, and the Nasdaq fell 50 percent. But we like gold for its future ahead, not for its past performance. Many see gold's rise in the past decade as another bubble. But as we see it, the bubble has barely started. We won't say how high we think it will go, but it could easily increase several times from where it is today before this bubble pops.

So why has gold dropped so far since late 2011? There are plenty of reasons why gold can go down in the short term, and we still expect some volatility between now and the dollar bubble burst. We've said before that there are signs of central bank manipulation, and we'll likely see more of that in the years to come. The drop in gold price may also have a lot to do with the situation in Europe, where liquidity problems increase demand for dollars and make it necessary for financial institutions to sell assets like gold. This is similar to what happened in 2008, when the liquidity crisis sent the price of gold tumbling 30 percent in a matter of months. The important thing to remember is that gold has more than doubled since that low point of around $700/ounce. Even if you had bought gold at its peak before the liquidity crisis, your investment would have increased 60 percent by now.

By comparison, the recent drop in the gold price, percentage-wise, was only about half what it was in 2008, and gold was still up about 10 percent last year. Among the factors driving gold in 2012 will be increased physical demand in China, continued buying by peripheral central banks such as Turkey, Korea, and others, and continued financial uncertainty. We see no reason why the growth trend in 2011 won't continue in 2012.

Note on gold ETF PHYS: PHYS doesn't always track the price of GLD, the biggest gold ETF. The reason is that PHYS typically trades at a premium to the price of gold (similar to gold bullion coins). In recent months, the premium has ranged from 1 percent to 6 percent. While the price of PHYS is predicated on the price of gold, it is also affected by the change in the premium. As an example, if the price of gold was up 1 percent and the premium on PHYS to gold was also up 1 percent from the prior day, PHYS would be up 2 percent. Had the premium dropped 1 percent, PHYS would be unchanged. Sprott Asset Management, which manages PHYS, does an excellent job putting this data on the following web site: www .sprottphysicalgoldtrust.com/NetAssetValue.aspx. Historical data can also be found at the site.

Silver and Commodities

In the long run, we expect silver to track gold pretty closely, meaning it will go up over time. In the short run, however, we expect silver to be more volatile than gold. This is partly because silver is an industrial metal as well as a monetary metal. Over half of silver's production each year is used for industrial purposes. Silver's long-term rise will be tempered over the next year by the declining demand for electronics, particularly from China.

Most commodities, including silver, are dependent on demand from China, which in recent years has radically increased its demand for food, coal, metals, and other commodities. This doesn't bode well for the commodities market, because there are signs the Chinese economy is slowing down dramatically. It's difficult to be precise because the Chinese government has a tendency to be less than truthful with its economic statistics. So don't expect economic readings from the Chinese government to indicate that. Most likely, as was the case this week with their GDP growth rate, Chinese government statistics will indicate perfect government management of a controlled slowing of economic growth from white hot to red hot. Would you expect anything less from a dictatorship and heavily state-run economy? Of course, many people on Wall Street will believe it because they want to believe it. Also, inaccurate inflation reporting, as here in the United States, can make many economic numbers look better than they are.

But given the dramatic slowdown of export-led economies like Brazil (whose growth has fallen to near U.S. levels), Canada, Australia, as well as Asian economies that are closely tied to China, especially Hong Kong (which is nearly in recession), it's very unlikely that the Chinese economy is really growing at nearly 9 percent as the government claims. Falling Chinese demand will take a big toll on commodities over the next few years, so we would expect some downward pressure on commodities in 2012. The International Energy Agency just announced that it expects very limited growth in oil demand this year due to the slowdown in the world economy. China is terribly important in commodities such as steel. As an example of that, China now consumes more steel for its construction industry alone than the demand for steel for all uses in the United States, Europe, and Japan *combined*. As further evidence of its voracious demand, it uses almost half of the cement production in the world. A big decline in Chinese construction demand would have a big effect on commodities.

Offsetting this to some degree will be money printing by the Fed, which could cause a temporary upturn in commodities. Of course, as inflation begins to get stronger, commodities will push upward even with declining demand.

A Note on Oil: The big variable with oil is Iran. Political tensions have been heating up between Iran and the West lately. As this escalates, it could lead Iran closer and closer to war. If war with

Iran does occur, oil prices will skyrocket. This could trigger a big downturn in the financial markets and force the Fed to print a lot of money immediately. Such printing could stabilize financial markets in the short term, but will make whatever upturn we see in the stock market this year much more tenuous.

The 2012 Presidential Election

No investment outlook written in mid-2012 would be complete without some mention of our upcoming presidential election. Of course, by the time you read this book, you will likely know much more than we do right now, so we (once again) are going out on a prediction limb to tell you what we think will happen and why—in this case, not about who will win in November, but how whoever wins will likely impact the economy in the short term.

While many people will find this disappointing, the truth is that the outcome of this election will likely have very little *long-term impact* on the fate of the U.S. economy. However, there are a few short-term potential impacts worth mentioning. Before we do, we would like to remind you once again that we have no political agenda in writing these books; we are simply trying to provide you with the correct macroeconomic point of view so you can come to your own logical conclusions about the direction of the economy and what you can do to protect yourself.

If the Republicans Win the White House

If Governor Romney becomes president, he will likely try to reduce the deficit by cutting spending. However, as he would soon discover, that is a lot easier said than done. What spending could Romney realistically cut? Will he try to cut Social Security? Not likely. What about cutting Medicare? No one is going to like that too much. How about trimming defense spending? That's definitely out. Romney will soon find that significantly cutting almost any government program will be politically very hard to do, hard even for a Republican Congress to go along with, if the Congress also happens to become mostly Republican.

Perhaps, if Congress is mostly Republican, they will try to cut some of the more Democrat-favored programs, such as welfare. But to get any real mileage out of just a few cuts, the spending reductions would have to be very deep, and the Democrats would surely fight that, using the same filibuster rules that allowed the Republicans to block so many Democratic initiatives in the past four years. Of course, if Congress remains mostly Democratic, as it is today, deep spending cuts will be even easier to block.

Meanwhile, it is very unlikely that any Republican president will try to increase revenues to the government with any new taxes. Instead, the money printing and the borrowing will continue. Money printing will continue because without it, the stock market and overall economy will continue to decline. Nobody wants that, least of all investors and the business community, who may have supported Romney. The borrowing will also continue because, as we explained in *Aftershock*, Second Edition, we can't quit borrowing or we won't be able to roll over the huge federal government debt. We have to keep borrowing to make our interest payments on the previous debt, so even if a Republican wins the White House, the debt ceiling will have to be raised again, and the borrowing will continue. The alternative would be to quit raising the debt ceiling and quit rolling over our debt, meaning we go into default on the debt, our credit rating drops to XXX overnight, the stock market crashes, and the Aftershock starts sooner rather than later. No one wants that, so even a Republican president and Republican Congress will kick the can down the road even more.

So, with continued money printing, continued borrowing, few spending cuts, and no new taxes, the longer-term outcome of having a Republican president, even with a Republican Congress, won't be much different than the outcome of not having a Republican win.

However, in the shorter term, many investors will likely feel more optimistic having a Republican in the White House, and we could easily see the stock market doing well right after the election and continuing to do well for perhaps several months, assuming there is no bad news coming in from Europe, Iran, China, or other negatives that could end the Romney stock market honeymoon early.

If the Democrats Win the White House

If President Obama retains the White House and the Democrats hang on to a majority in Congress, we can expect to see no big changes from today. The Federal Reserve will continue to print money, the government will continue to roll over the debt with more borrowed money, there will be no big spending cuts, and probably not much in the way of new taxes because, even as a minority in Congress, the Republicans will continue to block such attempts, as they have done before.

If Obama keeps the presidency but the Republicans become the majority in Congress, we can expect to see even less change, and nothing much new will get done that either side would like. The budget deficit will remain about the same, and our total debt will continue to grow.

If the Democrats keep the White House, investors will likely be less optimistic immediately after the election than they would be if Romney gets in. The stock market could become more volatile in the following months, and that could lead to an earlier next round of money printing by the Fed than we might have seen under Romney, but either way, the Fed will print more—it's only a question of how soon.

As we said, the 2012 election will make little difference for the falling multibubble economy in the *longer term.* No matter what happens this November, falling bubbles cannot be propped up forever. Various delaying tactics will be tried, and some—like massive money printing—will temporarily, marginally succeed in the short term. But none will be able to ultimately stop the coming multibubble pop and the Aftershock that will follow.

In Conclusion

Overall, 2012 should bring us short bouts of excitement followed by long periods of relative boredom—kind of like 2011. Europe will likely provide the biggest source of unwelcome financial excitement. China will play an increasingly sinister background role, slowing down the world economy, especially toward the end of the year. And American politics will likely provide some more financial excitement, with Congress trying to wrestle with the debt and our presidential election at the end of the year.

Of course, there is always the chance that the financial situation might get surprisingly bad this year. We don't think that will happen in 2012, but we certainly can't entirely rule it out. Also, there is always the chance for a Black Swan event, Iran being an obvious example. We'll be keeping our eyes wide open for any sign of a big surprise or for more incremental evidence that we are moving along toward the inevitable Aftershock head.

3

Conventional Wisdom
Won't Work This Time

INTRODUCING AFTERSHOCK
WISDOM INVESTING

For years, Conventional Wisdom (CW) money gurus have been telling us that buy-and-hold investing is the way to go. All you have to do to grow yourself a nice nest egg is get some high-quality stocks and bonds, in the right mix to match your age and goals, and then like those infomercial ovens on TV, you can "just set it and forget it."

The easy CW approach to investing naturally worked very well in an overall rising multibubble economy. As long as you stayed well diversified with a collection of average performing stocks and bonds, you could count on earning a good profit in the stock market and a steadily rising total return in the bond market, especially from the 1980s to 2000. With the Dow rising 1,100 percent in 20 years and falling interest rates pushing bond prices ever higher, investors could practically throw a dart at a stock page and end up with some good gains eventually. CW investing in a rising bubble economy is nearly effortless.

Then, beginning in 2000, all that started to change. Bonds still did okay, but that 1,100 percent growth in stocks got replaced by a big fat zero percent growth for the Dow and a 50 percent decline in Nasdaq stocks over the next decade. Nonetheless, the CW gurus seemed unfazed, plowing ahead with their CW investing as if America's multibubble economy would always continue to rise. They didn't see the bubbles, only the growth. And if that growth happened to occasionally experience a bit of a "down cycle," they could always just relax and wait for an inevitable "up cycle," because the rising bubble economy had convinced them that economic growth was virtually guaranteed if you just had patience and waited for a while. CW has faith and CW doesn't quit.

So when the real estate bubble started to pop in 2007 and kicked off a global financial crisis in 2008, along with a stock market drop of nearly 40 percent, many CW investment experts were quite shocked and confused. Without the correct macroeconomic view of what was occurring, they held even more tightly to their faithful buy-and-hold mantra. CW investing had simply not prepared them for moments like this. They used phrases like "Black Swan event" and "highly unpredictable" to describe the 2008 stock market crash and global economic downturn, when in fact it was all *very predictable* (and by the way, was predicted in our book *America's Bubble Economy* in 2006). CW, however, saw the entire global financial crisis as unpredictable and beyond our control—as if an unexpected asteroid suddenly hit us out of the blue in late 2008, not something we systematically created ourselves over the course of decades.

Then, just when it looked like economic Armageddon, the U.S. Federal Reserve came to our rescue—at least in the short term—with massive money printing beginning in early 2009, as well as massive federal government borrowing. The enormous expansion of the money supply directly boosted the stock market and helped support the overall economy. However, it also left us with the specter of future rising inflation and rising interest rates dangling over CW investing like an unseen guillotine hanging by a thread.

So now the question is *what's next?* Should we stick with the CW folks, like Warren Buffett and other previously highly successful investors, or does this new and evolving economy call for a new and evolving approach? Hmmm, can you tell which way we are going with this?

Before we get to the details of our Aftershock wisdom on how to invest in the new and changing economy, let's take a close look at CW investing and why it's so very hard for most people to give it up.

The Key to Conventional Wisdom: The Future Will Be Just Like the Past

The key assumption behind all CW investing is pretty simple: What worked well in the recent past will work well today. It's easy to understand, it's easy to follow, and, most of all, it's *very comfortable*. And for a very long time, it was also very true. Let's look at some recent history to see why CW investing still has such powerful appeal.

Over the past century or so, the U.S. stock market has experienced solid, albeit slow (by the standards of the 1980s and 1990s) growth. Even in the Great Depression—a big economic collapse by any measure—most major corporations survived (many major corporations such as Caterpillar were even able to maintain profitability), as did most major banking and investment banking firms. The government entered the Depression with relatively little debt and little inflation. In fact, they probably printed too little money, contributing to deflation during the Great Depression.

Also, for the first half of the twentieth century, the economy was much less capital dependent and, hence, much less vulnerable to changes in interest rates. Leverage was less common for corporations and was certainly less common for consumers buying homes or cars. Most of our grandparents would not have even considered having more than a 10-year mortgage on a home, and they did not use credit to buy cars (even though that was becoming increasingly common). Use of debt had grown enormously since the late 1800s, but it was far less than today. In addition, there was much less consumer spending, partly due to less credit for such activities. As an example, credit cards really weren't in heavy use until the 1970s and especially the 1980s. Thus, with less consumer spending, the earlier economy was more resistant to downturns in consumer spending.

The economy had also experienced only a few major bubbles prior to the Great Depression. The 1920s stock bubble was the biggest, but even that bubble was accompanied by huge real growth in the economy. Relatively speaking, it was a much smaller bubble than the combined stock, housing, private credit, and consumer spending bubbles that rose up beginning in the 1980s.

The inflation and flat stock market of the 1970s (due in large part to declining productivity growth) was a harbinger of future problems, but not enough to offset almost a century of solid growth. Gross domestic product (GDP) growth was still fairly good, even in the 1970s. Except for the period of the Depression, down cycles were limited. Any down cycles during the century were relatively modest and were far outweighed by the good to great up cycles.

All of this enormous growth in the economy provided a strong basis for solid, but slow, growth in the stock market, which helped people like Warren Buffett and others do very well (see Figure 3.1).

Then, beginning in the 1980s, all that slow and steady growth driven by real fundamental economic drivers was replaced by rapid growth driven by another kind of driver: rising bubbles. As we reviewed in Chapter 1, during this time we saw the rise of the . . .

- Stock market bubble
- Real estate bubble
- Private debt bubble
- Consumer spending bubble
- Government debt bubble
- Dollar bubble

However, since 2000, these bubbles have been stagnant and have started to fall:

- The Dow and the Standard & Poor's (S&P) index have been essentially flat, while the Nasdaq fell 50 percent.

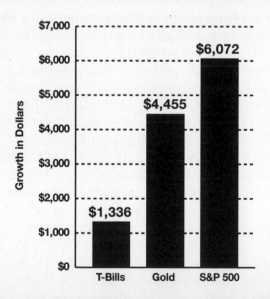

Figure 3.1   Stocks versus Six Month T-Bills and Gold, 1965 to 2011

What $100 invested in 1965 would be worth today.
Source: Bloomberg.

- Real estate has not recovered much since hitting bottom in 2008 and 2009.
- Private debt and consumer spending is still mostly down, with only marginal improvements.
- Meanwhile, gold (which, later in the Aftershock, will also become a bubble but is not there yet) is up more than 500 percent since 2000.

How does CW account for the changes described above? They say, "Don't worry, be happy. Just be patient and eventually everything will get better."

What in the world is giving CW so much sustained confidence? The answer is . . .

The Myth of a Natural Growth Rate

Inherent in CW is the deep faith that the U.S. economy possesses a reliable "natural" growth rate. This is somehow fundamental to our very existence and will never end. Hence, anytime we deviate from that natural growth rate and go into a recession temporarily, we will also, at some point, usually quickly, automatically return to our natural growth rate. That means that we can count on always having a rebound after every recession or, more to the point, after the recent financial crisis. This is also the fundamental basis for CW's thinking about investments in stocks, bonds, and real estate. CW says the economy has a natural growth rate and, hence, stocks, bonds, and real estate all have a natural growth rate, too. That is why buy-and-hold investing is at the heart of conventional investing: Just get in and hang on, and eventually that natural growth rate will kick back in.

CW makes no acknowledgment that we could be in a bubble economy or that the world could be in a bubble economy. All bubbles eventually pop, and they don't automatically reinflate. There is no "natural" growth rate that we can always count on to pull us through. Something has to actually *cause* a recovery; we don't just get one automatically if we wait long enough, like winter turning into spring.

The United States does not have a natural growth rate that is in effect at all times and will always save us. In fact, there never has been a natural growth rate—not for any country, not in the past, and not in the future. There is simply no such thing as "natural" economic growth. All economic growth has to be caused by something; it doesn't just happen automatically. That is why not all countries experience economic growth all the time.

Real (nonbubble) economic growth is driven by two forces: population growth and productivity growth. These two are related to some extent because higher agricultural productivity will lead to a larger population. However, our focus should be on productivity since we are primarily interested in becoming wealthier *per person*, not just having a larger economy with lots and lots of poor people. So, *productivity growth* is the source of economic growth. Hence, economies will grow only when productivity grows. An automatic increase in productivity is not natural or automatic. It has to come from changes in the way we produce goods and services. This involves changes in the way we do business, and that often involves changes in government and changes in technology.

China is a great example. What was China's "natural" growth rate in the 1960s? What was its "natural" growth rate in the 1990s? We all know China's growth rate was much higher in the 1990s than in the 1960s. Hence, there is no "natural" growth rate for China (or for any other country). It varies—quite a bit actually—depending on governmental and business actions. Growth was higher in the 1990s for China because they had made numerous important changes in the way they conducted business and in the way their government worked. Entrepreneurship was encouraged, free markets were encouraged, and more input from foreign investors and businesses was encouraged.

So, if China, or any other country, wants its economy to grow, it will have to continue to increase productivity. Yes, some of that productivity will continue to improve due to changes made in the past, but eventually the impact of those past improvements will diminish and economic growth will plateau if people don't continue to make *more* improvements in productivity.

This may sound a lot like us telling you "there's no free lunch," and that's true. But it has enormous importance for how many economists are looking at the economy. Many economists are assuming that any downturn in our economy is simply a diversion from our "natural" growth rate. In fact, you will even see that term used in many financial and economic articles. Nobody asks the most basic question: Where is that growth coming from? Instead, they simply assume it is always there and that our economy will naturally bounce back into growth mode. They are assuming that productivity is naturally growing all the time, even when economic history clearly shows it is not and that there is no "natural" or automatic growth rate.

Real Productivity Growth Is Slowing Down, Here and Around the World

Rather than staying the same or accelerating, productivity growth in this country and in the other major industrialized nations in Europe and in Japan has been slowing dramatically. Productivity growth in the last quarter of the twentieth century was much slower than in the first three quarters. These are long periods of time. That's how real productivity improvement works. It is a very long-term process.

By the way, you should almost completely ignore the government "productivity" statistics or "output per man-hour." Not that they are biased or wrong, but they don't give you a true idea of *real* productivity growth. For example, productivity by that measure can be improved enormously by simply stopping all research and development. That is a dumb measure of productivity.

So, instead of looking at misleading government figures of output per man-hour (although not intentionally misleading as much as just bad information), let's look at *real* productivity growth over a very long period of time. That's the only way to look at it, since significant productivity growth is a relatively slow process. For example, when we look at the productivity growth of food production in the United States over the longer term, we see that two centuries of advancements have made it possible for the number of people required to grow food to drop from 90 percent of the U.S. population to just 3 percent. Now that's real productivity growth!

Across many sectors, we had that kind of robust productivity growth in the United States for many decades. However, beginning in the 1970s (just before the bubbles started to inflate in the 1980s), overall productivity growth began to slow significantly (see Figure 3.2).

Here is another way to look at productivity. Under normal conditions, income generally goes up when productivity goes up. As Figure 3.3 shows, real income growth ("real" because adjusted for inflation) has slowed dramatically since 1970. The lack of large increases in real income is another indicator that productivity has not significantly grown since the 1970s.

By focusing on the big picture of productivity—which is the real fundamental driver of economic growth—it is easy to see that the CW idea that we are merely in a market "down cycle" that will soon be followed by an "up cycle" is wrong. This is not a short-term down cycle; it is a longer-term productivity slump and the more bearish

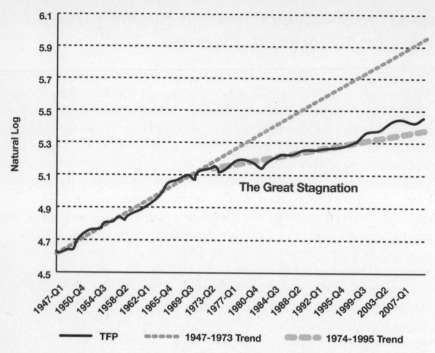

Figure 3.2   Slowing Productivity Growth (Using Total Factor Productivity)

Productivity growth was very rapid until the early 1970s and then grew very slowly afterward.

Source: John Fernald, San Francisco Federal Reserve.

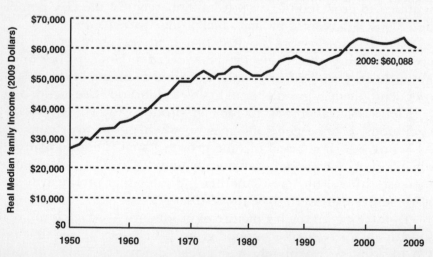

Figure 3.3   Real Median Family Income 1950–2009

Slowing growth in real family income after 1970 is another indicator of slowing productivity growth.

Source: U.S. Census Bureau.

analysts have it right when they say we are not going to get out of this economic downturn anytime soon.

But even the bears are wrong, too. They are correct to see doom and gloom ahead, but they don't see what is behind the doom and gloom, only that things are bad and will get worse. Having the *correct macroeconomic view* about stalled productivity growth is what separates the brains from the bears, and from CW, as well.

Warren Buffett: Master of Conventional Wisdom

Without a doubt one of the best, if not the best, CW investors is Warren Buffett. He is truly a CW master and his incredible success attests to that. If you invested $1,000 in his investment firm, Berkshire Hathaway, in 1990 it would be worth almost $30,000 by the beginning of 2000. That's pretty impressive.

However, after the beginning of 2000, his growth slowed considerably. Assuming you invested at the beginning of 2000, before the Internet bubble burst, a $1,000 investment would grow to about $2,300 at its peak in 2007 just before the housing bubble burst. That's still very good growth but nothing like the earlier growth of the booming 1980s and 1990s stock market. And, if you invested that $1,000 at Berkshire's peak in 2007 it would be worth about $900 today (see Figure 3.4).

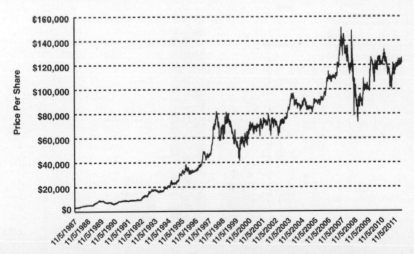

Figure 3.4   Berkshire Hathaway Performance, 1990 to Present

The price of Berkshire's stock (Warren Buffett's firm) did extremely well in the 1980s and 1990s, and very well until the financial crisis of 2008, but has struggled since then.

Some people would say Warren has lost his touch. We don't think so. We think he just lost his bubbles. Warren is still an excellent investor, but he tends to do very well during stock market bubbles and not so very well when there is no bubble.

So, is it any wonder that Warren doesn't want to believe we are in a bubble economy? Is it any wonder that he so fervently pushes stocks as a good investment? Remember Figure 3.1 at the beginning of this chapter that showed how well stocks had performed relative to gold and T-bills? He needs to push stocks because he desperately needs a bubble economy and a bubble stock market in order to show good growth. Now, of course, he doesn't say that, but clearly that is true.

And if the stock bubble were to continue to rise, you couldn't make a better choice than putting your money with Warren Buffett. But if the stock bubble does not continue to rise or if it pops, then you could be in real trouble betting on Warren. You could even end up like those who invested in another master of conventional wisdom investing, Bill Miller (see the sidebar that follows).

Buffett's reliance on CW is already showing problems because the stock market bubble is no longer rising. As Figure 3.5 shows, stocks don't look nearly as good now, while gold looks fantastic. Mr. Buffett would say this is simply a diversion from the longer-term pattern. We say the pattern is changing for all the reasons we discussed earlier in this chapter and in our previous books.

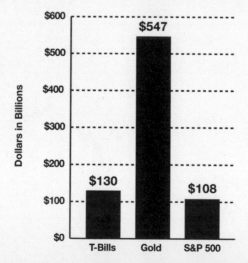

Figure 3.5   Stocks versus Six Month T-Bills and Gold, 2000 to 2011
What $100 invested in 2000 would be worth today.

Another CW Master: Bill Miller

Bill Miller wasn't as good as Warren at conventional wisdom investing, but he was still pretty darn good. His mutual fund, Legg Mason Capital Management Value Fund, beat the S&P 500 Index for 16 years in a row. However, with the fall in the stock market in 2007 things began to change. Bill saw housing-related companies falling fast—Companies like Fannie Mae and Freddie Mac. He didn't see any fundamental problems. He just saw lots of bargains, especially in a long-term growing U.S. housing market. He was a long-term value investor like Warren Buffett in some ways. He saw other stocks that had fallen and he snapped them up because this was just a down cycle in a long-term growth cycle. He knew he was doing what any smart investor should do—buy when everyone else runs away because that's when the money is made. In CW investing, that's exactly how you make money.

This kind of CW investing produced handsome returns for his mutual fund. At its peak, his fund had over $21 billion of assets under management.

Unfortunately, housing wasn't in a short down cycle but in a longer-term bubble burst. His performance collapsed. By 2011, he had lost money in four of the last five years. Fortunately, he was saved from even worse losses by the Fed's massive money printing with quantitative easing (QE1 and QE2). Still, it was all too much for Mr. Miller. He left the fund in 2011. As of June 2012, total assets under management were down to $1.8 billion and $10,000 invested in 1996 was worth about $8,300. The fund had lost everything it had made in over 15 years.

When the bubbles start to pop, CW investing is not the place to be.

Another Example of Conventional Wisdom Put to the Test: Hedge Funds

The people managing hedge funds are some of the best investors in the business. That's the Conventional Wisdom, and this time we agree with conventional wisdom. So, if CW is working, they would be some of the best practitioners of CW and would have some of the best returns to show for their CW investing.

So, let's look at hedge fund returns.

Fortunately, another John Wiley & Sons author, Simon Lack, recently published a book about hedge funds called *The Hedge*

Fund Mirage (2012) that reviewed the actual performance of hedge funds. Before we go on, we should clarify that not all hedge funds use conventional wisdom. Many are truly hedge funds and use a variety of non-CW strategies to get high returns.

However, most hedge funds are surprisingly unhedged and very conventional. They are essentially leveraged stock funds. You can see this clearly by looking at the correlation between stock market returns and hedge funds in Figure 3.6. As the chart shows, they really do make a good case study of the best in CW investing.

So, What did Simon Lack find in his research on hedge funds? Basically, what he found is that hedge funds did very well when they were first created in the early 1990s. They were smaller, which made it easier to find a good niche from which to extract higher profits. As they got bigger—much bigger—it became harder to find more or larger niches to properly invest their funds. And there was more opportunity when the stock bubble was just starting. Also, like any industry, they may have been a bit more creative when they were

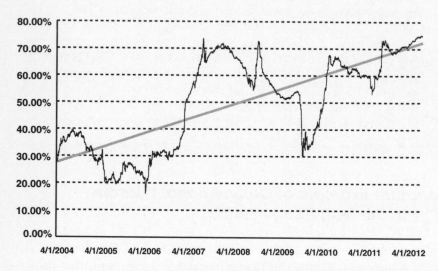

1 Yr. Correlation of the S&P 500 and the Hedge Fund Weighted Index

Figure 3.6   Increasing Correlation of Hedge Fund Returns and the Stock Market

Since 2004, hedge fund returns are becoming increasingly correlated with the stock market.
Source: Bloomberg.

first starting—they had to be to attract capital to a type of investing that was not well accepted.

So returns fell over time. However, fees did not.

That wasn't a big issue until the stock market collapsed in 2008. At that point, hedge funds lost an enormous amount of money. They weren't really hedged at all. Or at least a large number of them weren't. Let's keep in mind we're looking at an entire industry. There always have been outstanding performers and likely will be in the future. But, as an industry, it wasn't looking very good in 2008.

Mr. Lack made adjustments for this and found that, after deducting fees, hedge funds had lost almost *all* of the profits that the industry had *ever* made for investors in the stock market crash of 2008–2009. That's right, over 15 years of profits lost in less than 6 months, as shown in Table 3.1. Please note that this table does not take into account "survival bias" (when companies go under) and other reasons why these numbers are actually more conservative than reality. In other words, it was even worse than this.

So much for the best of CW investing. They had bet heavily on a rising stock market and had lost everything they had *ever* made in the few short months when the market took a big fall. And these people are the best in the business. The bottom line is that it's increasingly tough to make money with CW investing.

This short summary of Mr. Lack's groundbreaking work does it little justice. It's a great book, whether you have any interest in hedge funds or not. It's an honest and fascinating look at how modern American finance and investing is operating. Pick up a copy today—and hats off to another great John Wiley & Sons author.

The Key to Aftershock Wisdom Investing: The Future Is Not the Past!

The key to correct investing in the future is to recognize that the future will be significantly different from the past. Conventional Wisdom says that nothing is fundamentally different about the economy; we are just going through a rough spot. If we can just be patient and don't do anything rash with our investments, we can count on "natural growth" to eventually return and all will be

Table 3.1 Hedge Fund Returns after Fees

Year	Average HF AUM* (BNs)	Real Investor Profits (BNs)	Estimated HF Fees (BNs)**	Estimated FOF Fees (BNs)	Total Fees	Net Real Investor Profits (BNs)	Industry Share of Total Profits
1998	$131	$10	$7	$1	$7	$10	44%
1999	$166	$36	$14	$1	$15	$35	30%
2000	$213	$17	$12	$1	$13	$16	44%
2001	$279	$13	$12	$1	$13	$12	52%
2002	$414	$12	$13	$2	$15	$11	58%
2003	$666	$82	$36	$3	$38	$79	33%
2004	$1,027	$14	$27	$5	$32	$9	78%
2005	$1,295	–$ 6	$35	$7	$42	–$13	143%
2006	$1,537	$67	$66	$9	$75	$58	56%
2007	$1,925	–$11	$59	$11	$70	–$21	144%
2008	$1,797	–$448	$36	$10	$46	–$458	NM
2009	$1,506	$200	$30	$7	$37	$193	16%
2010	$1,624	$83	$32	$6	$38	$77	33%
Total		**$70**	**$379**	**$61**	**$440**	**$9**	**98%**

Source: BarclayHedge

**Assumes no incentive fees as many funds were still below their high water marks following 2008.

okay. Whereas, Aftershock wisdom says that there is no "natural growth," only real growth created by real productivity improvements. We have not had any significant real productivity improvements for many years. Instead, we had the rise and now the decline of multiple bubbles, and therefore the future is not the past, we are in a very different economy than before. In fact, the entire world is in a very different economy than before because we are in a worldwide bubble economy that is popping.

This is different from the past. We have seen bubbles before, such as the Internet bubble, and its demise really wasn't such a big deal, especially on a global level. *But it is different this time.* This time we have not one smallish bubble, but six, huge, interdependent bubbles, and when they fall fully, it is not going to be anything we have seen before—involving rising inflation, rising interest rates, and falling assets across the board.

We have also had inflation before, such as in the late 1970s and early 1980s, *but it is different this time.* This time, because we have so many colinked bubbles, high inflation and high interest rates are going to be the final blow to our multibubble economy and to the world's bubble economy, as well.

If the Future Is Not the Past, How Will It Be Different This Time? Future Inflation Is the Key

Our earlier books, *America's Bubble Economy* (2006) and *Aftershock* (2009 and 2011), described in detail what created the multibubble economy, and how the final two bubbles—the dollar and government debt bubbles—will be the next to pop, bringing on the Aftershock. Here is a quick summary:

Since the early 1980s, we have been borrowing more and more money (pumping up the government debt bubble). One of the key factors that made so much borrowing possible, especially in the past few years, has been the ability of the Federal Reserve to do massive money printing (pumping up the dollar bubble). This massive money printing worked to keep interest rates low and has allowed the government to borrow astronomical amounts to fund its deficit spending. In the years since the financial crisis of 2008, both the dollar and government debt bubbles have grown bigger than ever, in an effort to keep the rest of the multibubble economy afloat. All that was, and still is, okay—as long as the massive money printing can continue.

But here is the problem: massive money printing cannot continue forever. Why? Because massive money printing eventually causes rising inflation. Rising inflation eventually causes rising interest rates, and rising interest rates are not going to be good for maintaining this fake, stimulus-created "recovery." Instead, rising inflation and rising interest rates are going to be the final blows that pop the bubbles.

The dollar bubble will pop as a result of inflation spiking up, reducing the buying power of the dollar. There is no permanent way around this coming inflation, only short-term delaying tactics. If somehow massive money printing would never, ever cause rising future inflation, that would be great—in that case, we could forget about paying taxes or even earning money because we could all just print money instead. Clearly, that won't work.

High inflation and high interest rates will make dollar-denominated assets not so appealing, especially to foreign investors, who currently own more than $20 trillion in U.S. assets. When inflation comes, foreign investment will fall, and the dollar bubble will fall. Anyone who deludes himself into thinking foreign investors will stay in the United States because they "have nowhere else to go" is just being silly. Of course they will have other places to go. They will go back to their own countries' assets, such as their own short-term debt, which will be falling as well, but will not be falling as much as our dollar-denominated assets. Even today most money stays in other countries. It doesn't all come to the United States.

The decline in foreign investment in the United States would not have as much of an impact if there hadn't been so much inflow of foreign capital into our economy earlier. On the way in, that extra money helped pump up our bubbles, and on the way out, the drop in foreign investment will help pop the bubbles as well.

The combination of rising inflation and rising interest rates will pop the huge dollar and government debt bubbles, and will pull down what is left of the already falling real estate, stock, private debt, and consumer spending bubbles. With all our bubbles fully popped, the global Aftershock will begin.

Even if that is not something you can currently let yourself believe is possible, you must at least admit that rising inflation and rising interest rates will certainly not be good for any economic recovery. And once you let yourself see the bubbles, you will realize that, under these conditions, these bubbles cannot last.

Frankly, even without rising future inflation and rising interest rates, these bubbles cannot last. Why? Because they are bubbles! Bubbles don't last forever. What goes up must eventually come down because their rise was not driven by real productivity growth and other fundamental economic drivers. It was driven by speculation and a whole lot of borrowed and printed money.

Despite these facts, CW will try to deny, ignore, and happy-talk our way through an increasingly obvious falling bubble economy. But ask yourself this: How many CW-type analysts and economists predicted or anticipated our current economic situation? This is how CW tries to ignore the change. But, of course, that doesn't stop the reality of the current and future economy.

This enormous resistance by so many sophisticated economists and financial analysts to changing their CW economic outlook, even in the face of overwhelming evidence, is highly unusual in U.S. history. Although there has certainly been cheerleading in the past and blatant ignoring of reality by economists and financial analysts, this current period stands out as an extreme level of resistance to facing facts. CW has become blind as a bat, while insisting its eyes are wide open.

Key to the CW position that nothing too bad will happen next is their belief that inflation poses no threat. Some CW analysts (and even some bears) have gone so far as to say that future *deflation*, not inflation, is the real problem.

The Myth of Deflation Is the Last Refuge of the Deniers

Vital to the CW argument against our analysis is the wrong idea that instead of inflation, we are about to enter into a period of deflation. The idea that deflation is the real threat, not inflation, is the last refuge of the deniers. They want to deny that printing money is a problem. They want to be able to print all the money we need without any consequences, without inflation. So, instead, they say they are worried about deflation.

Let's start with a definition of inflation and then dissect the deflation arguments one at a time. As Nobel Prize–winning economist Milton Friedman famously stated:

"Inflation is always and everywhere a monetary phenomenon."

By using the word *monetary*, Friedman meant that inflation is a direct result of increasing the money supply. Increase the money supply, relative to the size of the economy, and you get inflation; decrease the money supply and you get deflation.

Wrong Deflation Argument #1: Prices Are Falling

A lot of people think that falling prices equals deflation. That is not true. Prices can fall when there is a change in supply and demand: falling demand and/or rising supply naturally reduces prices. That is not deflation. Deflation is caused by a contracting money supply and inflation is caused by an expanding money supply faster than the economy grows. We have a massively expanding money supply, and we are going to get significant future inflation, not deflation. Making matters more confusing, there is a difference between a change in the "nominal" price, which is the price paid, and a change in the "real" price, which is the price adjusted for inflation. The nominal price can rise due to inflation, while the real price can fall due to falling demand or rising supply. The fact that some asset values (in real dollars, adjusted for inflation) will fall due to popping bubbles does not mean we have deflation. What we have is falling bubbles.

Wrong Deflation Argument #2: Demographics Are Changing

Another argument we've heard for deflation is based on demographics. Some have said that as the Baby Boom generation reaches retirement, more people will be saving what money they have, which will make dollars scarcer and therefore more valuable. The problem with this is that, in the twenty-first century, when people save their money, they don't put it under their mattresses. They invest it. It circulates in the economy just like it always has.

Even if there were some truth to this idea, there's no way that a little extra penny pinching by the Baby Boomers could offset the massive money printing by the Fed that we've seen so far and will continue to see. Also, remember that we have had no periods of deflation in the United States since the end of the Great Depression when the government began to print more money. Inflation helped pull us out of the Depression. We simply cannot have significant deflation now or in the future when we are massively printing money.

Wrong Deflation Argument #3: Debt Write-Offs and Bankruptcies Reduce the Money Supply

Another common argument for deflation is that when debts cannot be repaid, the resulting write-offs and bankruptcies will effectively decrease the money supply. This argument seems to come from the fact that money is created as debt. But the argument goes one step too far in assuming that when debt is destroyed, that reduces the money supply. A simple thought experiment will show why this is untrue: If you lend me money and I can't repay you, the debt may be wiped out, but the money went wherever I spent it. It's still in circulation. Destroying the debt does not destroy the money.

It is true that when banks go under and cannot pay their debts, that debt is wiped out and it does reduce the money supply. But the reduction in the money supply by failing banks now or even later in the Aftershock, will certainly not reduce the money supply enough to offset the massive increase in the money supply due to massive money printing.

Wrong Deflation Argument #4: Available Credit Is Declining

A similar argument is that, when we talk about the increase in the money supply, we're not considering that credit effectively functions as money. So if the amount of credit goes down in a struggling economy, the money supply is effectively decreased, too. But decreasing credit doesn't cancel out any money already in the system—it just slows the rate of new money being introduced in the economy, which doesn't matter much if the economy has already been flooded with money. Whenever a purchase is made using credit (say, when you buy a TV with your credit card), sooner or later it ends up in a bank account somewhere. Once it's in a deposit account, it makes no difference where it came from. It's in the economy for good.

Wrong Deflation Argument #5: The Fed Can Get Rid of the Extra Printed Money before Serious Inflation Kicks In

There are two reasons why this will not happen. The first problem with this solution is that the economy is showing no signs of growing under its own steam. (Remember, there is no "natural" growth rate; the bubbles have been the growth engine, and without the bubbles, not much growth happens). Pulling money out of a no-growth economy would just make the recession far worse not better, so that won't work. The second problem is that even if the economy did recover somehow, not only would a contraction of the money supply jeopardize those gains, but the only way the Fed can pull that money out of the economy is by selling $1 to $2 trillion worth of government bonds. Not exactly a winning scenario in an already precarious public debt situation. If they tried to do this

Why We Look at the Monetary Base Instead of M_1 and M_2

When we talk about how money printing by the Federal Reserve is increasing the U.S. money supply, we are talking about the *U.S. monetary base*, not M_1 or M_2. That is because M_1 and M_2 are both impacted by market behavior, while the monetary base is not. The monetary base is the Federal Reserve's balance sheet. It includes the government's money holdings plus those of a few big banks. M_1 is all currency and demand deposits. M_2 is currency, demand deposits, and savings deposits. Because it is possible to have a rise in the monetary base while also having a decline in M_1 or M_2 due to other factors, such as market behavior, the size and growth of the *monetary base* is a more accurate predictor of potential future inflation.

by selling the bonds, interest rates would rise. Higher interest rates would have a negative impact on stocks, bonds, real estate, and other assets, which would hurt the economy. So the Fed won't pull the money out to spare us inflation later.

Not Only Will There Be No Contraction of the Money Supply, We Foresee a Lot More Money Printing Ahead

As the economy continues to struggle and markets fall, the Fed will do even *more* money printing, and this will result in even *more* inflation than anyone would expect. The Fed will do even more money printing in the future in order to cover the costs of . . .

- *Market stabilization.* Like the first rounds of quantitative easing that began in 2009, the next rounds will largely come from a need to prop up declining markets and a fragile banking system.
- *Stabilizing foreign currency markets.* The Fed can prop up the market and banking system only to a limited degree, especially as this goes on for a longer period of time. Foreign investors will still get nervous. Hence, the Fed will also need to print money to support the dollar in the foreign exchange markets.
- *Government spending deficit.* Long term, once the Aftershock hits, the Fed will have a very heavy burden of financing the government. We already fund about 40 percent of our spending with debt, and it will be much higher when the Aftershock occurs. The money to buy this debt will increasingly come from the Fed.

Keep in mind that this represents only the base money introduced by the Fed. Any loans created from these reserves will have a *multiplier effect* on that figure. So while we will not have inflation on the level of Zimbabwe or the Weimar Republic, we will certainly have very high inflation, and it will certainly have a very big impact on the future economy.

"I told you the Fed should have tightened."

This Debate Is Really Not About Inflation or Deflation, It's About Protecting the Status Quo with Denial

Because inflation will truly devastate the stock, bond, and real estate markets, people want to say it won't happen. If you own a stock, such as Bank of America, you desperately want to believe the problem is deflation, not inflation; otherwise, your investment is about to be wiped off the planet. For that reason, a lot of people want to believe we will have deflation, not inflation.

Maybe you believe it, too. If so, ask yourself this: If the Fed's buying massive amounts of government bonds with printed money doesn't create inflation, why don't we do more of it? Most economists agree that if we eliminated all taxes tomorrow, including corporate and Social Security taxes, while maintaining all federal government spending, that we would boost the economy right out of the current slump and into a period of enormous growth. All we have to do is borrow that money instead of taxing it. How do we borrow it? By selling bonds to the Federal Reserve. That's exactly what we did in the past with QE1 and QE2. With the Fed buying the bonds, it won't stress the bond markets. They just buy whatever it takes to fund the government each year. No more. No less.

Since the deflationists strongly assert that massive Federal Reserve purchases of government bonds (as they have done in the past few years with QE1 and QE2) won't create inflation, then what's the downside? We can just print all the money we want, whenever we want. We can quit paying taxes. In fact, why should anyone work at all? We can all just print money whenever we need it, just like the government. No taxes and lots of shopping would be a great boost to the economy, right?

But we all know in our gut that this is a fraud. We instinctively know that endless money printing is impossible and would eventually create problems. There really is no such thing as money from heaven, and having the Fed buy our government bonds with printed money is *not* money from heaven. It is the fuel for inflation.

Inflation doesn't start immediately, but that doesn't mean it doesn't happen. Inflation doesn't start at a high level, but that doesn't mean it won't get higher later. That's where we are today—we are far enough along that inflation has started, but it has not gotten to a high level yet. Ask anybody who's lived through an inflationary environment, and they will tell you that low inflation now is no protection from higher inflation later. Low inflation is simply the beginning of high inflation when you are printing massive amounts of money.

Let's also be clear that we have not had deflation in any way since the financial crisis. We have never had a negative Consumer Price Index (CPI), which would be a good indicator of deflation. We have always had a positive CPI. And most honest observers would say that the CPI significantly underestimates the true rate of inflation most consumers are facing.

The current denial of future inflation reminds us of the denial about the real estate bubble before it popped. In 2003, people believed that housing prices would keep going up at 10 percent per year for at least another decade, maybe longer. They were wrong, terribly wrong, but they admitted that only after the bubble popped. Until then, it was all perfectly reasonable and risk free, just like they say all this money printing is now. One of the proponents of believing that real estate was not in a bubble was then Federal

Reserve chairman Alan Greenspan (who famously said we had "just a bit of froth on the coasts"). Come to think of it, one of the proponents of the thinking that money printing won't cause future inflation is the current Federal Reserve chairman, Ben Bernanke. It seems that denying economic reality is one of the key job requirements for a Federal Reserve chairman. But denying reality won't change reality as much as Alan or Ben or many others would like to think. It helps people to justify bad investments, but it doesn't turn those bad investments into good investments. As much fun as it is in the short term, denial is not reality. Never was and never will be.

Why Don't More People See This?

Because they have so much to lose. The bubbles have brought us the greatest flow of easy money in our history. There is nothing better than easy money—it is *much* more fun than hard money; it's absolutely intoxicating.

The Internet bubble was a great example of how people can deny reality when there is so much easy money to be had. Even the most sophisticated investors—venture capitalists and investment bankers—fell victim to the siren song of easy money. Even today, how good is it when you can sell a firm, only a few years after starting it, and with no revenues and no profits, for $1 billion, as was the case when Instagram was sold to Facebook in March 2012. That's pretty good. John D. Rockefeller may have made a lot of money, but he never made so much money so fast as did Instagram.

Real estate has had similar tales. Seaside cottages purchased for $10,000 a few decades ago are now worth over $1 million. San Francisco, Boston, and New York have probably benefited the most from the combined real estate and stock bubbles. But there are lots of incredible tales of fast, big wealth in Los Angeles, Las Vegas, Phoenix, and Florida. The bubbles have been very, very good to us. Even if you weren't lucky enough to get a huge windfall and become a millionaire or billionaire from stocks or real estate, many people also benefited from businesses that prospered along with this enormous explosion of fast, enormous wealth.

Many of those people worked hard for their money, but they made a whole lot more money because of the bubbles than they would have otherwise. There was a lot of easy-money icing on top of the hard-money cake.

And finally, many, many more participated in the general increase of easy money in the form of a dartboard stock market that increased more than 1,000 percent no matter where you threw the darts at the stock page, or housing that doubled or tripled in value with little or no improvements.

It is good, very good. Admit it—easy money is a lot of fun. And, we might add, since it is a world bubble economy, there are lots of easy-money millionaires and billionaires around the world, and that has a big impact on Wall Street's thinking as well. They don't want to lose any easy money, whether it comes from the United States or some other country. Fast, big money from China, Russia, or the Middle East will do just fine to keep them happy. Right now in London, the best homes are selling for over $100 million, which is up from just a few million dollars several decades ago. And many are being bought by foreigners, not the Brits, with fast, big money, from Russia, the Middle East, and elsewhere.

Don't Expect Wall Street to Spotlight This Problem

How many Wall Street analysts or economists predicted the recent financial collapse or even the Internet collapse? They can't and won't see the next—and much bigger—one coming either.

Remember, these are the same firms that, in a period of low interest rates, low unemployment, and low inflation, basically went bankrupt during the financial crisis. In fact, almost *all* of the *best* and *biggest* investment banking firms would have failed without massive government assistance.

This *did not* happen in the Great Depression, despite record high unemployment and a devastated economy. Many firms survived the Depression without government bailouts. The reason for the incompetence today is that they have been blinded by easy money. They have more advanced degrees from top schools than in the past and the same basic genetic intelligence, but they are blinded by easy money.

So don't look to them to shine a spotlight on the problem— they are trying desperately to turn off the spotlight to save that easy money. Frankly, so are many of the rest of us who have stock and real estate investments. This willingness to overlook reality doesn't affect just the financially sophisticated, but the financially unsophisticated as well. We all want easy money.

People Who Want the Easy Money of the Past to Come Back Again Cannot Accept This Analysis

Those who keep hoping the easy money will return will say stocks and bonds have done well in the past 30 years and gold hasn't— and that is true!! Look at those charts at the start of this chapter. But, as we have said many times, *it is different this time*. We are in a bubble economy, and it will eventually pop. It's already started to pop in stocks and real estate, so the past 10 years are more indicative of their future performance than were the 20 years prior to that. Although the past 10 years have been good for bonds, that bubble is likely about to pop soon, too.

The bottom line is that the easy money is coming to an end and the cheerleaders on Wall Street and those outside the Street who cheer on the cheerleaders won't see this simply because they don't want to. Rather than face the decline and even demise of easy money, CW investors want to still believe in the magical powers of the mythical "natural growth rate" to bring us back to what we had before. The desire to hang on to CW investing, despite all evidence that it is no longer useful, is rooted in the basic human desire to avoid change and to believe in the past—especially when that past was so very, very good to us.

On some level, many CW investment experts know that something feels "different" this time, but they don't let themselves think about that too much and they don't radically change course. They may get very worked up over political debates about how the government is handling the economy, depending on which side they support, but they don't let themselves get too worked up about what will actually make a big difference in their future: their own willingness to see the bubbles and prepare for the pop.

Interestingly, when the bubbles do begin to fully burst, CW investors will instantly change their minds about "natural growth" and all the rest, and will completely understand that they need to get out of the popping bubbles as fast as they possibly can. There will be a stampede to sell, not buy, when the bubbles fall. If anyone really believed what they say they believe, wouldn't they want to stay in and buy up the so-called "bargains"? Some will do that, but most will not. At that point, most investors will be sellers, not buyers, and CW investing will be no more. Unfortunately, a whole lot of their money will have gone to Money Heaven. Until then, most CW investors just cannot let themselves see the falling bubble economy and the dangerous Aftershock ahead.

In Fairness to Current CW Investors

We have come down hard on conventional wisdom, but we do not want to be so hard on CW investors. To be fair, most CW investors simply do not know what else to do. There are not a lot of sensible alternative views of the markets and economy available, or wise advice as to what to do about it. If you have been a CW investor up to now, and most investors have been, then the first step is to allow yourself to consider the possibility that CW is not going to work for you forever. Most likely, you have already seen it fail you at least once, in 2008. That is just a small taste of what is to come.

If you are starting to think we may be onto something and you want to explore your options for changing your investment approach, please be prepared for your current CW financial advisers and others to shoot you down or at least not show too much interest in hearing about our macro view. Many CW advisers will go so far as to tell you to stop reading scary books because it's not good for you or your portfolio. Please remember that while these folks may know more than you about many investing details, only you can decide what overall big picture of the investment environment that you believe is correct. Your point of view is not trivial; it is essential to your investment decisions. Don't let others take the wheel. They are working for you, not the other way around.

In Fairness to the Cheerleaders

While we don't like CW cheerleaders because they are working to keep people in denial, we do understand why they do it. For financial analysts, they're just doing their job in being cheerleaders. That's what they are paid to do, whether they are stock and bond salespeople or the financial analysts who support them. There is a reason that financial analysts give a buy or a hold recommendation over 90 percent of the time. They are paid by and are supported by stock and bond salespeople. They are paid based on selling people stocks and bonds, not for pointing out the bubbles and telling you to go away. If they did that, they would be out of a job very quickly, and nobody wants to be out of a job, especially in this market.

But it is important for the rest of us to understand that financial analysts have that bias. We should not count on them to help us figure out what is really occurring or help us prepare for future protection. Never going to happen.

Cheerleading Money Managers Are Managing Other People's Money

Like financial analysts and stock and bond salesmen, many cheerleading money managers want to keep their jobs. And they don't keep their jobs by investing their money in money market funds. They need to invest their money in stocks—whether or not the risks are worth it. No one will hire a money manager just to invest in money market funds. Almost no one will hire a money manager just to invest in bonds. They have to invest in stocks to get the hope of a return to justify their high pay.

Even if the risks are far higher than the meager return from stocks justifies, it's absolutely critical that they invest in stocks to keep their jobs. There are certainly exceptions to this rule, but generally stocks are the stock-in-trade of money managers. When stocks are in a long-term bull market, being so focused on stocks is fine. But if they are in a bubble that is popping and turns into a long-term bear market, that's not so good.

Keep in mind that money managers are investing other people's money. Even if they lose money, as long as they are doing as well as other stock-oriented money managers, they will likely keep their jobs.

Of course, there are a minority of money managers who are not primarily salespeople. They are willing to manage money without a focus on stocks. This isn't easy, but in fairness to that group, we want to say that not all money managers are cheerleaders and salespeople. But an awful lot of them are.

An individual investor is very different from a money manager. An individual investor is investing his or her own money. His or her job is not dependent on investing in stocks. This is not "other people's money." If individual investors lose, they lose big—not just their bonuses at work but money that their families depend on.

Many CW advisers call individual investors "stupid money," and they call money managers "smart money." At this point we couldn't disagree more. The way we see it, they just have different goals. The people who play with other people's money are working to keep their jobs; the people who invest their own money are working to protect their assets. And the people who are investing their own money are voting with their feet. Even during the rebound of 2011 and early 2012, investors were moving their money out of stock mutual funds. The outflows since the 2008 crash have been enormous, despite the rebound, as Figure 3.7 shows.

Now you might say that means these people are being too cautious and the money managers are right. If the stock market bubble is rising, that is correct. But, if the stock market bubble is popping, reducing your stock market exposure is absolutely the right thing to do.

People who manage other people's money are biased to think the stock market bubble of the 1980s and 1990s will return. People

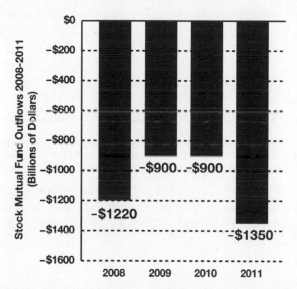

Figure 3.7   Outflows from Domestic Stock Mutual Funds Since 2008 Crash

Despite the big rebound in the stock market since the financial crisis of 2008, individual investors remain highly skeptical and have been pulling their money out of stock mutual funds every year since.

Source: Investment Company Institute.

who are risking their own money are more willing to see the reality that this market has not produced good returns for over a decade and the risks far outweigh the benefits. And they are reacting accordingly. It's not stupid money at all. It's people focused on protecting their own money rather than people playing with other people's money who are simply, and understandably, trying to keep their jobs.

However, We Give No Easy Pass to the Ostrich Economists

This is where our kid gloves come off. As we have often said, the financial crisis and the Aftershock represent a fundamental failure of the economics profession. Their job is not to be cheerleaders. Their job to create and support pathbreaking new methods of better understanding the economy.

But they don't, and, honestly, they don't even seem very interested. They aren't using their protected, tenured positions as university faculty as a base from which to attack the status quo and advocate uncomfortable but sensible alternatives. Rather, they desperately try to support their privileged station in life by supporting the status quo. Their attacks on the status quo are always muted, and their alternatives are often far less than reasonable. Printing more money and borrowing more money are not reasonable alternative policies in the long term.

It is the job of academics to question the status quo and offer reasonable and sensible alternatives. They don't always do that, but when academics are at their best, that is what they should do. In this task, academic economists have, for the most part, failed miserably. Of course, there are exceptions, but compared to financial analysts and money managers who have an obvious economic reason to support the status quo, there are far too few academics who are willing to seriously question and, most importantly, create good alternatives to the status quo economic policies.

How to Invest in a Falling Bubble Economy

This won't be a fun environment to invest in. Of course, it hasn't been that much fun for 10 years now. Maybe it's been fun for some investment bankers making big salaries, but for the rest of us, the past 10 years have been less than exciting.

Normally, in times of uncertainty or difficulty, Conventional Wisdom suggests that you add greater diversity to your portfolio. CW defines greater diversity as greater diversity across types of stocks, plus the addition of more bonds to create more safety. This was good advice in the past, when stocks and bonds were not in danger of significant long-term declines.

However, the correct view for investing in the future is to diversify by moving from endangered *asset classes* to safer asset classes. Stocks, bonds, and real estate are endangered asset classes and should be only short-term investments at this point. When to move out of those investments is tricky. Government intervention in the stock and bond markets through money printing and borrowing will work to maintain markets. Eventually, as we have said, these interventions will fail, especially as inflation grows beyond 5 percent. In the meantime, you can stay in if you really want to, but only with very careful and active management. Because of the massive amount of artificial stimulus keeping these markets going, there will be little underlying support for the markets once the stimulus fails. Hence, you need to be out before markets go down because when they do go down, they can go down very fast.

So the key to good timing will be to avoid trying to time it perfectly. Better to get out too early than too late. That means you need to begin diversifying early and continue to diversify as we get closer to the Aftershock. Of course, getting out early means you are guaranteed to leave some money on the table. But, again, better to be too early than too late. Don't try to time it perfectly.

How to Create a Proper "Dynamic Diversified Aftershock Portfolio"

To survive in an evolving economy, you must continue to diversify away from endangered asset classes to safer asset classes over time. Your portfolio isn't just diversified, it is diversifying—which means it is dynamic because it is actively changing over time. So the portfolio needs to be both dynamic and diversified, and hence the name Dynamic Diversified Aftershock Portfolio.

Again, you can hold stocks, bonds, and real estate for more time, but it is best to be reducing your exposure to those asset classes. In addition to outright sales of stocks and bonds, another way to reduce your exposure is to choose less vulnerable stocks and bonds. These are also known as defensive stocks and bonds. Defensive stocks tend to be in more boring companies that aren't as affected by the economy and sometimes produce good dividends. Electric utilities would be a good example of a defensive stock. The downside is that they won't go up as quickly as the market, like stock in Apple Computer, but they also don't go down as quickly either.

Defensive bonds are shorter term and have less credit risk. Short-term U.S. Treasurys would be a good example. Another example is Treasury inflation-protected securities (TIPS). These are Treasury bonds that adjust for inflation. Junk bonds have a great deal of credit risk, so they are not defensive. High-grade corporate bonds and municipal bonds are in between. The key for those bonds would be to keep them shorter term.

As you move out of these endangered asset classes, the key question is: What are the safer asset classes to move into? Unfortunately, due to the nature of investments over the next 10 years, there aren't a lot of long-term choices. This is further reason for active management. But even with active management, the number of options for many investors is more limited.

Very short-term debt or inflation-protected debt is clearly one of the options, especially as inflation goes higher. But, eventually, even government debt can get risky. Gold is an excellent option, but it will be highly volatile. Foreign currencies will also eventually do well but are hard for most investors to deal with. The same goes for agricultural commodities. Timing is hard, and they will be volatile. Shorting stock and bond markets will also work, but there is a great deal of risk in shorting and shouldn't be undertaken by most investors.

We will discuss the elements of the Dynamic Diversified Aftershock Portfolio in the rest of the book, including chapters on each of the key components. The key take-away point here is that *over time* your portfolio must move away from endangered asset classes, such as stocks and bonds, to safer asset classes, such as short-term debt and gold.

What if We Are Wrong and the Past 10 Years Were Like the 1970s and Maybe the Next Stock Boom Is Around the Corner?

That's actually a good question. Investors do tend to get more pessimistic when markets have been doing poorly, as they have in the past 10 years. The same sentiment occurred at the end of the 1970s.

Many investors thought that the market was entering a period of longer-term problems. None predicted an Aftershock-type situation, but few saw the enormous gains to be had in the 1980s and 1990s.

The difference is that we were just entering the stock, bond, and real estate bubbles at that point. There was also significant real growth in China and in Europe. Japan had troubles in the 1990s but was buoyed by the booming bubbles in the United States. All of these factors are not in existence going forward. Real growth in China will be hard to find once its massive construction bubble pops. Europe is already showing signs that its longer-term growth prospects are very limited. Japan is no longer growing off our bubbles since they are popping and will pop further. Real economic growth will be hard to find.

So maybe we could just find new bubbles to replace the old ones? Well, that is exactly what is happening. We are using the government debt and dollar bubbles to prop up the old bubbles. Will that last for another 20 years and keep the stock market moving up for another 20 years? The problem is that the government debt and dollar bubbles are best at maintaining old bubbles and not creating new ones. The reason is that if we powered up those bubbles to the point where they would create new bubbles, they would scare investors here and around the world. Tripling our money supply again and boosting our deficit to $3 trillion just to put the stock market into hyperdrive would quickly backfire because it would scare investors away.

So even if they won't take us back to the good old days of the 1980s and 1990s, maybe the government debt and dollar bubbles can at least help us keep our gains for another 20 years? If we only had a government debt bubble, it's possible we could keep it going for another 10 years or so. But, to help maintain the government debt bubble, we have had to create a dollar bubble. And that makes long-term viability an impossibility. If the government debt bubble could be maintained without money printing, then maybe we could make it another 10 years before it explodes in an Aftershock. Unfortunately, though, the money printing behind the dollar bubble has lit a fuse on the rest of the bubble economy, and that's why we can't keep maintaining the bubbles for another 20 years.

However, as we said before, it can maintain them for another two to four years. But that could be a very rocky road. Maintain doesn't mean a Dow of 12,000. The stock market could easily fall 30 percent or more while being maintained by the government debt and dollar bubbles.

Again, if we were willing to borrow a whole lot more and print a whole lot more, we could keep such declines from happening and even get the market growing rapidly again, but we won't. As we said, it could backfire pretty quickly. So even though government borrowing and printing will maintain the stock and bond bubbles, that doesn't mean they will be maintained at a high level.

Maybe we're not in a bubble at all? Maybe what we are seeing is real growth? If you still have your doubts about that, please go back and read Chapter 1.

What's a Savvy Aftershock Investor to Do?

Ideally, if you properly implement a good Aftershock investor strategy, your returns should look similar to the straight line in Figure 3.8. It should not look like the line that looks like a "W," which shows the stock market moving violently up and down. Of course, no one can hit a straight line, but that should be the goal.

Some people don't like that goal. They want to profit on every upswing and be protected from every drop. That is a lovely fantasy but not very achievable. You want to be the straight line, not the "W" line because you need to be prepared in case the downstroke

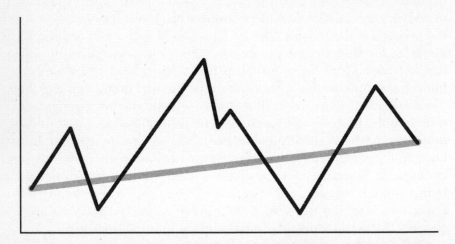

Figure 3.8 Ideal Aftershock Portfolio Performance in a Moderately Increasing, Volatile Stock Market

Shaded gray line is the performance of an Aftershock portfolio; the black line is stock market performance.

on the W doesn't rebound, which is what we think will eventually happen. So, right now, it's not so much a matter of beating stock market returns, although you may still do that; the more important short-term goal is to maintain your returns in a way that doesn't leave you exposed to the downstroke on the W.

Very high returns are probably not a smart goal right now because they carry too much risk and volatility. What you want is reasonable returns and limited exposure to what is potentially a big downside in the stock market and bond market. That's your biggest threat over the next five years. Maybe not this year and maybe not next year, but within the next five years, which is far more important for most investors, that's what you need to focus on.

It is almost impossible to perfectly time any market. But remember, even if you sell out early on stocks, you're not really losing out on future stock gains unless you would have sold at a later time when stocks are higher than when you sold. If you don't sell at the right time, you will have gained nothing because the stocks will come back down to levels where you sold earlier. So you have to sell at a higher level to lock in those gains, and almost nobody does that (otherwise, the market would fall dramatically). More important, if you get caught and don't sell before the stock bubble pops, stocks will go below today's level and you will take a significant loss over just selling today.

Again, the goal of the Aftershock investor is not perfect timing but reasonable returns with limited volatility and, most important, doing it without big exposure to a major downturn in stocks or bonds. It sounds simple, and it is. Implementing it is not so simple, but it is exactly what most investors need to do.

Even if there is no Aftershock as we think there will be, you still have to change your CW portfolio because this is a new investment environment and the old ways will no longer protect you. Our advice about what to do instead of the usual CW investing is contained in the rest of this book, with separate chapters on stocks, bonds, real estate, insurance, and more. The bottom line is, regardless of whether you believe we will have a full Aftershock, given the coming rising inflation and coming rising interest rates, if you have a conventional wisdom investment portfolio (and most people do), you essentially have two options:

Change It or Lose It

PART
II

AFTERSHOCK INVESTING

4

Taking Stock of Stocks

FACING THE FUTURE OF STOCKS, MUTUAL FUNDS, AND INDEX FUNDS

Over the course of half a century, the American investor has fallen deeply in love with stocks. Stocks occupy the heart of most investment portfolios and are at the heart of what has made so many Americans so much money over so many decades, especially in the 1980s and 1990s. And what's not to love? The stock market, as measured by the Dow Jones Industrial Average from 1980 to 2000, rose an astounding 1,000 percent. Not 100 percent, but *1,000 percent*. That's pretty darn good. It's especially good when you consider that the economy, as measured by gross domestic product (GDP), grew only 260 percent during that same time period. That's a whole lot less than 1,000 percent.

By contrast, in the prior period from 1928 to 1982, a time of huge growth of the U.S. economy, the Dow grew a more reasonable 300 percent in 54 years. And yet, in just 20 years during the 1980s and 1990s, the Dow shot up more than 1,000 percent. That is truly extraordinary!

It is also the quintessential definition of a bubble.

Like most bubbles, the stock bubble originally started to rise for good reasons. But as investors began to fall in love with the profits from stocks, those early gains just made them fall even deeper in love. And not just American investors were smitten; increasing numbers of foreign investors were joining the love-fest, as well. And not just individual investors. Big institutional investors who manage pensions, endowments, and life insurance funds fell in love, too.

But even love is not enough to keep a bubble going forever. Given enough time, economic gravity eventually kicks in and bubbles do pop. Knowing this is a bubble does not mean we have to exit it immediately because it is not going to pop today. But you must be aware that it is going to pop eventually, and if you choose to stay in this bubble a while longer, you will need to *actively manage* your portfolio.

There are big risks to staying in stocks and it's not clear exactly how much upside is left, although there could be some. Since 2000 there has been little upside (overall, the Dow has barely risen in the last decade) and there has been a huge amount of volatility. For Nasdaq stocks, the past decade has been even worse, with almost a loss of up to 50 percent. The short-term future is hard to predict, but if you time it right and get out before the stock bubble pops, you could also lock in some larger gains. Even if you decide to move entirely or heavily out of the stock market, or move to a more defensive stock position, you will still need to actively manage your portfolio to protect yourself and still make reasonable returns.

To understand our view of stocks and how to actively manage an investment portfolio containing stocks, you need to understand the Conventional Wisdom (CW) view of stocks. To understand the CW view of stocks, it's essential to understand the recent history of stocks. You don't need to know how stock markets were formed and other ancient history, but you do need to understand the more recent history upon which current conventional wisdom is based.

Love Story: How Stocks Became the Heart of Most Investment Portfolios

Stocks were not always the popular investment they have been for the past several decades. Before stocks became the darlings of the investment community, bonds had a more favored status. And before bonds, it was gold. As each asset class proved its reliability over time, it became more popular. Only when stocks began growing across the board for decades at a time did they become impossible to ignore for all but the most risk-averse investors.

Originally, stocks were primarily valued for the dividend payments that came with them. Rather than hoping to benefit from rising share prices, investors looked at stocks essentially as bonds with greater yields—payments could be variable, of course, but investors paid close attention to earnings and gravitated toward blue chip stocks with a consistent record of dividend payments.

It was only in the 1920s that many investors began to see the value in buying stocks with the intention of earning capital gains by selling them later at a higher price. At that point, the stock market became more speculative in nature and trading activity increased. This sent stock prices soaring. In a six-year span, the Dow Jones Industrial Average would quadruple in value, but it would take only a few days for everything to come crashing down in October 1929. Although it's worth noting that even after the crash ended the great speculation of the 1920s, it took several years for the stock market to fall during the Depression to its historic low point in 1932.

After the market crash and the Depression, stocks were naturally very unpopular. New Deal reforms, in particular the establishment of the Securities and Exchange Commission, sought to curb the unethical and manipulative behavior that had been rampant among publicly traded companies, and which had often left financially ruined stockholders in its wake. But it wasn't until the 1950s that stocks regained popularity among the general public. By the 1960s, the stock market was booming again, though that boom turned into a mini-bust in the next decade due to recession, and particularly high inflation (the natural enemy of the stock market).

What Is a Stock?

A stock is a certificate indicating that you own some small portion of a company. When you buy stock from a company, you are paying for part of everything owned by that company. If the company makes a profit in the future, the value of your stock goes up. As partial owners of the company, stockholders have the power to vote on decisions that may impact the future of the company. The more shares you own in a company, the more decision-making power you have.

Various types of stocks, mutual funds, and index funds are bought and sold on various stock markets around the world. Some readers may need or want more background on stocks, and some may not. So, in our attempt to keep the flow of the book moving, we have put some background material on stocks in the Appendix. Financial books can get a bit dull at times and we want to avoid that.

Irving Fisher: Stock Market Cheerleader of the Great Depression

Yes, stock market cheerleading didn't just start recently; it's been around for a while. It has simply gained an enormous number of practitioners recently with the massive boom in the stock market since the 1980s. One of the most memorable people to take up the cheerleading profession was Irving Fisher. The reason he's such an iconic figure is that he started with one of the earlier great stock market bubbles—in the 1920s. Of course, that was a mere pimple compared to our current bubble, but there are similarities.

The other characteristic that makes Irving so iconic is that he was not part of Wall Street. He didn't earn his money on the Street, and no one paid him to cheerlead. He was as pure a cheerleader as you can get. He actually believed it! And he had a lot of credibility. Irving was one of the most renowned economists from one of the most renowned universities in the nation: Yale.

He not only had good credentials. He actually did good economic work. He was one of the most outstanding and most respected economists of the time. His two books, *The Rate of Interest* and *The Theory of Interest,* both were important contributions to our current understanding of interest and capital.

However, Irving was not so great at predicting the Great Depression. In fact, he infamously said, just three days before the 1929 crash, *"Stock prices have reached what looks like a permanently high plateau."*

Of course, no one at the time thought that statement would later become infamous; they just thought Fisher was a very smart economist who made very smart observations that were right. That quote was reflective of a great deal of stock market cheerleading Mr. Fisher did in the late 1920s. We know now that his very smart observations turned out to be absolutely wrong, and he himself lost quite a bit of money because of it. Just getting popular support for your economic predictions doesn't make them *right*—it just makes them *comfortable.* The stock market collapsed and did not become fully vibrant again for decades and the economy sank into the Great Depression.

So Irving Fisher was one of those really smart economists with great credentials who everyone wanted to believe was right, who was not right. And he won't be the last incredibly smart economist or financial analyst with good credentials who is a market cheerleader. Irving Fisher serves as a wonderful cautionary tale to today's financial analysts and economists who keep cheerleading, but it is a cautionary tale that goes largely ignored today and will likely come back to haunt them later when they lose both their historical respect and their jobs.

As we mentioned earlier, for most of the past few decades, an investor could make money in the stock market just by throwing darts at a dartboard and watching his portfolio grow. And in today's era of 24-hour stock market analysis on TV and the Internet, there's a temptation to divorce stocks as a commodity from the companies whose ownership they represent.

When investors are willing to pay more for assets than their inherent value justifies—particularly if that investment is fueled by debt—we have an asset bubble. But how do we assign an accurate, nonbubble value to a stock? It really comes down to earnings. But how to translate earnings into share price can be tricky. We'll look at some of the traditional ways and then at the ways we think are more reflective of a company's value.

How Are Stocks Valued? It's All about Earnings

Earnings, fundamentally, are what you are buying when you buy a stock. You're usually not buying assets; you're buying all of the company's future earnings. Not just next year's earnings but *all* its future earnings—forever. But how do you put a value on something so long term and something so unknowable? Well, that's the trick. It is a bet you are making. You, of course, hope that bet is more than just a guess. At the very least, you want it to be an educated guess.

Before we can tell you about how we look at stocks, you have to understand the conventional wisdom approach to valuing stocks. Again, you have to know CW before you can understand any deviation.

Price-to-Earnings Ratio

One of the most commonly used methods to value earnings is to determine a price-to-earnings ratio (P/E ratio or just P/E). This is basically a measure of how many years' worth of earnings you are willing to pay for the company's stock. For example, a P/E of 10 to 1 (often shortened to just 10 by financial writers) means you are willing to pay 10 times the company's current annual earnings for the stock. So if the company's annual earnings (not revenues) are $10 million, the company is worth $100 million at a P/E of 10. If you want to calculate the price of a share of stock, you just use the earnings per share. So if the earnings per share is $10 and the P/E is 10, a share of stock is worth $100.

There is no magic rule as to how many years' worth of earnings investors should to pay for a stock. For S&P 500 stocks the P/E has varied from 8 in 1980 to 22 in 2000. Generally, P/Es are higher for companies with higher growth.

Although the ratio is simple, what goes into determining the correct ratio can be very complex. One of the key issues that has to be considered is the cost of capital. You're paying now for earnings coming later. Those earnings in the future are not worth as much as the same amount of cash now (the time value of money).

Also, there is uncertainty regarding those earnings. What if the company's earnings decline quite a bit in the next few years? What if it goes out of business? What if revenues grow but earnings decline? Lots of things can happen to a company's earnings over a period of 10 or 20 years. Hence, the more years' worth of earnings you are willing to pay, the greater your risk because the likelihood of bad things happening to a company's earnings are much greater over a 20-year period than a 10-year period.

Finally, what if the stock market values those earnings less in the next few years? Your company may have exactly the earnings you hoped for, but the market values them less and, hence, your stock is worth less.

Valuing uncertain future earnings in an uncertain stock market is a very tricky game. That's part of the reason why valuations can vary so much over time. There's no certainty in the calculations.

Most important, partly because of all this uncertainty, psychology plays a huge role. Some people may see fewer risks in a company's future than others. Some people may see fewer risks in the future economy than others. Who knows who's right and what the right P/E should be.

However, if the economy slows, expect P/Es to decline. Some of that decline may have been anticipated, but lately, stock market analysts have been none too good in predicting economic slowdowns. Hence, the P/Es fall only when the economy has proven to be in a slowdown. That also means that P/Es could fall a lot if the economy slows down a lot.

Of course, in a down economy not just P/Es are falling, but the actual earnings are often falling as well. This will cause further damage to a stock's price. In addition, earnings can fall substantially if interest rates rise substantially. These are two key vulnerabilities that the stock market faces in the future as we near the Aftershock. We will talk more about these issues later in the chapter.

It's easy to see how psychology can enter the stock valuation game. There's a lot of uncertainty and judgment that are a key part of valuing stocks. In addition, if bubble psychology enters the game, it often doesn't matter what the "correct" P/E should be. All that matters is that stocks have been going up in price and investors want to get on board that rising boat. Earnings valuation and analysis is needed only to make investors feel good about their decision to jump on the bubble boat.

To make matters even worse, earnings themselves are not always easy to define and therefore the correct P/E is not a certainty. Hence, different people look at the history of P/Es differently. Robert Shiller, the person who helped create the Case/Shiller Home Price Index and did great work in tracking real historical home prices, has also done a good job in tracking historical P/Es. His historical chart of P/Es is presented in Figure 4.1.

Many people will have different views of historical P/Es, just as they have different views of historical homes prices. However, we think Dr. Shiller has done the best job at giving us a good idea of what historical P/Es have been.

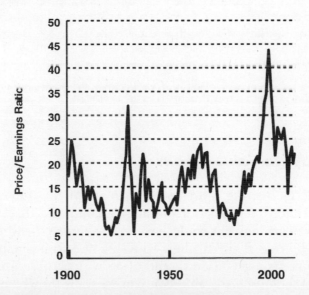

Figure 4.1   Historical Price-to-Earnings Ratios

Notice the high points were right before the crashes of 1929 and 2008.

Source: Robert Shiller, Yale University.

Discounted Cash Flow Models

When you buy a stock, you are buying the company's future earnings. The question analysts face is how to model that. One of the most commonly used methods to calculate the value of those earnings is a discounted cash flow (DCF) model (it actually uses the free cash flow instead of profits, but the concept is the same). Although this is a very simple model and high-powered financial analysts use more sophisticated models to calculate a company's value, it contains the key elements of many valuation models and serves to quickly illustrate what is involved in such a model.

Essentially, a DCF model attempts to capitalize all of a company's future earnings and thus calculate the current value of the company and its stock price. Of course, that's not as simple as just adding up the future earnings of the company. Those earnings have to be "discounted" to their current value. That discount is determined based on a number of factors, including the cost of capital, the uncertainty of the earnings, and the uncertainty of the stock market valuation. That discount rate is then applied to the company's future earnings.

However, since you can't add up the earnings of a company forever (how long is forever?), a typical DCF model only adds up the earnings for, say, five years in the future. To capture the "forever" part of the company's value, a "terminal value" is calculated. Much of the value of a company in a DCF model is in the terminal value. Needless to say, this model isn't perfect. What it does is try to put numbers behind all the intangible issues of uncertainty in earnings and in valuing the company's earnings forever. It also illustrates just how tricky it can be to calculate the correct value of a stock and how much is always left to the judgment of the financial analyst.

Other Ways to Value Stocks

Although P/Es are the most common method for valuing stocks, there are other methods for valuing a company that currently doesn't have earnings but could have in the future, or whose assets have value beyond their earnings (possibly due to mismanagement of the company's assets). We should also say that there are a multitude of methods used to value companies, some of which are proprietary and many of which are much more complex than those discussed in this book. What we are trying to give you is a basic overview of how stocks are valued, as a background to understand conventional wisdom and why it is wrong, not a course in equity valuation and analysis.

Price-to-revenue ratio. If a company doesn't have earnings due to mismanagement or an economic downturn, or for a variety of reasons the company's earnings are not a good measure of the company's future or potential health, a different measure of value could be used, which is the price-to-revenue ratio. In this valuation method the investor simply looks at the price of the stock relative to its revenues to determine its value. The clear risk in this analysis is that by ignoring earnings you could be getting yourself into an investment that ultimately doesn't pay off. Even very large companies and investors have made big mistakes relying on such analysis to make investments. It is also much easier to get a bubble valuation when you ignore earnings.

Book value or liquidation value. Sometimes a company mismanages its assets. Maybe it's an older retail chain that isn't very good at retailing anymore but owns a lot of good retail real estate. Maybe it's an oil company that is not well managed and is just riding on the earnings from oil and gas wells drilled many years ago. In this case, valuing the company at its liquidation value makes sense. A liquidation value is the value of the company's assets, not its earnings or revenues. This may help an investor see what may be the hidden value in a mismanaged company. A comparison of the company's stock price to its liquidation or "book value" is also one way to measure how the market views the quality of a company's management and its assets. Currently, many large banks are valued below book value, indicating that many investors think the bank is overvaluing its assets and is possibly managing what assets it has very poorly.

Private-company valuation. Private companies are usually valued at a significant discount to public companies. This is largely because they are less liquid (harder to sell) than public companies. You can sell a share of public company stock very easily. Not so with a private company. This is often referred to as the marketability or liquidity discount. However, today a big part of the reason that private companies are valued significantly less is that they are not participating in the public stock market bubble.

As a comparison to public companies, private-company valuations don't usually vary that much over time, unless they happen to be in a hot industry, such as social media. In fact, they usually trade for about 4 to 6 times earnings. That means that private buyers are willing to pay about 4 to 6 years of profits to buy a company. That actually makes sense given all the uncertainties in any company's future earnings. But notice how much lower that is than public company stocks, which often have valuations of 15 to 20 times annual earnings. A normal marketability discount might be 20 to 30 percent. But the actual discount for being private is much higher, which is a partial indication of a bubble stock market.

In addition, many private companies are bought with borrowed money based on paying back that loan from the company's earnings. Hence, many people buying a company don't want to buy a company that will take more than four to six years to pay off its loans. They don't plan to flip the company. They plan to make money from it, and they want to make money from it as soon as possible. This type of valuation makes a lot more fundamental sense than a bubble valuation. It is also similar to the leveraged buyout (LBO) valuation model used in Aftershock wisdom, which we will describe later in this chapter.

Benjamin Graham

No discussion about stock valuation would be complete without some mention of the bible of stock valuation, Benjamin Graham's classic book *Security Analysis*. Published in 1934, this landmark book on stock valuation is what Warren Buffett most often refers to when speaking about his own views on company valuation. Graham's book offers investors three guiding principles. First, always invest with a margin of safety by buying at a discount to a stock's "intrinsic value." That way, if the market value falls a bit, you are still ahead. Second, expect market volatility and find ways to profit from it. Options for doing this include dollar-cost averaging and diversification. And, third, know your investing style: actively involved and willing to research and learn on your own over time or more passively involved and in need of professional assistance and lower risk.

Conventional Wisdom on Stocks

The overriding mantra of the recent stock market CW cheerleader is that stocks are always poised for growth, while gold is at its peak and ready for a fall. Never mind that since 2000 exactly the opposite has been true. The goal of the stock market cheerleader is to *sell stocks,* not to do proper historical analysis. Of course, as we always say, CW faith in more growth ahead is grounded in history—at least the part of history they like best (i.e., the rising bubbles). CW says the future will be like the good past. Yes, the CW cheerleader would agree that the recent past has not been kind to stocks, but if you look farther back in history, the performance in stocks has been quite good. On this, the cheerleader is correct. Just like real estate, stocks have been a good buy over the long term, especially if we define the long term as since 1950. If we ignore the Great Depression and the long, slow recovery of the market during World War II, stocks look pretty good historically.

If you look at the Warren Buffett chart on stocks since 1965 that we presented in Chapter 3, it looks even better. So if the future is like the past, especially those golden years of 1980 to 2000, when the stock market was up over 1,000 percent, the future is pretty bright. It's also easier to overlook the past 10 years and assume that this is more like the 1970s—just a prelude to another stock market explosion of 1,000 percent or more.

CW Stock Cheerleading Is Based More on Salesmanship than Rigorous Analysis

However, none of this analysis looks at the fundamentals. In fact, it really isn't even analysis. It's just saying that the good part of the past will inevitably continue and the bad part will inevitably give way to the good part. As we said in Chapter 3, there are fundamental economic reasons why the future will be different from the past, especially the good parts of the past. Actually, if you go back over the past 200 years of financial and economic history, it's easy to see that big change is the real pattern of financial history—not just endless and enormous growth in the stock market as far as the eye can see.

That type of analysis is not analysis, it's just salesmanship. And even hard-nosed stock market analysts are primarily employed by firms that all started as stock and bond sales firms and which to this day are heavily driven by the sales of various stock- and bond-related securities. So it's no surprise that when the financial analysts employed by these firms are asked to rate stocks, they usually rate them as a buy or a hold. In fact, research on analysts' opinions shows that they rate stocks as buy or holds over 95 percent of the time, as indicated in Figure 4.2.

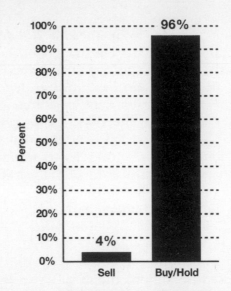

Figure 4.2   Stock Analysts' Buy/Sell Recommendations, November 2011

Very few analysts recommend selling stocks. Mostly they suggest buying or holding.

Source: Fact Set Research Systems.

This seems a whole lot less like analysis and a whole lot more like salesmanship. And that salesmanship mentality pervades Wall Street and the financial press. In one way or another, the livelihoods of all these people often depend, in one way or another, on good sales of stocks and bonds. We're not trying to be critical—it's just the truth. Everybody has to make money. But that means it's not the best environment for hard-nosed and objective analysis. Ask someone who knows and has tried to do objective analysis, like Mike Mayo, who recently wrote *Exile on Wall Street* (see sidebar on next page) about his work analyzing the banking industry. The financial press doesn't always like someone who challenges the prevailing CW on Wall Street and neither does Wall Street.

When Applying Valuation Methods Just Discussed, Analysts Make Key Assumptions

Many financial analysts would say in protest that they are doing proper analysis and not cheerleading. They are applying the valuation methods just discussed in one form or another and those methods, although improved, haven't fundamentally changed

Mike Mayo: The Courageous Stock Analyst

Mike Mayo is no stranger to controversy. A stock analyst for 25 years, Mayo has worked for some of the world's largest financial firms, including Deutsche Bank, Credit Suisse, and Lehman Brothers. His frank analysis has led to some shaky tenures and in some cases his departure. "Eventually, when I left [Lehman Brothers]," Mayo says, "I was literally escorted out of the office." In late 2011, he wrote a book detailing the fundamental problems with the financial industry, *Exile On Wall Street*.

In 1999, while working at Credit Suisse First Boston, Mayo made waves by writing a report advising the sale of all bank stocks, citing lowered standards for loan procedures across the board. The response was less than welcoming. He was skewered by the financial community and mocked on cable news programs. He recounts in his book: "One trader . . . printed out my photo and stuck it to her bulletin board with the word 'WANTED' scribbled over it."

Clearly, Mayo had touched a nerve, but his analysis was prescient. In 2007, Mayo was one of the few analysts who saw the impending crisis in the financial sector, predicting that the crisis could cost as much as $400 billion, "a number that was much higher than anyone else's estimate to that point though one that still turned out to be too low."

Mayo argues that the culture of the financial industry gives analysts, ratings agencies, and regulators little incentive to provide investors with honest assessments. "Less than 5 percent of stock ratings on Wall Street are a negative rating," says Mayo. "Any first-year business school student can tell you that not 95 percent of stocks are worth buying."

Today, Mayo continues to send ripples through the financial community. In May 2012, now working at CLSA, he downgraded his rating of JP Morgan Chase, widely considered the industry's sturdiest firm, to the industry's only negative rating. Just before this move, he downgraded Bank of America, and then later he issued a warning about Morgan Stanley's reputation after it mismanaged Facebook's IPO.

Clearly, Mike Mayo has never been afraid of calling it like it is, even at great personal risk. And for that we give him an ABE Award for Intellectual Courage.

during the stock market bubble. That's true, but as we pointed out in that discussion, assumptions of future economic conditions and company earnings are absolutely fundamental to that analysis. And the current analysis depends on two key assumptions, which we discussed in Chapter 3: (1) the assumption of a natural growth rate and (2) the assumption that we are not in a multibubble economy.

Stock analysts and cheerleaders naturally assume (almost unconsciously) that there is a natural economic growth rate. That means an economic growth rate that always goes up no matter what, and that means a stock market that always goes up. We discussed earlier why there is no such thing as a natural economic growth rate—there is simply no theoretical or historical basis for a natural growth rate in any country at any time. All economic growth is basically derived from productivity improvements, and those happen only when people make changes to improve their productivity. Even during periods of high-productivity growth, like the twentieth century, the growth rates can change dramatically because productivity improvements are not being made all the time. Just look at China over the past century or even the United States over the past century. It's hardly been one solid straight line of growth.

The second assumption is harder to refute since we are still living in a multibubble economy and it is very hard for people to see bubbles until they pop—especially people who don't want to see it. We made the case for the multibubble economy quite a while ago in *America's Bubble Economy* in 2006, but don't expect the cheerleaders to see it. It's simply not in their stock and bond salesmen's interest.

Why Conventional Wisdom Is Wrong

Aftershock wisdom is clearly different from conventional wisdom on stocks. It looks at some basics. As discussed in Chapter 3, GDP grew 260 percent between 1980 and 2006, yet the stock market grew over 1,000 percent. That just doesn't make economic sense. Big growth that is not firmly based on real fundamental economic drivers adds up to a bubble. Research by the eminent economist Milton Friedman showed that over a longer period of time, company earnings don't outpace growth in GDP. That's because any excess company earnings above economic growth are eliminated.

As we mentioned earlier, if you look at a longer-term historical perspective, the stock market grew 300 percent from 1928 to 1980—a period of more than 50 years of massive economic growth and population growth—whereas in just 20 short years, from 1980 to 2000, it grew more than *1,000 percent*. We think you will agree that Figure 4.3 even looks like a bubble. Why else would there be so much growth in the stock market so quickly, compared to the past? And, economic growth was stronger in the past, not weaker.

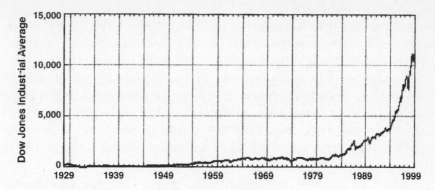

Figure 4.3 Growth of the Dow, 1928–1999

The stock market had modest but reasonable growth until the 1980s and 90s when growth just exploded.

Source: Bloomberg.

Also, it's not just the rocket rise of stocks, it's the whole rising multibubble U.S. economy and the rising multibubble world economy that makes an even greater case for calling this a stock market bubble. We discussed this in Chapter 1 and in more detail in *America's Bubble Economy* and *Aftershock*, Second Edition, so we won't go over it again here. Suffice it to say that Aftershock wisdom calls this a stock market bubble. And as you already know, bubbles eventually pop.

But if this is a bubble, how big is that bubble and how much of it is nonbubble? In other words, how much do stocks have to fall to be more properly valued? Another way to look at it is what is the correct way to value stocks?

The problem with the way CW currently values stocks (as described earlier in this chapter) is that all the CW valuations rely heavily on assumptions about the future economy, future earnings, future interest rates, and other variables that are highly subject to optimistic and bubble-infused interpretation.

So how can we get a valuation method that isn't so easily influenced by bubble-think?

Introducing the Leveraged Buyout Model of Stock Valuation

Aftershock wisdom gives us an effective and realistic method for valuing public companies on a nonbubble basis. We call this method the leveraged buyout model of valuation. It's not a perfect name because it conjures up an image of the outrageously overpriced LBOs that drove up the private-equity bubble of 2007. However, we still use it because it is technically correct.

Unlike the LBOs that drove up the private-equity bubble of 2007, which essentially relied on private-equity firms paying the highest possible price for a company fueled by incredibly stupid bank loans and then hopefully flipping it for an even crazier public price down the road, the LBO valuation model we are talking about is entirely different.

What we are talking about here is the leverage that would be used for purchasing a normal private company where a bank lends money for the purchase and that loan is paid back to the bank out of the company's earning over a period of several years. The assumption is that the entire price of the company is determined by *what a bank is willing to lend* to buy the company, assuming the bank is paid back entirely out of the company's earnings. In this model, there is *no* assumption that the bank loan will be paid off by the sale of the company. The loan can only be paid back to the bank *out of future company earnings*; therefore, the bank will lend only the amount that can be paid back in this way. That really limits the potential for false bubble valuation.

By definition, a company's LBO valuation will be a low valuation by today's standards. However, we believe this is correct now and later it will be the *only* valuation for any company in the Aftershock. This is the "how low it can go" valuation below which the stock market will not go. If the stock market values it for less, investors can then buy the company for the LBO valuation amount and make money by buying the company at a low price. They pay back the bank loans in a few years and keep any profits to be had after that time. In the Aftershock, the payback time banks will require will be very short, probably no more than two to three years, because the uncertainty of earnings is great enough that many banks won't want to take the risk of loaning more money than can be paid back easily in a short period of time.

For example, if the stock market values a company at $40 million dollars and its earnings are $20 million dollars a year, a bank (or other group of lenders) will likely be willing to make a loan of $40 million to buy the company under the assumption that it is quite likely it will recoup the $40 million in a short period of time (two years). Hence, the value of any public company has a floor, and that floor represents the *nonbubble* valuation of the company, which is the amount a lender will lend to purchase the company over a short period of about two to three years. Any value above that LBO valuation is a bubble value.

This method of valuation will produce very low valuations of companies, but they will be nonbubble valuations. This will be the model used once the Aftershock hits. It's also where potentially a lot of money will be made by those few investors who are still active enough to participate in the market. Needless to say, banks will want hefty equity on the part of the buyer for any of their loans, and when the Aftershock is at its worst, there will be very few loans of this type. The point is that in order to correctly value companies on a nonbubble basis, this method will be the only reliable way of accessing a companies worth. There has to be enough future earnings to pay off a loan in a reasonable amount of time, otherwise the loan is not justified—and neither is the company valuation.

Normal Valuation Methods Are Irrelevant, Only Bubble Valuation Matters

As discussed earlier, the normal valuation methods are highly subject to economic and financial assumptions that are changing and are about to change even more. What matters now is bubble-think and the ability of various economists and financial analysts to make people feel more comfortable believing that bubble valuations are real valuations.

Investor attitudes are key to stock market valuations today. However, investor attitudes can and will change. Bubble blindness, after all, is only a temporary condition. All bubble blindness has a cure: *time.* Over time, it becomes increasingly obvious that we really are in a multibubble worldwide economy and there is no "natural" economic growth rate to save us. Over time, it will also become increasingly obvious that the government cannot borrow enormous amounts of money that is enabled by enormous amounts of money printing without creating inflation.

Most important, bubble blindness is quickly cured by others who lose their blindness. If only 20 percent of the investing public loses their blindness, that is enough to pop the bubbles. As with all bubbles, only a few investors will get out the door before this bubble pops. Most investors will stay blind until the bubbles pop and their money suddenly goes to Money Heaven.

So, bubble blindness is always temporary. The only question is whether it is cured before the bubbles pop or it is cured when the bubbles pop.

Stocks Will Fail in Three Stages

Investors will not all run out and stay out of the stock market at the first signs of trouble. That's why the stock market will not fall all at once but will decline in stages, leading up to the Aftershock, before the biggest crash. Here is our best approximation of how that will happen.

Stage 1: The Recent Past and Now

During the global financial crisis of late 2008, stock markets around the world fell 40 percent and more. Since then, massive money printing by the Fed and massive borrowing by the U.S. government have been helping to boost and support the stock market. But the fact that stock investors are generally still trusting current stock valuations doesn't mean those valuations are worthy of that trust. Lots of things can temporarily sell at the "wrong" price for a while until investors figure it out. But at that point, investors' views of trustworthiness can change very quickly.

Stage 2: The Short-Term Future

Stocks will likely not fall dramatically in the immediate future, although investors are getting more skittish and the Dow could easily drop 100 to 200 points or more in a day, depending on the news. However, in the recent past, it seems that even very negative news does not always create as big a drop as one might expect. When stocks do fall, prices will not drop in a straight line. In the short term, each time stocks fall a bit, there are some investors who see bargains rather than a falling bubble, and they begin to buy those "bargains," which prevents a deeper fall. Also, there is some reason to question whether this market is occasionally manipulated to some extent.

As long as the Fed is able to continue massive money printing without significant inflation (yet) and as long as the government is able to continue its massive borrowing, the United States will continue to be viewed as a relative safe haven, especially compared to Europe, U.S. stocks still have appeal for both foreign and domestic investors. Remember, these people are in love with stocks, and it will take some time to give that up.

Stage 3: Medium-Term Future

Over time, as inflation and interest rates rise, the bloom of love will begin to wilt. Certainly, rising inflation and rising interest rates will not be good for companies or their stocks (or for any of the other bubbles). That's because massive stimulus is not the same thing as massive growth. And, increasingly, the stimulus will have less of an impact, over shorter and shorter periods. "Green shoots," if any, will turn brown faster and faster. Without a real recovery, there will be lots of stock market oscillations.

Stocks Just Before and During the Aftershock

Even if the Fed were to stop all money printing today (and they certainly will not), we have already increased the money supply threefold since March 2009. That is more than enough to give us plenty of future inflation and rising interest rates to damage the future economy and the stock market. High inflation and high interest rates are not going to occur overnight. It will happen over time. So the more time that goes by, the greater the risk to stocks.

However, time is not the only risk factor. There are a number of other potential triggers that could push things along sooner. Among these possibilities are further problems with the European debt crisis, an economic downturn in China, or a potential Israeli strike on Iran. These were discussed in more detail in Chapter 2.

Because so much of any bubble is driven by investor psychology (both on the way up and on the way down), bubbles can pop very, very quickly. Please see Chapter 11 for details about how the stock market may crash.

Before the Aftershock, the federal government can, and will, ease the pain of this for as long as it can with more money printing. But as we've said, eventually this medicine becomes a poison, and there will be little the Fed or anyone else can do without just making things worse. Right now, the Fed can put money into the system with very few short term consequences, as any potential inflation will lag at least by a couple of years behind money printing.

But once inflation gets going (in the 5 to 10 percent range), the lag time behind any new money printing will get shorter and shorter, and investors will become increasingly concerned. Once enough investors, particularly foreign investors who now own so

"A TEMPORARY SOLUTION WOULD BE TO WHITE OUT THIS PART OF THE CHART."

many dollar-denominated assets, begin to exit, the bubble will suddenly burst as more and more investors try to flee.

What's a Savvy Aftershock Investor to Do?

Clearly, being 100 percent out of all stocks *before* the Aftershock hits is essential. However, we are not there yet. That means there is still time before inflation moves up high enough and interest rates rise high enough to kick off the coming multibubble pop and the Aftershock that will follow. Before that occurs, some stocks will hold up better than others. So in the shorter term, it is still okay to own some stocks—as long as they are part of a *well-diversified, Aftershock-based, actively managed portfolio.*

As we say throughout this book, conventional wisdom will no longer protect you. So the first thing every stock investor must face is the fact that this is a bubble and it is going to pop. Once you have a firm grasp of that, the next logical questions are what to do about it and when.

The Case for Active Management

In a rising bubble economy or in a growing nonbubble economy, successful investing means picking stocks that are going up or about to, and then hanging on to those stocks until you are ready for some profit taking. However, that kind of buy-and-hold or set-it-and-forget-it investing, based on the old ways of valuing stocks, doesn't work too well in a falling bubble, even if that bubble's fall has been temporarily slowed and boosted by massive government stimulus. In a falling bubble or in a temporarily supported bubble that will fall again soon, that is not going to fly.

Instead, if you are going to own any stocks between now and the Aftershock, then your portfolio requires *active management*. The word *management* seems pretty straightforward. It means you have to make some good decisions and execute those decisions correctly. That is tricky enough. But it gets even more challenging because you also need "active" management, meaning you have to *keep* making correct decisions and keep executing those decisions correctly, again and again, as the economy and the investment environment evolve over time.

How to Temporarily Own Stocks in an Actively Managed Aftershock Portfolio

For the next year, stocks will be driven by more money printing. When the Fed prints more money, such as a QE3, stocks will go up. It might only require talk of more money printing to push the market up, but if there is no printing, just talk, it will go back down. Also, QE3 will only work for so long to keep up the market, just like QE1 and QE2. It is a temporary fix. Eventually, the QE money tree will have less impact on stock values because more people see it as just a temporary fix. That could easily happen as soon as a QE4—it may not work very well to boost stock prices. Hence, QE-driven stock prices will only last so long, and playing the QE trade by buying when QE is announced won't work as well in the future. The decreasing impact of money printing on the stock market will also ultimately lead to a long-term decline in stock prices.

So what about exiting stocks after QE3? Unfortunately, exiting stocks is a bit different from exiting bonds. Ideally, we wanted to do a chart, just like we did for bonds in Chapter 5, that broke stocks down into different categories and we would tell you what is a good time to exit each category. Unfortunately for stocks, there is an enormous level of correlation between all types of stocks.

Because of this high degree of correlation, it is likely that when stocks fall, they will all fall at the same time. Some stocks have a higher beta, meaning they will both rise faster and fall faster than average. These include financial stocks, high-technology stocks, and other stocks that are often placed in the "high-growth" category. But that does not in any way change the overall direction for all stocks just before and during the Aftershock. There will be no safe havens in the stock market when the stock bubble pops. There will be no "timed exits" where we can say hold on to these stocks for a while longer but sell these other stocks now. Yes, some will take less of a hit than others, but *all* will decline.

Our Current Recommendations

Currently, we recommend high-dividend stocks, such as electric utilities, as a temporary safe haven because they are defensive and pay good dividends, but when the market falls a lot, they will fall, too. They work best in a market that is moving upward at a slow rate but with high volatility, as has been the case in the past couple of years. Also, high-dividend stocks are becoming high priced because many investors are looking for their dividends and safety. Hence, there may not be a lot of upside left, and the good returns from high-dividend stocks are likely to fall.

Given what we now know about stocks and what's going to happen to them, it would be wise to keep up on economic conditions and especially watching for rising inflation. The Consumer Price Index can be followed on the web site for the Bureau of Labor Statistics at www.bls.gov. (You can also keep up with us at www.after shockpublishing.com, and even register for our Aftershock IRP newsletter.)

As we mentioned, we expect plenty of stock manipulation from the Fed to prop the markets up, and while this is bad news for the long term, it will be good for stocks in the short term. So keeping a portion of your portfolio in the stock market for the time being can be a good move. There's nothing wrong with riding a bubble while it's inflating (or reinflating), as long as you get out before it pops. But as we have said repeatedly, it's far better to be out of stocks too early rather than too late. If you are particularly risk-averse, don't worry too much about missing the last boost in the stock market before the crash. In the long run, you'll still be much better off than most.

A good way to move out of stocks is to move out a little bit at a time, selling off more and more each month and moving into gold and other safe investments as we approach the Aftershock in the next couple years. This way, you can benefit from temporary rises in the stock market without exposing yourself to too much risk. It's also a good strategy to stay diversified while the Aftershock is less imminent, allowing you to protect yourself more only as you become more convinced of the crash ahead.

In the meantime, stocks in safer sectors like health care and electric utilities will generally be a safer bet than stocks in the volatile financial or technology sectors. Also, choosing stocks that pay high dividends can mitigate potential drops, and it will be easier to pull out of these stocks before suffering big losses.

We mentioned before that selling short can be a risky practice. The big problem is timing. We know stock prices will fall, but we don't always know exactly when. This is one reason we like long-term equity anticipation securities (LEAPS), which can be used to short stocks over a period of up to two years. Timing is still sensitive here though. If we're still two to four years away from the Aftershock, it might be a little early right now to begin investing in LEAPS. This is an advanced type of investment and not for people with little knowledge of the market.

An easier option than shorting specific stocks or buying put options and LEAPS is to invest in inverse index exchange-traded funds (ETFs). There are ETFs that short various indices like the S&P 500, so when those indices fall, these funds rise. While timing is still sensitive here, inverse ETFs can be a good way to hedge stock positions in the meantime before pulling out completely. However, please be cautious with inverse ETFs that are double leveraged. These funds will drop a whole a lot whenever the market temporarily moves up.

The bottom line for stocks is that in the long run, they will all drop sharply in the Aftershock. In the shorter term, if you want to be in the market, you must limit your risks with active portfolio management, based on the correct macroeconomic view of what is occurring and what will happen next. (Please see Chapter 11 for more details about creating a diversified, actively managed Aftershock portfolio.)

5

Bye-Bye Bonds

WHY BONDS ARE GETTING RISKY
AND WHEN TO GET OUT

Why do investors buy bonds? To radically oversimplify, the main appeal of bonds is that they are not stocks. Investors buy bonds to preserve capital (also known as avoiding losing money on stocks) and to earn some fixed income (because you can't count on steady profits from stocks). If the stock market were a jackrabbit, full of excitement and profit potential, bonds would be your steadfast turtle—slow, reliable, and safe.

Financial advisers tell us to have a greater ratio of bonds to stocks as we get older. While a younger person's portfolio might be 30 to 40 percent bonds, older investors usually go for 60 percent or more bonds, especially as they near retirement. Because the profit potential for bonds is limited, there is a broad assumption that their risk potential is limited as well. Under normal conditions, this is usually true; bonds are generally less risky than stocks. But, as you know by this stage of the book, future conditions will be anything but normal. As inflation and interest rates significantly rise in the lead up to and during the Aftershock, our steadfast turtle will inevitably become investment road kill.

Conventional wisdom (CW) says stick with bonds; they were good to us before and they will remain good to us in the future. The new Aftershock investing wisdom says some bonds may be okay for now, but you better keep your eyes open and get ready to get out as the investment environment continues to evolve. Just as we explained in the previous chapter about stocks, it is not necessary to give up on bonds immediately. However, please do not fool yourself into thinking bonds will provide you with lasting safety. Just as with stocks, owning bonds requires *active portfolio management* based on a clear and correct macroeconomic view of what is occurring and will happen next.

The big problem that investors will face in the future, as inflation and interest rates rise, is that *both* the stock market and the bond market will become increasingly less attractive. So far, that has not generally been the case, and most conventional investors who look to recent history as their guide will not be prepared for what is ahead. That's why we keep telling you throughout this book that it's time to trade in your old conventional investing for a new Aftershock-aware, actively managed portfolio.

Remember: "Past performance does not predict future results."

What Are Bonds?

Basically, a bond is a loan. Bonds are fixed-income securities issued by private or public entities in exchange for your lending them money. But unlike a typical loan you might make to a friend or a bank might make to you, a bond can also be bought and sold for a profit or a loss on the bond market. This makes bonds more than a loan; a bond is a security that can be traded.

Based on the type of borrower, there are several types of bonds. The most common of these are:

- *United States Treasurys,* issued by the federal government. These come in many varieties, based on maturity dates (short, medium, or long term) and other features, such as inflation protection (Treasury inflation-protected securities or TIPS).
- *Municipal bonds,* issued by states and local government.
- *Corporate bonds,* issued by private companies.
- *Mortgage-backed securities,* issued by government-sponsored agencies, such as Fannie Mae (Federal National Mortgage Association), as well as by private corporations.
- *Savings bonds,* issued by the federal government.
- *Certificates of deposit,* issued by private financial institutions.

- *Money market funds,* a collection of short-term securities pooled together, issued by financial institutions.
- *Floating-rate notes,* change as an interest rate index changes. With some corporate bonds, the coupon changes, while with TIPS, the principal changes.

As we mentioned in the previous chapter on stocks, some of our readers may need or want more background on bonds and some may not. To keep the book from becoming too boring, we have put some additional background material on bonds in the Appendix. This chapter will focus on how bonds make money and how to avoid losing money on bonds as we approach the Aftershock.

How Do Bonds Make Money? "Total Return" Is the Key

Bonds earn money two ways:

1. Over time, the issuer of the bond pays the bondholder a set percentage of interest on the loan, called the *coupon.*
2. At any point, the bondholder may choose to sell the bond on the bond market for a potential profit, called *capital gain* (or *loss*).

Together, the net of the coupon (the interest rate) plus the capital gain (gain or loss) equals a bond's total return.

Total Return Component #1: The Coupon

When you buy a bond, you agree to lend the issuer a certain amount of money over a certain length of time. In return, the bond issuer agrees to make regular interest payments to you over the life of the loan until its maturity date. This is called the *coupon.* Interestingly, the interest payment to bondholders is called the *coupon* because, decades ago, bonds were issued on actual paper and interest was paid when investors literally clipped coupons off their paper bonds and took them to the bank to receive each interest payment. This inconvenient and risky procedure was eventually replaced by electronically issued bonds and interest payments, but the old name remains.

The amount of the coupon (fixed-interest rate) depends on a number of factors, such as:

- The current market interest rate at the time the bond was issued.
- The creditworthiness of the borrower—typically, higher-grade bonds have lower coupons than lower-grade bonds, which are considered riskier.
- The length of time until maturity—generally, the longer the maturity date, the higher the coupon.

Except in the case of floating-rate bonds, once the bond is issued, its coupon usually does not change over time, which is why bonds are called "fixed-income" investments.

Total Return Component #2: Capital Gains

Turn on the news or read the business section of any newspaper or financial web site, and you will hear a lot about stocks: What's up, what's down, and what might go up or down next. Bonds are hardly mentioned. Yet bonds make up a much larger market than stocks.

Bond prices change daily on the bond market depending on several factors, primarily changes in interest rates and any positive or negative news about the creditworthiness of the bond issuer. That means if you buy an already issued bond on the bond market, its value may be greater than it was at the time the bond was first issued. Depending on the market value at any given moment, you may have a potential capital gain or a potential capital loss. This new value of the bond changes the total return you will make on the bond. Why? Because total return is the sum of both the coupon and the capital gain (or loss).

How to Calculate Expected Total Return

Following are three common measures that combine the coupon and the current market price to help calculate the expected capital gain (or loss) at maturity.

- *Current yield.* Because the latest price of the bond on the bond market also matters to investors, the current yield is the bond's interest rate as a percentage of the current price of the bond on the bond market.

- *Yield to maturity.* This is the total potential income return of both price and coupon of the bond if it is held to its maturity date.
- *Tax-equivalent yield.* Only in the case of nontaxable municipal bonds, the interest earned on your bond is based on your tax bracket.

In addition to your regular coupon payments, bonds have another nice feature: The bond issuer agrees to repay the principal of the loan at its maturity date, which may range from just a few months to as much as 30 years or longer after the issue date. If you hold a bond until maturity, you get the full coupon. For example, if you purchase a 10-year bond for $1,000 with a 5 percent coupon, you would earn $50 per year (with payments of $25 made twice a year) for 10 years.

On top of earning its fixed-income payment, a bond has another nice feature: The bond issuer *guarantees* to pay back your principal in full. Not too many other investments offer such a reassuring promise. So, going back to the example of a 10-year bond of $1,000 with a 5 percent coupon, you would receive a total of $500 in fixed-income coupon payments ($50/year for 10 years), plus full repayment of your original $1,000 principal, for a total of $1,500!

But the story does not end there. In addition to the potential yield of the bond over time, based on its fixed-interest rate, there is also the option of earning a profit (or a loss) by selling your bond on the *bond market.* Here is where bonds get a bit trickier.

Your Bond's Total Return Is Always Changing

As mentioned before, a bond's total return is the sum of the capital gain and the coupon. Because bonds are traded on the bond market and their prices continuously change, the bond's effective or current yield also changes, regardless of its original coupon.

For example, if you buy a 10-year $1,000 bond with a 5 percent coupon for $1,200, you are no longer getting a 5 percent yield from it. You will still get the same fixed 5 percent coupon of $25 twice per year. But because you paid $1,200 for the bond, not $1,000, this coupon *effectively* represents a 4.2 percent annual yield. Therefore, its effective or current yield is 4.2 percent.

But wait a second. You also have to consider that when the bond matures, you will not get your $1,200 back. You will get $1,000, which was the original price of the bond. **That's a $200 capital loss to take into account, which is why it's a good idea to calculate a bond's *yield to maturity*.** Yield to maturity spreads the discount or premium paid for a bond across the length of time you own it.

For example, if you bought this 10-year $1,000 bond 2 years after it was issued, spreading that $200 loss over the time you own it gives you a yield to maturity of only 2.25 percent. You may be getting $25 every 6 months, but when the bond matures, you are effectively losing half of that yield (getting 2.1 percent instead of 5 percent) because of that $200 loss on the premium price. Of course, this is the case only if you paid a premium for the bond. If you paid a discount for the bond (meaning you paid less than $1,000 for a $1,000 bond), then the current yield and yield to maturity *add* to the value of your bond.

Your total return (the coupon plus the capital gain) is the *real value* of your bond at any given time, whether you sell it or not. It may be tempting to think that your fixed-rate bond is just plodding along, earning you a steady stream of income, and it is. But bonds are much more than their coupon value. Every minute that

What's a Better Bond Bet?

Which bond would you rather buy: a 10-year bond with a higher coupon selling at a premium or a lower-coupon bond that you can buy at a discount?

At first, it may seem as if the higher-coupon bond is a better investment because of its better interest rate. But that is not always the case. Sometimes a lower-coupon bond, bought at a discount, is your better choice. Why? Because the only thing that matters is the bond's *total return*, which is the sum of the coupon plus the capital gain. Paying a premium for a bond (because it has a higher coupon) is an expense that must be considered when determining the capital gain. So if the higher coupon is not enough to offset the cost of the premium during the time you own the bond, then the lower-coupon bond, which can be purchased at a discount, is actually the better deal.

the bond market is open, the total return value of your bond is changing. In addition, your options for putting your money into other investments are also changing. All these factors must be considered when you decide if owning bonds is in your best interest. If you look only at the bond's coupon interest rate, you are missing the bigger picture of the total return. And as we will see shortly, missing the bigger picture can lose you a lot of money very, very quickly.

Higher Risk, Higher Yields

Bonds may be less risky than stocks because, unlike stocks, they pay interest and also guarantee the return of principal, but they are not risk free. The level of perceived risk affects how much interest bond issuers are willing to pay when a bond is first issued. After a bond is issued, any changes in the level of risk will impact how much investors are willing to pay for that bond on the bond market. These risk factors include changes in interest rates, changes in creditworthiness, and the passage of time.

Interest Rate Risk

The bond market is ultra-sensitive to changes, even very small changes, in interest rates. Depending on current interest rates, bonds may trade at a premium or at a discount to their par or face value (i.e., the principal for which it was originally purchased and will be paid at maturity). If interest rates have gone up since a bond has been issued, the bond will trade at a discount to make up for the lower coupon payments, compared to the currently higher rates one can get on newly issued bonds. However, if interest rates have gone down since the bond was issued, that bond will trade at a premium because of its higher coupon, compared to current interest rates.

In general, the longer the bond has to maturity or the lower the coupon, the more price sensitivity that bond has to yield changes. The degree of this price sensitivity is measured in terms of something called *duration*. The greater a bond's duration, the more sensitive the price of the bond is to interest rate changes. For example, a bond with a duration of two will move 2 percent in price for every 1 percent change in yield. A bond with a duration of four will move

4 percent for every 1 percent in price change in yield, and so on. Clearly, when interest rates rise, the prices of bonds with the highest duration will fall the fastest.

As in all markets, what investors believe may happen in the future affects how they value or discount any asset. In the case of bonds, if investors foresee a decline in interest rates in the future, they will want to buy bonds now in order to sell them at a profit later. However, if investors believe that interest rates may rise in the future, they will not be too eager to buy lower interest rate bonds now unless they can get them cheaply. When interest rates rise more and more, demand for already existing bonds will decline more and more, and bond prices will fall more and more.

This is why investor beliefs about the future direction of interest rate changes make a difference in the current market value of bonds. Just as we discussed in the previous chapter on stocks, *investor psychology matters*.

Credit Risk

In addition to being ultra-sensitive to interest rate changes, bond values are also responsive to changes in perceived credit risk. As with any loan, higher perceived risk of the creditor comes with higher rewards to the lender (meaning higher interest rates), while lower perceived risk loans come with smaller rewards (lower interest rates). Thus, the safest bonds tend to have the lowest yields, and riskier bonds from the least creditworthy companies, or junk bonds, come with the highest yields.

Under normal conditions, credit risk typically does not radically change from the time a bond is issued until the time of its maturity, but that is not always the case. A once creditworthy bond issuer can become not so creditworthy over time. That is the credit risk. Even without a big change in creditworthiness, this risk does change somewhat over time.

If investors feel that the creditworthiness of the bond issuer has gone down since the bond was first issued—meaning the borrower has for some reason become less likely to pay the coupon or return the principal—then bondholders are more likely to want to get rid of these bonds, and their market prices will decline.

However, when investors feel confident in the bond issuer, they are willing to pay more for a bond that appears to be a lower risk than for a bond that seems to be at higher risk. Of course, the lower risk also means a lower coupon.

The degree of credit risk is not a permanent feature of a bond. Just like interest rates, creditworthiness changes over time and investor psychology plays an important role. Because the coupon is higher for the higher-risk bond, investors may want to take a bet on them, hoping the bond issuer's poor public image may improve down the road. When investors feel less confident about the future, they may feel less eager to own even currently high-rated bonds if investors become concerned about future credit risk.

Time Risk

All risk, including interest rate risk and credit risk, increases over time. The longer the maturity date, the greater the odds of either interest rates going up or the bond issuer's creditworthiness going down. So the greater the amount of time to maturity, the greater the risk, and therefore the higher the interest rate paid. By tying up your principal for a longer time, you are making a bigger sacrifice by not having your money available for other purposes (the time value of money), and you are taking on greater interest rate and credit risk. So, generally speaking, long-term bonds come with higher coupons than medium-term bonds, which come with higher coupons than short-term bonds.

But it doesn't always work that way, particularly if interest rates are expected to go down, not up. In that case, long-term bonds may come with lower coupons than short-term bonds. A long-term bond that does not come with a higher yield than a short-term bond can be a losing proposition for the bondholder unless you feel confident that interest rates will fall.

However, if interest rates rise—as we know they will when inflation increases—then long-term bonds are a very bad bet because the future interest rates will likely be much higher than what these long-term bonds currently pay, making the market value of the long-term bonds fall.

The Bond Ladder

One traditional way to protect yourself from fluctuating interest rates is by creating a *bond ladder*. This is done by buying a variety of bonds with staggered maturity dates, so that you have bonds maturing at least every year, with the longest bonds maturing at later dates. Bond ladders can be as short as 30 days to 6 months or as long as 30 days to 30 years. As you get some of your principal back each year, you can reassess the current financial circumstances and reinvest accordingly. If interest rates rise, you won't be hurt as badly as if you had all one kind of bond, and if interest rates fall, at least you will have some portion of your bond portfolio that will benefit.

This is a great plan—under normal conditions. But, as we keep saying, these are not normal conditions. We aren't saying you should abandon the bond ladder strategy entirely now, but please proceed with caution and take note of the caveats raised in this chapter, especially with longer-term bonds.

Investors Have Three Good Reasons to Feel Confident in Bonds

In general, investors have considered bonds to be among the safest of all investments. The reasons for this are rock solid:

1. *Bonds issued by private entities are backed by the assets of the bond issuer*, so even if they become less creditworthy or go into bankruptcy, as a creditor, you have the right to collect on this debt. Bonds are safer than stocks in this situation because bondholders get paid before shareholders.
2. *The bond issuer guarantees repayment of the principal.* No stock issuer can make that claim.
3. *Bonds issued by public entities are backed by state and federal governments*. These entities have the ability to raise taxes to make good on their payments.

Given these three very nice safety features, investors tend to think of many bonds as nearly risk free. However, nothing could be further from the truth in a falling bubble economy in which the government is massively printing money. As we will explain in more detail shortly, as inflation goes up and interest rates rise, bond values will quickly fall. While there is a bit of concern that interest rates cannot stay this low forever, in general, investors are not too concerned about rising interest rates or a big downturn for bonds. This is the key reason that so many individual and institutional investors who follow conventional wisdom on bonds will get hurt so badly in the coming Aftershock: *They aren't expecting it.* Any investor who is younger than 50 years old has been in a bull bond market their entire adult life. That's a large percentage of our investing community, and they will be very much taken by surprise. When inflation and interest rates rise significantly, long-term bonds—and *all bonds*—are going to take a terrible beating. Many large institutions are heavily invested in bonds, especially long-term bonds, and a significant chunk of their assets will go to Money Heaven.

Conventional Wisdom on Bonds: The Safety of the Recent Past Means We Can Count on More Safety Ahead

Almost all conventional wisdom–type thinking usually has a good historical basis. So to understand CW we need to look at recent history. Only by understanding CW can we understand the Aftershock view on bonds and why CW is wrong.

Like stocks, we don't need to go back to the beginning of the bond market; we just need to take a brief look at the more recent history of bonds because that's what CW focuses on. So, if we look back at the beginning of the modern bond market in the late 1800s and early 1900s, we see that bonds dominated the investment landscape. Stocks were not very important. As we discussed in the previous chapter, they were considered too risky, even for institutional pension funds. Eventually, as we moved into the 1960s, stocks became more acceptable, but bonds maintained their position as a much less risky and more stable alternative to stocks. Bonds were the way to reduce risk in a stock portfolio.

However, by the beginning of the 1980s, bonds had entered a new era. Three major changes were about to occur:

1. Interest rates were very high and about to start falling lower, heating up the bond market.

2. Looser government regulations made it possible for the banking sector to issue more bonds.
3. The government was starting to run large deficits and needed to issue enormous numbers of bonds. This was also part of an overall massive increase in consumer lending (often backed by bonds, such as mortgage bonds) and corporate borrowing. And it wasn't just a U.S. phenomenon—borrowing was rising all around the world. There was a worldwide massive increase in debt and exposure to debt.

The first factor, declining interest rates, made bonds a particularly good investment. Remember what we said earlier about the importance of looking at the total return of the bond, not just the interest rate. As interest rates fell, bonds were showing excellent capital gains. As you can see from Figure 5.1, this bond bull due to falling interest rates has continued to this day and will likely continue for a while longer in the future.

Of course, that's where the second big change in the 1980s gets more important. Since the 1980s, the amount of outstanding debt has exploded, as Figure 5.2 indicates. This is not just government

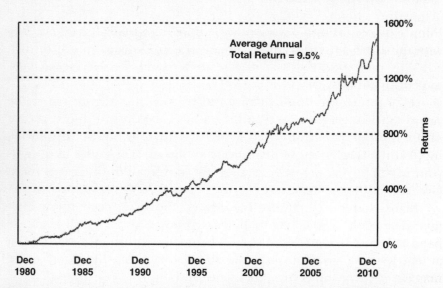

Figure 5.1   Falling Interest Rates Have Pumped Up Bond Prices Since 1980

Bonds have been a very good investment since 1980.

Source: Bloomberg and Bain Capital.

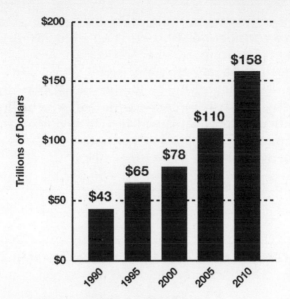

Figure 5.2   Bond Market Growth, 1990–2010
The size of the bond market has exploded since 1980.

debt but all debt, including corporate, mortgage, and consumer debt. When the bubble economy pops, this massive debt will be absolutely explosive. We saw a preview on a small scale of what's to come with the mortgage debt–fueled financial meltdown in 2008.

The mortgage meltdown was only a small preview because mortgage debt is only a small part of the world's overall debt. Also, the U.S. government, through its massive borrowing and money-printing powers, was able to step in and essentially take over much of the mortgage debt market. In Europe the same thing is happening, with a combination of increased borrowing and some money printing being used to stabilize the government debt situation for Greece, Spain, and Italy.

Many people think that because the government was able to take over the mortgage market, and governments in Europe have been able to keep the European debt situation from melting down, at least so far, that there isn't a much larger debt problem. But the massive debt problem is still there; it just can't be as easily seen. And if it can't be easily seen, you can bet that CW won't see it. The last thing CW wants to spot is problems.

What can be easily seen is that bonds have performed very well over the past few decades, and even before then they were certainly quite safe. Yes, there were some problems in 2008, but they were solved. Hence, bonds still seem safe and their investment performance has been amazing. So, needless to say, CW is very happy with bonds. History proves they are right. Right?

But what if the underlying conditions of the past change in the future? What if that massive increase in debt is actually undermining the ability of governments and people to pay off these bonds? Most important, what if the world's bubble economy pops and inflation and interest rates rise substantially?

With those questions in mind, let's look at the Aftershock view of what will happen to the bond market in the future. Needless to say, it isn't what CW sees now—or ever wants to see.

Why Conventional Wisdom on Bonds Is Wrong

Conventional wisdom on investing in bonds is wrong because it relies on two key assumptions that, unfortunately, are dead wrong:

1. The recent past is a good reason to trust the near future.
2. If all else fails, the federal government will somehow save us (as it did for the mortgage bond market).

Let's tackle each of these wrong assumptions one at a time.

Wrong Assumption #1: The Recent Past Is a Good Reason to Trust the Near Future

First of all, and most importantly, the future is not the past! It never was and it never will be. *Markets always evolve.* There is never a question of *if* a market will evolve; it is always only a question of *when*. The bond market has enjoyed an amazing run, beginning in the 1980s. As great as it has been, what justification or evidence do we have right now to believe that somehow that great run will never end? Right now, interest rates are ridiculously low. Is it reasonable from here to expect interest rates to fall even lower? Logic tells us that interest rates are far more likely to eventually rise than to fall even further.

You don't have to buy our macroeconomic point of view to see this eventually happening. As a general rule, interest rates tend to run about 2 to 3 percent above the inflation rate. That is certainly not the case today. Interest rates are very low, relative to inflation, and some interest rates have actually gone so low that they are now in negative territory. For example, as of this writing in June 2012, the Swiss two-year bond had a coupon of −0.5 percent. That means investors who buy this bond are not only willing to make no profit on the bond, they are also willing to lose money, just for the safety of "parking" capital in what they view as a safe haven.

With current interest rates so atypically low and even negative, the odds are that interest rates will eventually rise, or not fall much further, in the future. Right now, massive money printing is keeping interest rates low, but massive money printing cannot go on forever.

Why can't money printing go on forever? At the risk of driving you crazy from repeating ourselves in every chapter, it is because *massive money printing eventually causes massive inflation.* You simply cannot print money without end and avoid devaluing the dollar. If we could escape that basic truth, we could just keep printing without end and forget all our money problems forever. Can't do that.

Expanding the monetary base will cause rising inflation (for details, please see Chapter 3 and also see *Aftershock*, Second Edition), and rising inflation will cause rising high interest rates. Remember, you don't need too much of an increase in interest rates to get a *big drop in bonds.* Even a small increase pushes bond values down (see sidebar and Table 5.1). Therefore, a big rise in future inflation and interest rates will create a massive downside for bonds.

Wrong Assumption #2: If All Else Fails, the Federal Government Will Somehow Save Us

This will be true, right up until the minute it is no longer true. Certainly, the federal government will do all it can to protect bondholders, if for no other reason than as soon as it stops protecting bondholders, it can no longer issue any more bonds because no investors will be willing to buy those bonds.

But as we approach the coming Aftershock, the government will not be able to save the bond market. Why? Because . . .

Moderately Rising Interest Rates Equal Sharply Falling Bond Prices

Think U.S. Treasury bonds are a safe investment? Sure, the U.S. Treasury may not default on bonds in the next couple of years, but bonds can still lose a lot of value when inflation goes up and forces interest rates to rise. To give you some idea of how much a Treasury bond can lose with relatively small interest rate increases, we offer you the following example. Let's assume you just bought a 10-year Treasury bond that is earning 3 percent. If the interest rate rises from 3 percent to just 4 percent, your bond loses a whopping 12 percent of its value. Table 5.1 shows what happens if interest rates go even higher.

Table 5.1 Interest Rates Up, Bond Values Down

Interest rate	Lost bond value
5%	18% lost
6%	25% lost
7%	31% lost
10%	46% lost
15%	63% lost

The Final Two Bubbles in America's Multibubble Economy Will Pop

The dollar bubble and the government debt bubble will be the last of our six conjoined bubbles to burst. The first four (stocks, real estate, private debt, and discretionary spending) bubbles have already begun to fall, and they will all fully pop when the last two finally go.

To support the falling economy since the real estate bubble popped and the stock market crashed in late 2008, the government has been employing two powerful types of temporary stimuli: huge deficit spending (borrowing money) and massive money printing (which makes that huge borrowing possible by keeping interest rates low). This has worked in the short term. Without these types of stimulus, the stock market and economy would have crashed by now.

However, as we have pointed out again and again, the stimulus itself will soon add to, not cure, the problem. That's because huge deficit spending, while a temporary boost to the economy, adds to our already huge government debt bubble; and massive money printing, while a temporary boost to the stock market, will create rising future inflation (eventually popping the dollar bubble). And when inflation rises significantly, interest rates will rise. Also, the value of the dollar will fall—and so will the value of most dollar-denominated assets, as investors make a mad dash to get out of them.

Rising inflation and rising interest rates would be bad for any economy, but they are especially bad for a multibubble economy already in decline. High interest rates will be bad for stocks, bonds, real estate, and businesses. And high interest rates will be especially bad for the government debt bubble. That's because the government never actually pays back the principal of its debt, only the interest payments, and it makes these interest-only payments by borrowing more money. Therefore, each time interest rates rise, the government has to borrow again and again at the new, higher interest rate, adding exponentially to the debt.

As inflation and interest rates rise and the government debt spikes ever upward, investor psychology will turn increasingly negative. It is hard to believe now, but eventually investors won't want to buy any of our debt. At that point, we will continue to make our interest-only payments with more printed money, but soon that will not work either because more money printing will push inflation higher and higher and interest rates higher and higher, too. At some point, massive money printing will have to end and our interest-only payments will not be made, and the U.S. government will be in default on its debt.

As of this writing in June 2012, Standard & Poor's (S&P) rates the United States at AA+, while Fitch and Moody's still maintains its AAA credit rating for the United States. But that could change with the next big federal budget showdown. Also, inflation and interest rates are low. But later, when inflation and interest rates rise enough to force an end to massive money printing, and when the government can no longer make its interest payments on the debt, U.S. government bonds will drop to XXX credit score very quickly, just like the mortgage market crash, because investor psychology will change very quickly.

" THANK GOODNESS WE INVESTED IN LONG TERM BONDS. "

Why Aren't Bond Investors Worried About This Now?

Investors have some comforting reasons for not being too concerned about bonds (yet). First, as explained earlier, recent history has been very good for bonds. That is hard to ignore, especially when you want that good recent history to continue. In addition, investors draw comfort from the many nice safety features of bonds, such as the guaranteed return of the original principal, which other investments generally do not have. And, of course, bond investors draw deep comfort from their faith that the federal government can always print more money and buy more bonds, keeping the demand for bonds strong.

But even more than these reasons for their comfort with bonds, investors' unwavering confidence in bonds comes from an even deeper and more powerful source: The *psychology of denial.*

It is natural to want good things to last forever; that's just human nature. It is also human nature to not want to face certain facts that might threaten the current good status quo until those facts absolutely have to be faced. However, we actually often quietly know more than we want to openly face. We lie to ourselves, but to a certain extent we sort of already know that it is a lie.

In the case of bonds, most investors actually already know on some level the very thing that they don't want to face. Most of them know that quantitative easing (QE) causes inflation, that rising inflation causes rising interest rates, and that rising interest rates cause bonds to fall. Because they would rather not face these facts, they are highly motivated to believe that whatever the current level of money printing we are now doing is just the right amount. Like Goldilocks with her favorite bowl of porridge, the amount of QE is always "just right"—not too hot, not too cold, not too little, not too much. Each time more massive money printing occurs, CW investors and analysts declare it is just the right amount. No matter what is happening, it is all "doable," it is all just fine because *the government will not let us fail.*

Denial is what will keep the party going in the stock market and the bond market right up until the moment when the denial suddenly evaporates and everyone wants out. *That is how you know it is denial.* If investors don't already know on some level that things are not as wonderful as they seem, why is it so easy for them to change their minds on a moment's notice and head for the door? Clearly, deep down, investors are more skittish than they let on, even perhaps to themselves. But when the time comes, they generally don't take very long to figure out that they all want out. (This denial stage is the first of the six psychological stages of dealing with the coming Aftershock, described in more detail in our 2011 book *Aftershock*, Second Edition).

Bonds Will Fail in Three Stages

Investors will not all run out and stay out of the bond market at the first signs of trouble. That's why the bond market will not fall all at once, but will decline in stages leading up to the Aftershock, before the biggest crash. Here is our best approximation of how that will happen.

Bill Gross: King of Bonds

Bill Gross is the founder and co-chief investment officer of PIMCO, an investment firm based in Los Angeles (Newport Beach). He manages the largest bond fund in the world, the PIMCO Total Return Fund with over $1.4 *trillion* in assets. That's also the largest mutual fund or exchange-traded fund in the world. So, needless to say, when Bill Gross speaks about bonds, people listen. He can literally move the markets. Of course, since he has a vested interest in what he is saying, you have to keep in mind he may want to move the markets in whatever direction benefits him. But, even with that caveat, he is well worth listening to, as he one of the best of the big bond fund managers.

One pronouncement he made in the spring of 2011 was most interesting. He said he was moving out of U.S. Treasurys. That's a bold statement for a big bond manager. He said he thought the risks were increasing and it was time to move.

As it turned out, it was not time to move. His fund suffered and missed out on the big bond rally caused in part by the downgrade of U.S. bonds by S&P. Yes, the logic of the bond market is pretty screwy right now, but that's the way it is when so many people are increasingly afraid of stocks. His fundamental instincts about problems with Treasurys were right, but his timing was off. It serves as a good lesson about Aftershock investing. Even if you can see a bubble as clear as day, that doesn't mean it is immediately going to pop. It will pop, it just may not pop tomorrow or even next year.

Stage 1: The Recent Past and Now

As you may have noticed, during the global financial crisis of late 2008, while stock markets around the world were falling 40 percent and more, the bond markets remained generally unfazed. If anything, bonds benefited to a certain extent from the crisis because investors viewed bonds as a safe haven as they fled from stocks. This just provided more evidence to the CW cheerleaders that bonds are very low risk. But the fact that the bond market is currently trusting bonds, which is keeping interest rates low, doesn't mean bonds actually are worthy of that investor trust. Lots of things can temporarily sell at the "wrong" price until investors figure it out. At that point, investors' views of trustworthiness can change very quickly.

Stage 2: The Short-Term Future

As long as the United States is still viewed as a safe haven, especially compared to Europe, and as long as massive money printing by the Federal Reserve keeps working to keep interest rates low, bonds will do okay. But bonds will become increasingly vulnerable over time. Clearly, any future rise in interest rates will hurt bonds, so the big question is what will happen next for interest rates? How much lower can they go?

With U.S. interest rates already so low, it is hard to see them going much lower, although they could temporarily. Interest rates could even fall below zero, but that clearly would not be sustainable. (An interest rate below zero means that the bond holder is guaranteed to lose money over time. Even if investors were willing to put up with that for a while, they certainly don't want that over the longer term.)

It is much more likely that interest rates will rise, not fall, over time. In the short term (2012 and 2013), interest rates will not likely rise too dramatically. But remember, any rise in interest rates will have a negative impact on bond prices. Please go back and take another look at Table 5.1 if you need any further convincing about how fast bond values drop as interest rates rise. Even a small rise in interest rates will hurt bonds. The saving grace for bonds in the short term is that whenever stocks take a significant dip, investors typically like to move temporarily into bonds in a flight to safety. This will help keep up demand for bonds, even if interest rates start to creep up a bit.

Stage 3: The Medium-Term Future

As time goes on, interest rates will creep up even further. What will make interest rates rise further? Well, by now you know all too well what we are about to say: Massive money printing will lead to rising inflation, and rising inflation will eventually bring us rising interest rates. This is not something we can get out of by pretending it isn't there. Even if the Fed were to stop all money printing today (and they already said clearly that they will not), we have already increased the money supply threefold since March 2009. That is more than enough to give us plenty of future inflation and rising interest rates.

High inflation and high interest rates are not going to occur overnight. It will happen over time. The more time that goes by, the greater the risk to bonds. Rising interest rates will clearly make bonds fall more and more.

As money printing and other manipulations begin to backfire, inflation and interest rates will rise, and bond prices will decline much further. But not every bond will crash in value overnight. Bonds from weaker issuers—the ones with higher interest rates that some investors thought would pay off big—fail first, as those companies can no longer secure cheap debt to prop up their earnings and are forced to default.

Bonds Just Before and During the Aftershock

Leading up to and during the Aftershock, companies will be forced to liquidate, but with so many going on the market at the same time, they will have little value, and hordes of bondholders will line up for their many pieces of a very small pie.

Bankruptcies, decreased lending, and a mass exodus of foreign investment will lead to a collapse in the stock market, and suddenly even the most rock-solid companies will start to look like another Lehman Brothers. While a stock market holiday may be declared (see Chapter 11), there will be no need to declare a bond holiday. The bond market will effectively shut itself down.

The federal government can, and will, ease the pain of this for as long as it can with more money printing. But as we've said, eventually this medicine becomes the poison, and there will be little the Fed or anyone else can do without just making things worse. Right now, the Fed can put money into the system with very few short-term consequences, as any potential inflation will lag at least by a couple of years behind QE. But once inflation gets going (in the 5 to 10 percent range), the lag time behind any new money printing will become shorter and shorter, until eventually the economy responds almost instantly to any additional money printing by the Fed by raising prices.

This is truly being stuck between a rock and a hard place for the federal government. With tax revenues dropping due to high unemployment and expenses skyrocketing due not just to inflation but to bailouts and covering guarantees on pensions, insurance, and other debt obligations, the government has no choice but to go deeper and deeper into debt. But with inflation at exorbitant levels, no one wants to put their money into Treasury debt without significantly higher interest rates. Traditionally, here is where the Treasury could turn to the Fed to print money and finance its debt, but with any increase in the money supply leading to near-instant inflation—not to mention terrifying investors everywhere—that "solution" becomes self-defeating.

Treasury debt can't be paid. Guarantees can't be covered. Expenditures are out of control. When the federal government can no longer borrow money, there's no longer any need to worry about its credit rating. They'll probably call it something like "repudiating payment," but make no mistake: This is where the most rock-solid of debtors, the U.S. government, goes into default. Not all government obligations will be repudiated, but it's likely that most outstanding bonds will cease to be paid. Cases of hardship will be given priority, but then that's not a position that most investors will want to be in.

In the Aftershock, the government safety nets for bonds of all kinds will fail because the government will not have the money to cover them. We will not be able to print money forever due to the rising inflation. Once we can no longer print money, the government will no longer be able to make its interest payments on the federal debt and the government debt bubble will pop. Needless to say, at that point, nearly all dollar-denominated bonds and other assets will crash.

What's a Savvy Aftershock Investor to Do?

Clearly, just as for stocks, being *100 percent out of all bonds* before the Aftershock hits is essential. If U.S. Treasurys are in trouble, no bond of any kind will be safe. However, remember that we are not there yet. That means there is still time before inflation moves up high enough and interest rates rise high enough to kick off the coming multibubble pop and the Aftershock that will follow. Before that occurs, some bonds will hold up better than others. So in the shorter term, it is still okay to own some bonds, *but only if they are part of a well-diversified, Aftershock-based, actively managed portfolio* that includes a variety of asset types, such as stocks, bonds, gold, foreign currencies, and more (see Chapter 11).

What, Me Worry? How Dangerous Are Your Bonds?

Many investors make the mistake of thinking that if interest rates go up, they can still get some benefit from holding on to their bonds because at least they are earning *some* interest on the bond, and earning *some* interest is better than no interest at all, even if they aren't getting the highest possible interest rate.

But there is much more to the story than that. The problem is not merely that you will earn a lower interest rate. The problem is that the *value* of your money tied up in the bond will be falling due to rising inflation. For example, if you are holding on to a 2 percent bond because you think that earning 2 percent is better than earning zero percent, and if inflation is 12 percent, then you are losing 10 percent per year. If inflation is 22 percent, you are losing 20 percent per year.

Even if you don't believe inflation will go that high, you are already losing money today because inflation is already more than the 2 percent you are getting on your bond. And if interest rates rise, as they likely will even if we don't have an Aftershock, your bond is only going to drop in value. So a low-percent bond is *not* better than no bond at all because if you have no bond at all, you have that money available to invest in something that keeps up with inflation—or, even better, earns you a profit.

Remember, as we have said in every chapter of this book, buy-and-hold investing is over. Completely over! If you stick with a conventional buy-and-hold portfolio, you will eventually experience *buy-and-lose*.

How to Temporarily Own Bonds in an Actively Managed Aftershock Portfolio

Let's start with what *not* to own. First, we know that weaker bonds will be the first to crash. This includes less creditworthy *corporate bonds, municipal bonds* that are not government insured, and *high-yield bonds*. Don't be lured in by their higher coupon rates. The very real risks are not worth the potential rewards.

The next big red flag is all *long-term bonds*, which are more sensitive to interest rate changes than short-term bonds. Interest rates

Don't Be Overly Impressed by Credit Ratings

While credit ratings can be a good measure of a bond issuer's credit-worthiness at the moment, these ratings are not necessarily good indicators of true future risk. That is because the ratings agencies generally are assuming the continuation of a stable economy and do not foresee any major changes ahead. They are not predicting significant future inflation and rising interest rates, let alone a world-wide, multibubble burst. Once that happens, credit ratings in general are not going to mean very much.

Keep in mind that credit ratings have really only been tested during relatively good and stable economic conditions. And the few occasions when hard times have hit, these ratings systems have not fared particularly well. Case in point: Standard & Poor's, Fitch, and Moody's all gave Lehman Brothers an A rating—right up until just before Lehman collapsed. So much for the value of credit ratings!

are probably already as low as they can realistically go. This is due to the artificial demand for bonds created by the huge number of government bonds purchased by the Fed in recent years via QE (money printing). Any increase in interest rates is going to hurt long-term bonds the most, so sticking with shorter-term bonds works to limit risk and can ease the pain when interest rates do rise.

So with these caveats, what does that leave us?

Generally speaking, we want to stick with the lowest-risk, government-backed, short-term bonds for the sake of capital preservation. The point here is not to chase high interest rates, but to maintain wealth in a well-diversified, actively managed portfolio between now and the Aftershock. In the short term, before the Aftershock, bonds to consider are:

1. Mortgage-backed securities
2. Short-term T-bills and Treasury notes
3. TIPS (Treasury inflation-protected securities)

Mortgage-Backed Securities

We said that real estate would be the first area hit and that many mortgages would go under. But remember that Ginnie Mae bonds

Which Is Better, Buying Individual Bonds or Bond Funds?

Whether you're in the market for newly issued or secondhand bonds, the most common way to purchase bonds is through a broker. Just like with stocks, you can use a full-service broker or discount broker, depending on how much help you need in choosing bonds. If you use a full-service broker, be sure that you understand how the commission is charged. It is often included in the price of the bond, meaning that you won't receive that part back when your principal is returned. You can also buy U.S. savings bonds from your local bank.

However, individual bonds are harder to sell. You will take a discount when you sell them. For some types of bonds, like smaller-entity municipal bonds, you may have to take a substantial discount of up to 5 percent or more to sell them. Hence, we recommend buying bonds using exchange-traded funds (ETFs) or mutual funds. ETFs and mutual funds are a convenient way to buy and sell bonds and are as liquid as buying and selling a stock. You will get the market value of the bonds whenever you sell, just like selling a bond, but with less of a discount because the ETF or mutual fund is more liquid. But, unlike a bond ETF or mutual fund, if you hold a bond to maturity and it doesn't default, you will get your entire principal back, but you will be paid with less valuable dollars depending on the level of inflation. Even if you hold to maturity, you're not getting paid more with a bond than with a bond fund, it's just that the true market value is hidden.

in particular are federally guaranteed, and while that guarantee won't mean much down the road in the Aftershock, it will be helpful before the federal government comes close to default. There will be plenty of warning signs in the meantime. So government-sponsored mortgage-backed securities can actually be a good option for capital preservation *in the short term.*

Short-Term T-bills and Treasury Notes

Again, these won't have the most attractive rates, but they are much more reliable than corporate or municipal bonds. While the Fed cannot print money forever, it can keep it up long enough to make these investments very safe from credit risk in the shorter term. They may still lose some value from inflation, but because these mature faster, than shorter term bonds, that helps to limit the negative impact. Also, because they roll over so frequently, you can repurchase them at the new higher interest rates.

TIPS

Should be among the most resilient bonds. Since the principal is indexed to the CPI, their value will go up as inflation rises, both in principal and in market value. Even if the yield is very low, these bonds can hold up very well and for significantly longer than other types of bonds. But even TIPS will eventually be a bad idea. Most important, the CPI may significantly understate the true rate of inflation, so you will be losing some purchasing power. Also, when the government eventually does default on its debt, adjustable-rate loans, such as TIPS, will be among the first to be repudiated. So it's important to keep an eye on the situation and get out of TIPS before it is too late. In other words, even TIPS require active investment management.

Timing Your Exits Out of Bonds before the Aftershock

Timing each stage of the demise of bonds is tricky and depends on many moving parts that are hard to predict in a book that will be published before many of these events will take place. We know what will happen but we don't know the exact moment that each new development will occur. In the short term, you can reasonably assume that getting the timing perfectly right is unlikely. That means you are either going to be a bit too early or a bit too late. Too early seems like a much better choice. Therefore, exiting all bonds sooner rather than later is not such a bad idea.

But if you are not ready to get out of all bonds yet, Table 5.2 summarizes our current thinking about bond risk, with a ranking of A, B, and C at each stage prior to the rapid crash of bonds to XXX at the start of the Aftershock.

Bonds in the Aftershock and Beyond

Most previously issued bonds will be essentially worthless in the Aftershock. Clearly, you will want to be out of *all bonds* before their

Table 5.2   When to Exit Bonds

Type of Bond	Stage 1 Now	Stage 2 Short-Term Future Best Guess: 2012–2013	Stage 3 Medium-Term Future Best Guess: 2014–2015
Short-term U.S. Treasurys	A	A	B
Medium-term U.S. Treasurys	A	B	C
Long-term U.S. Treasurys	B	C	C
TIPS	A	A	B
High-grade corporate bonds	B	B	C
High yield	C	C	C
Municipal bonds	B	B to C	C
CDs/money markets	A	A	B
Savings bonds	A	A	C
Mortgage-backed bonds	A	B	C

A = good, B = OK, C = more vulnerable

A, B, or C score crashes to XXX. Please don't let all your bond investment capital go to Money Heaven before then. Remember to keep your eyes open and stay alert as these vulnerable markets evolve. You can also follow our thinking in real time by visiting our web site at www.aftershockpublishing.com.

CHAPTER 6

Getting Real about Real Estate

When the U.S. real estate bubble began to burst in 2007 and 2008, a lot of people were taken by surprise. We were not among them. Our first book, *America's Bubble Economy*, warned in 2006 that home prices were rising too rapidly relative to incomes, and that of our six big fat, colinked bubbles, the real estate bubble would likely be the one to pop first.

At first, the conventional wisdom (CW) "experts" said it was nothing more than a subprime mortgage problem, but soon the subprime mortgage problems spread to non-subprime mortgages and then to real estate in general, as prices began to fall. No subprime mortgage problem could have done that if we didn't already have a big fat real estate bubble, vulnerable to a pop.

And even when that happened, the CW experts *still* told us not to worry; recovery, they promised, was imminent.

So far, that has not happened. Instead, the falling real estate bubble has been very painful. Disappearing equity has put many mortgages underwater. Shockingly, 15.7 million mortgages in May 2012 were underwater, according to Zillow. That is nearly one out of every three mortgages in the United States! The falling real estate bubble has also pulled the plug on the housing-bubble-driven consumer spending bubble, and kicked off the domino multi-bubble fall that led to the global financial crisis of late 2008 and is continuing to put downward pressure on the bubble economy.

While all real estate is unique to your particular location and situation, in general, home values have not returned to previous highs. Prices have recently stabilized or picked up slightly in some areas, while in other areas prices continue to fall.

It may be tempting to think that falling real estate prices have hit bottom, but unfortunately that isn't true. The primary reason that home prices have not dropped much lower yet is that massive money printing by the Fed and massive government borrowing are helping to keep the partially popped bubbles temporarily afloat. When this massive stimulus begins to cause serious inflation and rising interest rates, the bubbles, including the real estate bubble, will fall.

This is not a comforting thought for real estate owners, but avoiding reality will not help. If you own property of any kind, you have two choices: see the falling real estate bubble before it's too late to protect your equity; or see it later, after the value of your property falls further and there are far fewer willing and able potential buyers. We are not saying that you must sell now; we are saying that you must face reality now, so you can make your own wise decisions about what to do.

What Really Drives Real Estate Prices?

It's easy to think that real estate prices should always go up over time. But there are real fundamental economic drivers behind rising real estate prices, and without those fundamental drivers, the only way to push up prices is by inflating a bubble. What fundamental economic drivers moved real estate prices up in the past, and what changed to create an overblown real estate bubble?

Centuries ago, most people lived on farms, with more or less everything they needed within close proximity, even if a great deal of labor was required to keep it going. This arrangement changed dramatically in the nineteenth and twentieth centuries, with three fundamental economic drivers giving us a period of long, sustained growth in real estate prices that continued nearly uninterrupted for generations:

1. *Population growth.* As Will Rogers once said, "Buy land. They ain't making any more of the stuff." The amount of land on this Earth does not increase. So when population grows rapidly as it did in the nineteenth and twentieth centuries, it is a simple matter of supply and demand for real estate. Demand goes up, supply stays about the same, and therefore prices rise.

2. *Urban migration.* Increases in population and changes in the economy led to the growth of cities as people moved away from farms and competed for living space in relatively small areas. Again, the forces of supply and demand made real estate prices rise.

3. *Wage increases.* Technology and economic changes led to improvements in productivity, and massive productivity growth drove a corresponding growth in people's incomes, giving them more money to spend on their homes. That was more good news for real estate prices.

All three of these fundamental economic drivers contributed to each other and contributed tremendously to the rise of real estate prices over more than a century. Adding to this feedback loop was the increasing popularity of vacation homes. As cities became more and more congested, people sought refuge in quieter, far-away places. Vacation houses were cheap, but over time more and more people with more and more money were chasing the more desirable vacation spots, which of course just drove real estate prices up even more.

The Real Estate Bubble Rises

Beginning in the early 1970s, those three key factors of population growth, urban migration, and wage increases all started to slow down substantially after more than 100 years of high growth. Nonetheless, real estate prices continued to climb. The late 1970s and early 1980s were a time of relatively high inflation, so at first the price increases in real estate did not reflect much change in real value, just higher prices due to a cheapening dollar (inflation). It is important to also note that income growth—a strong fundamental driver of nonbubble real estate prices—did not rise much during this time. In fact, since the 1970s, real wage growth has been essentially flat for more than a generation. So the primary driver of rising real estate prices in the 1970s was inflation, certainly not income.

Then, in the early 1980s, things changed. As inflation declined, real estate prices began to take off due to something else: *low interest rates and a booming economy*. During the high inflation of the late 1970s and early 1980s, mortgage rates had been as high as 18 percent, so when interest rates fell, the cost of borrowing money decreased a lot. And not only real estate got a big shot in the arm from this. Lower interest rates and easy credit for consumers in the 1980s helped launch the beginnings of our rising multibubble economy, of which the real estate bubble was just one.

The beauty of all this cheap, easy credit was that lots of money was available to make all kinds of purchases, real estate included, with a lovely perk: Instead of spending one's *own* limited and hard-earned cash, home buyers and consumers got to play with the bank's money. And, my goodness, is other people's money a whole lot easier to spend!

Naturally, as more and more people bought homes and other properties, real estate prices went up and up. This created a bubble-inflating feedback loop: When home prices went up, people were then able to refinance their mortgages and pull out some of the increased equity in their homes—making it possible to go shopping for *even more stuff*, including more real estate, not to mention all sorts of other bubble economy goodies, from new cars to vacations to home improvement projects and more.

Cheap loans, easy credit, and rising real estate values became a wonderful win-win for the banks and consumers. Soon the banks and

"We sold our two-bedroom in the village at a great price and bought the Virgin Islands."

other lenders were aggressively seeking more and more mortgage buyers, especially mortgage refinancing, which began to grow rapidly. In fact, by the early 2000s, homeowners were routinely using their rising home equity like personal ATMs, withdrawing essentially "free" money that helped pump up the rest of rising bubble economy.

Without the low interest rates, the easy access to credit, and the overall rising bubble economy, real estate prices would not have risen much over the past three decades, because during that time we had nearly no growth in real wages (adjusted for inflation). It has been almost all pure bubble growth.

Conventional Wisdom about Real Estate: Continued Low Interest Rates for as Far as the Eye Can See

Conventional wisdom says that, despite the recent downturn, rising real estate prices are bound to return, even if that takes a while. And prior to its happening, home values will certainly not fall too much lower. The worst is behind us. It is just a matter of time before we get back on track to the assumed "natural growth" of real estate values—just like we've had for more than 100 years.

Conventional wisdom not only believes we will "get back on track" soon, they also believe that the main problem that caused the real estate drop and financial crisis in 2008 was a lot of subprime mortgages going bad, and that it was not due to any other problems.

Now that we have begun to solve those subprime-related problems, CW expects to see real estate gradually recover. They acknowledge that the economy faces some temporary headwinds that are keeping the real estate rebound from happening sooner. But, in time, demand will pick up and all will be well again, as the overall U.S. economy continues to recover.

One reason CW feels so very confident in this point of view is that they fully believe that *low interest rates will last forever*. Low interest rates are what helped make home buying so affordable, and low interest rates will continue forever, ensuring that real estate remains the fabulous investment that it has already proved itself to be for so many, many years.

CW sees no fatal future flaw in this logic—primarily because they desperately do not want to see it. They don't want to face the fact that future inflation is coming and interest rates will rise. They want to see low interest rates forever.

Over the long haul of time, real estate has been a great investment, not just for a few decades but for many generations. More recently, especially between 2001 and 2006, real estate profits had become enormous, morphing into a supercharged investment. Not only could you earn a cool 10 to 15 percent or more (in some cases even 25 percent) per year in increasing equity, you could *leverage* that investment with other people's money at super low interest rates.

It used to be that only the big players, like hedge funds and big real estate developers, had easy access to leverage, and they used it well to create massive profits. It was rare for average American consumers to get access to so much leverage, and now they, too, were using it to create huge returns. And, of course, the bigger real estate investors were using leverage, too. Why spend $100,000 to earn a 10 percent return equaling $10,000 when you can put down just $10,000, borrow the other $90,000, and earn 100 percent equaling $10,000. Wow, what a bonanza!

The profits from leveraged real estate investments were absolutely astronomical, and CW absolutely does not want that to ever end.

Why Conventional Wisdom about Real Estate Is Wrong

Conventional wisdom on real estate is wrong for the same reasons that CW is wrong about all the other falling bubbles—*it's a bubble!* As explained earlier, the growth of real estate prices since 1980 was no longer driven by fundamental economic drivers but instead by low interest rates, easy access to credit, and the rest of the rising bubble economy. Bubble prices don't last forever because bubbles eventually pop.

Let's go a little deeper now, to dissect the CW myth of "always rising" real estate values.

First, the idea that real estate prices always grow is just plain historically wrong. In fact, we have had many periods of slow growth, no growth, and even negative growth in real estate prices. For example, from 1930 to 1950, the growth of land prices was a dismal *negative* 3.27 percent. Then, from 1960 to 1970, we had a modest

The Myth of Limited Land

Population growth may be slowing down, but the U.S. population is still increasing. And if the amount of land is constant, some would argue that means land prices should always go up because demand for land (due to population growth) is rising while the supply of land remains the same.

This seems logical, but actually this logic is flawed. The issue is not the amount of land, but the *use of the land* that matters most, and land use is not a fixed quantity.

Two centuries ago, Thomas Robert Malthus predicted that population growth with a fixed supply of land would inevitably lead to starvation. We now know that he was wrong: After he said that, farms in Great Britain became much more productive, and improved sea travel made importing food much easier. Some might argue that technological developments like that are in the past, and we won't see anything like them again, but we'd say that's pretty short-sighted. It's not that hard to imagine us making better use of our land in the near future than we do now, and the result will mean lower land prices, not higher.

What the government does to limit or expand use of land has a big impact. For example, propping up the value of farmland, through farm subsidies and market protections, makes owning farmland more profitable and thus more valuable. The government can also place restrictions on land use to discourage new development, creating scarcity and thus raising prices for other land. The government can limit access to roads and schools, make permits difficult to acquire, or even offer tax advantages for undeveloped land.

Just as land can be limited in these ways, it can be made less limited by curbing or reversing these actions. Any time development is encouraged—highways are built to provide easy access, for example, or zoning restrictions are eased—the effect is to *lower* the price of real estate. Much like increasing productivity, the end result might be better in the long run, but government can stand in the way, at least temporarily.

growth rate of 1.76 percent. Even during the period from 1990 to 2000, land prices rose only 1.08 percent. So the whole idea of endless growth is just not borne out by the historical facts.

Second, the idea that real estate values always rise because population is always growing and land is limited enough to always drive up prices is also not correct (see the sidebar on the myth of limited land).

Finally, the striking contrast between the *lack of increase in incomes* (in inflation-adjusted dollars), compared to the dramatic rise in home prices during this time, confirms beyond anything else that real estate has been a *rising bubble*, not driven by real fundamentals. We would expect to see median home prices to rise with a corresponding rise in median incomes. However, if incomes are up 2 percent and real estate is up 80 percent, by definition you have a bubble.

Future Rising Interest Rates Will Pop What Is Left of the Real Estate Bubble

The biggest flaw with conventional wisdom on real estate is the idea that interest rates always will stay low, as they have for decades. Instead, we will have rising interest rates. Rising future inflation (due to massive money printing to support the falling bubbles) will drive interest rates up significantly, and without an endless supply of low interest rates, the whole CW argument—not to mention the bubble itself—falls apart.

As interest rates rise and mortgages become more expensive, we can kiss what is left of the falling real estate bubble goodbye. On the way up, this bubble was fueled by low interest rates and easy lending, allowing people to buy houses they would not be able to afford under normal conditions. But with higher mortgage rates, more money will go toward the buyer's interest payments, leaving less money available to pay for the property. When people cannot afford something, they buy less of it and prices go down.

Remember, at the same time that mortgage rates rise, employment will also fall further, so there will be fewer potential buyers. Fewer buyers means even more inventory for sale. Increasing supply and falling demand means falling home prices and a big real estate bubble pop.

How Can People Be So Blind?

We certainly do not blame people for believing that real estate prices should always generally go up. That is what most of us have seen, and it is an awfully nice idea to believe in. Aside from occasional dips due to recessions and one depression, home prices have generally risen, not only since most of us were born, but since our parents and even our grandparents and great grandparents were born. So we don't blame homeowners for having faith that real estate will eventually rise again and will generally keep rising forever.

But we do blame the so-called "experts" (investment analysts, economists, government officials, etc.) who should have known better. By looking at the facts rationally, it was not all that hard for us to describe the rising real estate bubble in our first book, written in 2005 and published in 2006. Nor was it so terribly hard for us to predict that the real estate bubble would be the first of our six big colinked bubbles to blow, putting downward pressure on the others. This took insight and analysis, but mostly it took a *willingness* to see it. Without a willingness to see it, the *correct* macroeconomic view is a lot harder to see.

The correct macroeconomic view is that real estate prices *do not* just go up automatically and endlessly without cause. There are real economic forces that push real estate prices up, and if those forces are absent and if real estate goes up anyway, then we have a rising bubble. But bubbles do not rise forever. Eventually, bubbles pop. It is as simple (and as painful) as that.

The popping real estate bubble is an excellent example of what all the other falling bubbles will look like when their time finally comes. At first, we maintain complete bubble blindness for as long as possible, until the rising bubble begins to level off and fall a bit. Then begins the excuse making, aimed at rationalizing what is assumed to be just a temporary downturn. Next, when things don't dramatically improve, there is more minimizing of the facts and more happy talk about the good old days soon returning. The denial-fest continues and the cheerleading carries on, right up until the moment of the final pop. At that point, it all seems so obvious and the "experts" pretend they have been expecting it all along.

It is only a distant memory now, but prior to 2007 rarely did the media even mention the term *real estate bubble*. Now, of course, it is a household phrase.

What's a Savvy Aftershock Investor to Do?

If you want to spare yourself any further losses from the falling real estate bubble, the first thing you must do is be willing to face facts, without influence by the CW cheerleaders who want you to believe we are on the verge of a lasting recovery. While falling prices may have stabilized or even risen a bit in your area, there is no credible reason to believe that there will be a big rebound to previous real estate values in the near future. Instead, prices will eventually fall even further. This bubble has not fully popped.

Between now and then, real estate owners have a choice: See the falling bubble before it's too late to protect what is left of your equity, or see it later, after everyone else sees it, too, leaving very few buyers to whom to sell your property. At that point, you will either have to sell at a significant loss or hold on to the property for many, many years.

Unlike stocks or bonds, real estate is more than just an investment; it is often an important part of our personal lives. We may live and raise our families in these properties, or perhaps our parents did. We may have built businesses under some of these roofs. So there is often more to making real estate decisions than just a consideration of finances. You may also need to think about sentimental value, school districts, distance to work, and a variety of other issues. In a book, we can't really help you much with that. However, we can help you analyze the future prospects for real estate and your current options. Our advice depends on the type of real estate you own:

- Your primary home
- Second homes and vacation properties
- Income-producing rental properties
- Commercial real estate
- Farmland

Your Primary Home—Keep It or Sell It?

Everyone has to live someplace. If you decide to keep your current home, be sure that you understand that you will not be able to sell it in the next 5 to 10 years without taking a big loss compared to what you could have sold it for earlier or today. Its price may remain stable or even go up a little in the next couple of years, but after that, the next big drop is coming.

Therefore, from this point forward, think of your mortgage payment as if it were rent because, just like rent, you are not going to get it back later. Even though paying a mortgage does have some advantages over paying rent, the basic point here is that you are *no longer building equity*; you are simply paying for a place to live. Therefore, ask yourself, "Is this someplace I would like to live for the next several years at my current mortgage payment, without building equity and without the ability to leave unless I take a big equity loss?" If your answer is yes, you might as well stay. If the answer is no, you will do better to sell now and find a rental so you will have the flexibility to move later if you wish, without a big equity loss.

But it's really not that simple, is it? You may have children in a school district you like or a good job nearby, and a suitable rental in your area may be hard to find. Maybe this house was your parents' home, or maybe you just love the place and want to spend the rest of your life there. We understand there are many good non-financial reasons for keeping your current home. (All three coauthors of this book own their homes and don't plan to sell, each for different reasons.)

But whether you decide to stay or to sell, here are some important points to keep in mind:

- *All mortgages should be fixed-rate loans, not adjustable rate.* As inflation rises, you will pay back fixed-rate loans with cheaper and cheaper dollars as the value of the dollar falls, while adjustable-rate loans will become increasingly more expensive. If you currently have an adjustable-rate mortgage that you don't intend to pay off in the next two years, now would be a good time to refinance to a low *fixed-rate* loan.
- *Don't make more than your minimum payment.* Inflation will allow you to pay off your loan later with cheaper dollars. Accelerating your payments means you are paying off your loan with more expensive dollars. No point in doing that.
- *Avoid an adjustable-rate home equity line of credit (HELOC) for more than short-term loans.* If your HELOC loan is at an adjustable rate, your payments will get increasingly larger as inflation and interest rates rise. If you have a fixed-rate HELOC loan, your monthly payments will remain the same. So if you have an adjustable-rate HELOC loan, either pay it off in the next couple of years or refinance it as soon as you can to a low fixed-rate loan.
- *Don't exaggerate the value of the mortgage interest tax benefit.* Since the amount of interest paid declines as you pay down your loan, the tax benefit also decreases over time. More important,

the gain of that tax benefit will be entirely erased by the loss of your home's value as real estate continues to fall, before and during the Aftershock.

- *Don't assume that a reverse mortgage is a good idea.* The equity in your house will decline as the real estate bubble falls further, so borrowing against your equity now and using it for living expenses over the next few years could leave you with a lien against a greatly reduced-value house. Even worse than the lien, your payments will likely stop because the company won't be able to keep them up when things go bad in the Aftershock. However, if you borrow money against your current equity and invest it well, you could come out ahead. The key is investing it well, not living on it.

Your Pool of Potential Buyers Is Not Infinite

It is easy to assume that whenever we want to sell something, there will always be a buyer. If you are considering selling your home or other real estate in the future, here's a new way to think about it. Your pool of potential buyers for your property is not infinite. At any given moment, there is only a finite number of people who might want to buy your property, and as the bubbles continue to fall, that pool of potential buyers will shrink.

While it is true that you only need to find one buyer to sell your property, the smaller your pool of potential buyers, the less likely you are to find that person. As time goes on, your pool will shrink each time someone figures out that this "recovery" is not real. Your pool shrinks when they can't get credit or they don't have the down payment. Your pool will shrink each time someone climbs out of the pool because they don't want to risk more price drops later. And, eventually, as inflation and interest rates go up, your pool will shrink each time someone gets kicked out of the pool by higher mortgage rates and stricter credit terms. The longer you wait to sell, the smaller your pool of potential buyers will become. Eventually, the only way to get someone to jump back into the pool is to drastically lower your asking price, which, if you need to sell, you will eventually do.

So if you are thinking of selling, you can either go fishing in your pool now, while it is still stocked with potential buyers, luring them in with a reasonable selling price, or you can wait too long to go fishing or not make the bait attractive enough, and never catch a buyer.

- *If you decide to sell, don't stubbornly hold out for your top price.* Lower your asking price sooner rather than later so you can find a willing and able buyer while there are more of them still around (see the sidebar on the following page). There is no panic now, and you can still hold off for a while if you wish, but selling sooner is better than waiting too long.

What if I Am "Underwater" in My Mortgage?

Depending on your circumstances, you may qualify for one of the new programs now available to help homeowners refinance if their mortgages are greater than their homes are currently worth, especially if you can't make your payments. The web site www.makinghomeaffordable .gov has information about government programs.

If you don't qualify for any government help and you are behind on your payments, you may be able to fight foreclosure and eviction on technical grounds. This could involve spending some money on legal services, but it may be worth doing because sometimes homeowners discover that their loan documents were not properly created or procedures were not properly followed by the lender, which makes it very difficult for a bank to foreclose.

Even without a technicality like that, it takes a lot of time for foreclosures to finalize. The national average is 674 days. In New York, the average time is 900 days, and in Florida, the average time period is now 1,000 days. Banks are not enthusiastic to foreclose because it forces them to try to sell the real estate and take a loss. So you may be able to negotiate with the bank to give you a new and better arrangement, perhaps making smaller, fixed payments over time.

Failing that, you may have to walk away from the property, but only when eviction is imminent. If you do that, the bank may be able to get a deficiency judgment against you, which varies from state to state. In a deficiency judgment, the lender can come after you for any losses they sustained in the foreclosure proceedings. Of course, this may not matter much if you don't have any assets to be seized. Not paying your mortgage will certainly damage your credit score, but during the Aftershock lots of previously creditworthy people will have poor credit scores, and there won't be much credit available anyway.

If fighting foreclosure or walking away is not for you, another option is to try to get the bank or lender to agree to a "short sale." It's called a short sale because the property is sold for less than the loan, and the lender forgives the difference. Banks won't always agree to this, but if they think the only other option is foreclosure, they may consider it the cheaper of the two losses. If you do a short sale, keep in mind that the amount of debt that has been forgiven is typically counted as *taxable income* when you file your federal and state tax returns.

Should I Keep Paying My Underwater Mortgage?

There are two schools of thought on this. Some people decide to stop making payments on an underwater mortgage and do one of the options described in the previous section so they can get away from their bad investment and stop throwing good money after bad. Others decide to stay in their homes and keep making their payments. If you can make your payments without hardship, and if you have a low, *fixed-rate* loan (or can get one), you will find that rising inflation over the next 5 to 10 years will eat away your mortgage payment. This assumes that your income will go up more or less with inflation, while your mortgage payment stays the same, making it relatively easy to pay off your home, despite its being underwater now. But remember, you may not be able to count on uninterrupted income for the life of your mortgage, so having a cash cushion is important. (Also, having a diversified Aftershock portfolio of other investments that keep pace with or outpace rising inflation is important, too.)

Won't Inflation Push Up the Price of My Real Estate?

Yes, inflation will make the *nominal price* in dollars rise. But high interest rates and the crashing real estate bubble will make the *real value* of homes (in inflation-adjusted dollars) go down. For example, it won't really matter if your home is worth twice as many dollars as it used to be if it costs four times as many dollars to buy groceries or fill up your car. Furthermore, when the real estate bubble fully pops, expect it to happen very quickly. Inflation may push up prices over time, but the crash could easily devastate the value of your real estate nearly overnight.

The Reality of Real Estate

The reality of real estate, if the Aftershock happens, is that you won't need to worry quite so much about the decision you make today. Many people will simply stop paying their mortgages because fore-closures will be slow and difficult to enforce. It already takes a long time today, and it will get much longer then. To the extent the bank moves to foreclose, it will likely be quite willing to simply work out a rental arrangement at a very low rental rate. They can't sell the house since there are few buyers and almost no mortgage money to be found with reasonable terms. The upside to all of this is that the cost of housing will be very low—and that will be an important plus in the Aftershock when money is tight. Like all real estate, there will be differ-ences depending on where you live, but the same large macroeco-nomic factors will affect all real estate and it will be surprising just how much effect it has, even on high-end real estate.

Is Now a Good Time to Buy?

In general, we say *stay away* from buying real estate now. This bub-ble is still popping and prices will only fall lower later. Don't let the cheerleaders talk you into seeing bargains where there really aren't any. Premature real estate "bargains" are the false mirages of the bubble blind.

However, there are two exceptions to our general Don't Buy rule:

- If you want or need to buy a primary residence (not invest-ment property), then this could be a good time to buy, while mortgage interest rates are still very low. But only do this if you are prepared to own the property for at least 10 years; otherwise, you will take a big hit later when you have to sell it at a loss or walk away. And, of course, take out only a *fixed-rate* loan, no adjustable-rate debt.
- In the rare case when you can buy a property at well below current market value and resell it quickly to a willing and able buyer for a profit, then this could be a good time to buy. The danger is that you will get stuck holding the property for too long, prices will drop again, and your potential profit will evaporate. If you never flipped a property before, now is not

the time to start your learning curve. If you are a seasoned flipper, it would be wise to tighten up your criteria for what you identify as a "good deal."

Second Homes and Vacation Properties

As we have already seen in the first phase of the real estate bubble pop, second homes and vacation properties lose value even faster than primary residences. They are a discretionary purchase that is not needed in the same way that one's primary home is needed. The market value of these less needed homes will be devastated in the Aftershock, and before then they will drop in stages as the other bubbles fall.

So unless you have strong sentimental or other reasons for keeping it, selling all second homes and vacation properties as soon as possible is a good idea. Don't wait for more evidence that the real estate market is not recovering. By then, the pool of potential buyers will be even smaller than it is now and you will likely have to sell for a lot less than you could sell for today.

In the shorter term, the value of some vacation properties in certain areas of the country may be somewhat protected, especially at the higher end of the market where some potential real estate buyers may be temporarily buoyed by the stock market bubble. In the longer term, however, all real estate will fall.

If you want to sell now but have been unable to get a buyer, lower your asking price if necessary to make the sale. Remember, if you don't lower your price now, you will only have to lower it even more later.

Please cheer up! There will be many wonderful second homes and vacation properties available for pennies on the dollar during the Aftershock—but only for those who were savvy enough to protect and grow their assets now so they have money available to buy those bargains later.

Income-Producing Rental Properties

Right now, it may seem like owning rental property is a good idea. In some areas of the country, demand for residential rentals has gone up as the real estate bubble has come down. More people are renting because they have lost their homes to foreclosure or have put off buying, either because they are waiting to see if real estate falls further or they cannot get a loan. In the short term, this higher demand for rentals has led to higher rents in some areas, and will likely continue for a while longer.

However, in the longer term, these higher rents will not last. Future rents will decline because . . .

- Rents always eventually track real estate values. As real estate falls further, rents will eventually fall, too.
- Later, as unemployment climbs, rents will fall because a growing number of renters will lose their jobs and will stop paying rent altogether. Renters are usually the first to get hit in a downturn. In the Aftershock, the courts will be too backed up for a quick eviction and your renters will simply squat in your property without paying anything, perhaps for years.
- When enough people are squatting without paying rent, those who do still pay rent will not be willing to pay too much.

If you are willing to own these properties after they no longer produce significant rental income, then there is no reason to worry about any of this. Maybe you will use it for other purposes by then (perhaps as future rent-free homes for your friends and relatives who didn't read our books).

But if you don't want to hold on to rental properties when they no longer bring you income, then you will at some point want to sell these while you still can.

It is hard to let go of income-producing real estate while the money is still coming in, especially if you count on that income. So it's understandable that you would want to put off selling for as long as possible. However, the longer you wait to sell, the harder it may be to find a buyer who is willing and able to pay your asking price. And if you wait too long to sell, you may not be able to find a buyer at all. Our ideas about timing your exit from income-producing real estate are offered later in this chapter.

Income-Producing Commercial Real Estate

As the bubbles fall, commercial real estate will decline for the same reasons that residential real estate will decline: rising supply (because more properties will be up for sale) and falling demand (because there will be fewer willing and able buyers). Right now and in the near-term future, commercial real estate values are not dropping significantly, if at all. Some have dropped a lot but have more recently rebounded. So now is the best time to sell, while there are still potential buyers who think we are on the verge of an economic recovery. As we keep saying, if you wait until there is a lot of proof that there is no recovery, there will be far fewer potential buyers.

In the long term, commercial real estate values will decline substantially in the Aftershock because unemployment will rise, consumer spending will drop, and demand for rental space will fall dramatically. Retail, wholesale, warehouse, and office space will simply not be needed at current levels.

We don't have to be 100 percent right about this for you to be 100 percent out of luck. Even a 20 percent drop in your occupancy rate could kill your profits.

We agree with conventional wisom that *medical* commercial real estate is different—but not that different. Medical commercial real estate will take longer to fall in value but will not be immune. Some medical practices will be more Aftershock-proof, but many will not, particularly discretionary practices, such as cosmetic surgery and medically supervised weight loss centers, as well as high-end boutique practices in general. Even basic medical and dental practices will sustain a big income loss and will seek lower-cost leases in order to stay in business. At first, you may see only a slight decline in medical real estate values, and then as the bubble economy falls further and pops, a faster exit of high-end medical practices and then other medical practices, as they can no longer pay their leases.

We also don't recommend that you count on government programs, such as "Section 8" housing payments, to hold up forever. Even if they continue, they will not keep pace with rising inflation, and in time your costs will outstrip your income on these rentals.

Farmland

There are two very separate types of farmland: income-producing farms and non-income-producing farms. Our advice depends greatly on which one of these you have.

For farmland that is non-income-producing, the value of the land will fall with the rest of the real estate bubble. Most family farms that are currently being used for residential homes and perhaps family recreation (hunting, fishing, etc.) should be considered as any residential property, rather than a "farm." If the farmland does not have a house or other usable structures, it is essentially raw land that will rapidly fall in value as the bubbles pop.

However, if you have farmland that is producing an income, either from crops or livestock, then you have more than just a piece of real estate; you have a business. In valuing that business, the general trend of falling land values is only one consideration. A larger consideration is the current and future business income, plus the value of the equipment the business may own.

As inflation rises, the price of agricultural commodities in the United States will increase as well, so if you own farmland that produces food, your gross income should rise with inflation—which is much better than most businesses will do as inflation rises. More importantly, as the dollar falls exports of agricultural goods will increase and real prices (adjusted for inflation) will rise. However, your expenses will also go up, at the same time that government agricultural financial support declines and credit becomes increasingly tight. With real estate values down, the selling of farmland will be mostly on a cash basis during the Aftershock, based almost entirely on the value of the agricultural business. For owners of farmland and those looking into it, the land value itself will be far less important than the value of the commodities produced on the land.

Timing Your Exits Out of Real Estate

Regardless of the type of real estate you may wish to sell, our general advice for exiting is the same:

Sooner Is Better than Later

Unlike stocks and bonds, you cannot unload real estate at the click of a mouse. It takes time to sell real estate, so you have to plan ahead. Remember that evaporating pool of potential buyers we described earlier. The longer you wait to sell, the more potential buyers will figure out that real estate prices are not going back up and are continuing to go down.

Also, the longer you wait to sell, the higher mortgage rates will rise, which will have a very negative impact on real estate prices (see Figure 6.1). As mortgage interest rates rise, buyers with a set monthly payment for real estate can only afford cheaper and cheaper purchases.

Now that you have read this chapter, you know that the combination of falling demand and rising mortgage rates will push real estate prices down dramatically in the longer term. However, in the shorter term, most people don't know this yet. Therefore, while the economy is still relatively strong, the sooner you begin the process of trying to sell your real estate, the more likely it is that you will be able to find a willing and able buyer.

If you already know that you want to sell your primary home or vacation home, put it up for sale as soon as you can. If you are still thinking about it, don't think about it for too long.

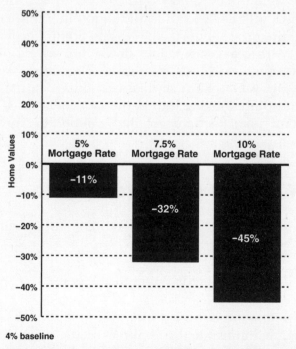

Figure 6.1   Home Values Decrease as Mortgage Interest Rates Rise

This chart assumes the current mortgage rate is 4 percent. An increase to 5 percent would force home prices down 11 percent to maintain the same monthly payment.

Source: Aftershock Publishing.

Help! My Property Isn't Selling!

We often hear people complain that they can't sell their homes or other real estate. Here are some potential solutions for upping the odds of attracting a buyer:

- *Engage a real estate agent who will do more than just take their commission.* Get recommendations from friends or from good customer reviews on the Internet for an agent who is willing to work hard to help sell your property. The right agent can make the difference between selling quickly or stalling out. If your home has been on the market for more than a few months, consider taking it off the market for a while and trying a new agent.
- *Make your property stand out from the pack.* You can distinguish your place from others for sale by offering something extra or unusual that gets you noticed. For example, throw in a flat-screen TV in the living room. Or offer to include a paid vacation, cruise, or one-year membership to the local pool or country club for the buyer and their family. For higher-end homes, we've seen sellers include a brand new car in the driveway or a six-pack of tickets to the Super Bowl. Don't laugh—sometimes this works.
- *The number one fix for a property that isn't selling: Lower your price.* Nobody likes to hear this but it works extremely well. Find out what similar places are selling for in your area and cut it by 5 to 10 percent. As time goes on, you will likely lower your price anyway, along with all the other sellers. By doing it before the other sellers, you increase your odds of finding a buyer before the other sellers.

Exiting Out of Income-Producing Real Estate Is Trickier

In an ideal world, you would naturally want to continue to collect your income for as long as you could and then sell your property later when it is no longer producing a profit. The problem with this plan is that by the time the property stops being profitable, the value of the property will have fallen significantly. So each month that you continue to earn income on your real estate, you are one month closer to the time when you cannot sell your property without taking a loss.

How do you time your exit out of something that brings ongoing income now but will fall in value later? On one hand, you want to wait as long as you can so you can keep getting that income; on the other hand, you want to sell before the price declines enough to wipe out the gain for that income. If we knew exactly how much the selling price would fall and we knew the rate of the fall over time, we could create a formula to figure out the golden moment when it makes the most sense to sell, in a way that will maximize both your income and your selling price.

Unfortunately, we don't have that level of precision when predicting the rate of decline of various real estate prices in each local area. So the first thing you must do when deciding when to exit your income-producing real estate is to come to grips with the fact that it is nearly impossible to time this perfectly. Therefore, you are either going to be a bit too early or a bit too late. No one wants to be way too early, but a bit too early is clearly better than a bit too late. The closer we get to the Aftershock, the faster real estate prices will fall. Given that we expect to see inflation and interest rates begin to rise significantly in the next couple of years, selling before that occurs would be ideal—or just as it begins to occur is okay too.

What about Investing in REITs?

A real estate investment trust (REIT) is essentially a holding company that invests in real estate, and investors can buy shares of a REIT just like a stock or mutual fund. Obviously, if we're advising against owning real estate, REITs would not be at the top of our list of safe investments. However, for savvy investors who want to put a small portion of their portfolio in REITs in the short term, there still may be some good opportunities for growth. However, the same caveat applies here as it does to any other real estate investment: It's better to get out too early than too late.

Once you make the decision to sell, don't make the mistake of holding out too long for a high price. If you can't get a buyer within a reasonable amount of time (a few months, not years), lower your asking price if necessary to make the sale. As we mentioned earlier, if you don't lower your price now, you will only have to lower it even more later.

The High Cost of Doing Nothing

Many people find that owning real estate makes them feel comfortable and safe. This is understandable. Owning your own home feels, well, like home. Change, especially when it involves leaving home or losing income, takes courage. Remember that good decision making helped you acquire the real estate you have today and good decision making will also help you create your future during this unusual time. If you choose not to sell your real estate now or soon, while you can get the most for it, that's perfectly fine as long as you are fully aware of what you are doing and its consequences. Over the next several years, your real estate equity is going to Money Heaven and it's not coming back.

Please also know that the biggest cost of hanging on to falling real estate is not just the loss of your current equity; it is the much bigger *opportunity costs* of losing wealth when you could have been protecting and growing your money elsewhere.

Staying Afloat in a Sinking Economy

It's one thing to read about the changing macro economy; it's another to actually *do* something about it. Most people will take no new actions until it's too late. For those who want to prepare for, not just react to the coming Aftershock, we offer the following services:

You are welcome to visit our website www.aftershockpublishing .com for more information as we approach the Aftershock. While you are there, you may sign up for a two-month free trial of our popular

Aftershock Investor's Resource Package (IRP), which includes our monthly newsletter, live conference calls, and more. Or you may reach us at **703-787-0139** or info@aftershockpublishing.com.

We also offer **Private Consulting** for individuals, businesses, and groups. Please contact coauthor Cindy Spitzer at **443-980-7367** for more information.

Through our investment management firm, **Absolute Investment Management**, we provide hands-on, Aftershock-focused asset management services on an individually managed account basis. For details, please call **703-774-3520** or e-mail absolute@aftershock publishing.com.

CHAPTER

Threats to the Safety Nets

THE FUTURE OF WHOLE LIFE INSURANCE
AND ANNUITIES

Why do people buy whole life insurance and annuities? Our faith in these products is so solid that the question seems almost silly. We buy them for protection, of course! If bonds are considered safer than stocks, then insurance and annuities are supposed to be even safer than bonds. The universal assumption is that, even in the rare event that the company goes under, these policies *always pay out*. These are the bedrock safety instruments that allow even the most anxious investors to sleep soundly at night. Like the old Prudential ad that calmly reassures us: you can always count on "The Rock."

Where did this "rock solid" mentality come from? Like most of our ideas about money and investing, it came from the past. Today, people don't worry too much about the safety of their money in banks, but before the Federal Deposit Insurance Corporation (FDIC) was established so that the government insured depositors' money, banks were not always so safe. If you lived in New York or Chicago, you might have access to some very reputable financial institutions. But if you lived in more remote parts of the country, the pickings were slim. If you had a nest egg to protect, keeping it under your mattress or burying gold in your backyard may have seemed like a better option than risking it at the bank.

Enter whole life insurance and annuities. These could be bought from a national company with a solid reputation. An annuity could provide investors with the income they needed for the remainder of their lives. And with whole life insurance, the policyholder had reliable savings that could be borrowed against when necessary, not to mention the protection for his or her heirs. For many people, this made whole life insurance and annuities more attractive options than a savings account at a potentially less reliable local bank. Why take a risk when you could own a piece of The Rock?

But this long history of comfort that people have derived from owning whole life insurance and annuities has kept most of us from thinking about the deeper and riskier realities of these policies. That is because . . .

All Insurance and Annuities Are Essentially Investments in Bonds, Stocks, Even Real Estate

When you pay your premiums to an insurance or annuity company, they are not just stashing that cash under a mattress; these companies are *investing* it. Therefore, whether you know it or not, *you* are investing it. When you buy an annuity, whole life insurance, or long-term care insurance, you are buying exposure to the investments that these companies own.

What do these companies invest in? For many years, they invested primarily in long-term corporate bonds. One of the main reasons that insurance and annuity companies have the reputation for being so very safe is that traditionally they invested almost exclusively in safe, highly rated bonds. By pooling the policies of their clients into what is called a general account, insurance companies typically invest in a highly diversified portfolio of bonds, providing protection against default and related risks in the bond market.

In the past few decades, insurance companies have also begun investing in some stocks, and more recently they have been providing permanent financing to commercial real estate development, and even to some large-scale residential real estate projects.

If you have a whole life insurance policy, it is easy to think of it like car insurance—something you can count on if an unfortunate event occurs. But, really, your whole life insurance policy is an investment, with bonds making up the biggest piece of your company's investment pie.

As a good example of this, we looked at the investment portfolio of Northwestern Mutual (see Figure 7.1). We chose Northwestern because it is such a highly rated and well-managed company. Interestingly, they invest in almost no government bonds due to their lower coupon rates. They prefer mostly long-term corporate bonds, which carry a higher risk and therefore offer higher yields, as can be seen in Figure 7.2.

Conventional Wisdom on Whole Life Insurance and Annuities: Perfectly Safe and Worth Every Penny!

Based on past performance, today's conventional wisdom tells us these policies are rock solid and safe. The top insurance companies in the United States have high ratings based on their historical reliability and creditworthiness. Many of these companies have been in business since before the Great Depression, and they have

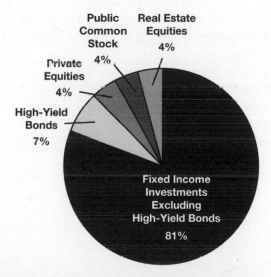

Figure 7.1 Northwestern Mutual Mostly Invests in Bonds

Bonds make up the lion's share of most insurance company investments.

Source: www.northwesternmutual.com.

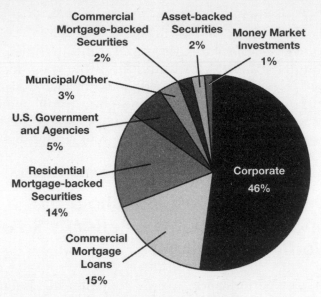

Figure 7.2   Northwestern Mutual's Bond Portfolio

Government bonds are only a small proportion of Northwestern Mutual's bond portfolio.

Source: www.northwesternmutual.com.

weathered every recession, every market fall, and every inflationary period along the way. This certainly inspires the full and long-term confidence of investors who want to hold on to their policies for 20 or 30 years or more.

The insurance industry's primary rating agency, A. M. Best, analyzes and grades insurance companies regarding their credit-worthiness, debt, overall financial strength, and other factors. Like a report card, they rate each insurance company from A++ for those considered the most superior, to F for those in liquidation (see Table 7.1).

As an additional way of spreading out and limiting risk, insurance companies may also use reinsurance. Many insurance companies also have very large reserves and are well capitalized, further adding to their strength. This type of strength is part of what A. M. Best is looking at when determining its insurance company ratings.

Adding to the overall sense of security, each state maintains a fund (funded primarily by an insurance policy premium tax) standing ready to cover insurance policyholders in the event that an individual insurance company happens to fail. And if necessary,

Table 7.1   A. M. Best Rating Scale for Overall Financial Strength

Secure	Vulnerable
A++, A+ (Superior)	B, B− (Fair)
A, A− (Excellent)	C++, C+ (Marginal)
B++, B+ (Good)	C, C− (Weak)
	D (Poor)
	E (Under Regulatory Supervision)
	F (In Liquidation)
	S (Suspended)

Source: www.ambest.com

even the federal government could potentially step in to bail out insurance companies, as it did with AIG.

All This Provides a Deep Sense of Safety, but Comfort Comes at a Premium Price

With the support of seemingly rock solid credit ratings and the potential for government backup if necessary, it is understandable that insurance and annuities provide a deep sense of safety. Not surprisingly, that comes at a price. Here is a brief description of these policies and the relatively higher premiums you must pay in order to feel safe.

Whole Life Insurance

There are two general types of life insurance: term and whole life. Term life insurance provides your beneficiary a set payout amount in the event of your death if it occurs within a limited "term" of time. When that time period is up, your term policy ends. If you want to buy another one at that point, the new term policy will likely be at a higher premium because of your greater age. And if you have also developed a medical problem since you bought the first policy, you may not be able to buy another policy or you may have to pay a much higher price.

In the case of whole life insurance, you are buying a combination of what you would get with a term life insurance policy except that, rather than terminating, it lasts your "whole" life. In addition, whole life insurance acts as a forced savings account. Whole life insurance gives some people the peace of mind that comes from feeling that they are guaranteed coverage for life, and it provides a tax-free death benefit to the beneficiaries. It also often provides for the payment of a certain amount of money later, under certain conditions or at specific times. Most policies also usually allow loans to be made against the policy. A third type of insurance, called universal life, is a hybrid of both term and whole life.

Whole life insurance policies (and to a lesser extent, universal life) are significantly more expensive than term life insurance. You are paying for the feeling of safety of lifetime coverage, whether you need it or not, and the feeling of safety that you have a forced savings account (even though you could earn more by investing it on your own). Whole life insurance is much more of an investment than term life insurance and, accordingly, it costs more.

Annuities

An annuity is a contract between you and an insurance company, in which you give them either a one-time or series of payments in exchange for a guarantee of periodic payments to you, beginning now or in the future. Annuities are popular in retirement plans because earnings are usually tax deferred. When withdrawals are later taken, the gains are taxed as ordinary income, not capital gains.

There are three types of annuities: fixed, indexed, and variable. In all three cases, the annuity is basically an investment in some type of asset (typically bonds, but also stocks), plus the addition of insurance that provides some minimum payout in the event that your investment falls below a set amount. A fixed annuity is essentially the purchase of a fixed-interest-rate bond with the addition of bond insurance, plus perhaps some life insurance. An indexed annuity pays based on changes in an index, such as the Standard & Poor's 500, and provides insurance that earnings will not fall below some specified minimum, regardless of index performance. A variable annuity pays based on the performance of a variety of investment options, each with different levels of risk and return, similar to a variety of mutual funds. It also provides insurance that earnings will not fall below some specified minimum.

Buying an investment plus some insurance for that investment costs more than simply buying the investment directly, so whenever you hear the word *annuity*, it really means investment and *insurance* because that is the extra feature you are buying. Annuities can be complicated and come in many varieties, but the bottom line is that annuities are essentially investments with some level of insurance protecting those investments.

Many annuities are heavily invested in bonds. In the case of a fixed annuity, this is especially ironic because you are buying a bond and you are insuring your bond investment with some insurance that itself is an investment in bonds. The annuity uses the safety of one set of bonds (the bonds the insurance company owns) to insure the safety of another set of bonds (the bonds you own in your annuity).

Like all forms of insurance, your bond insurance is limited. It generally covers a relatively narrow range of conditions, such as only a certain change in interest rates. It does not cover you under all conditions. In the last few decades, that has not been a problem. Bonds have done very well as interest rates have dropped since the early 1980s. And even if interest rates rise a bit in the future, your annuity is still safe because that narrow range of change would still be covered by your bond insurance. As long as conditions do not significantly change, all is well for annuities.

Just as with whole life insurance, when you buy an annuity, you are buying a level of comfort. Rather than simply buying the investment directly at a lower price, you are buying an investment plus some investment insurance. You are paying a premium in order to feel safe.

Long-Term Care and Disability Insurance

Long-term care (LTC) insurance covers some of the costs of health care that is needed over an extended period, such as in old age, in particular, nursing home care. The younger you are when you buy LTC insurance, the cheaper the payments will be, but the longer you will probably have to make payments before you need it.

There are three basic types of LTC insurance: indemnity, expense-incurred, or cash policies. Indemnity plans pay a fixed daily rate regardless of what you spend on care. Expense-incurred policies reimburse you for actual expenses, up to a fixed amount. Cash-based policies pay you a fixed amount even if you incur no expenses (for example, if a relative provides your care). For an additional cost, your LTC insurance may also provide a limited inflation rider, a return-of-payment rider in case you don't use it, and simple or compound interest earned on your payments.

Like whole life and annuities, buying long-term care insurance is purchasing a feeling of safety.

Are These Policies a Good Deal?

Conventional wisdom says absolutely yes! Their track records in the past have ranged from okay to great, in large part because their main underlying investment—bonds—have done so well, especially since the early 1980s. All that profit has helped insurance companies grow, adding to their "rock solid" image.

In addition to their investments growing, selling whole life and other insurance products has been quite profitable for these companies. With the sale of a whole life insurance policy, the company gets a customer for life. Even when that customer eventually dies and they pay the death benefit, most of that payout will come from the policyholder's own premium payment. And even if the payments don't fully cover it, whatever difference they have to make up will almost always be only a fraction of the total income the company made by investing their customer's money over the life of the policy. In the case of annuities, the companies also do well, selling bonds plus bond insurance. So naturally, these companies push pretty hard to sell whole life insurance and annuities.

But are they a good deal for you?

While not fantastic investments, these policies have been okay investments (and even good investments) in the past, depending on your age, income, family situation, and goals at the time. And they are still okay investments now. These policies are generally very safe under the current conditions. And even in a deeper recession, there would be little reason for concern.

The question is will these policies continue to be okay going forward, as the economy continues to evolve and we approach the coming Aftershock?

Threats to the Safety Nets   179

Why Conventional Wisdom Is Wrong: Facing the Real 800-Pound Gorilla in the Room

Do you remember the recent television commercial in which a very large gorilla extols the virtues of annuities? A seemingly well-informed giant gorilla sits next to an average-looking American, perhaps on an airplane or in an open convertible, begging his bewildered human companion to consider the many must-have benefits of buying an annuity.

"You could have guaranteed income for life!!" pleads the passionate primate, as the person stares off anxiously into the unknown. "But, hey, what do I know. I'm just the 800-pound gorilla in the room."

Clever ad. However, the *real* 800-pound gorilla in the room is actually a multitrillion-dollar monkey on our backs, in form of the ballooning U.S. money supply (more than $2.8 trillion, as of mid-2012) and massive federal debt (nearly $16 trillion and continuing to rise rapidly). By this point in the book we probably don't have to remind you that we believe this massive money printing by the Fed, driven in part by our massive debt, will eventually cause significant rising inflation. Rising inflation will cause rising interest rates. And rising interest rates will help pop what is left of our already falling bubbles—especially the dollar and the government debt bubbles—and bring on the Aftershock.

Conventional wisdom (CW) on insurance is wrong because CW is making the usual mistake of assuming that inflation and interest rates will never significantly rise. As we said in the previous chapter on real estate, CW imagines low interest rates for as far as the eye can see.

How Will Rising Inflation and Rising Interest Rates Impact My Insurance or Annuity Policies?

As we mentioned earlier, one of the biggest misconceptions about whole life insurance, annuities, long-term care insurance, and the like, is that these are just insurance policies, and therefore they are somehow separate and protected from the dangers of the markets. But that is completely false. These instruments are *investments* and they must be analyzed and managed as such, as these markets evolve.

The safety of whole life insurance, annuities, and the like is directly tied to the safety of bonds, and to a lesser extent, the safety of stocks and real estate. This is not just our point of view. Even the credit rating agencies know this is true. Why else would the safety of these instruments be assessed and graded *using similar indicators to ones used to assess the safety of bonds?*

So far, the rating agency we mentioned earlier, A. M. Best, has had a good track record for rating the stability of insurance companies. But just like the other rating agencies, such as Moody's and S&P, they have never really faced an Aftershock-type situation in the markets, and their ratings do not reflect how a given company might hold up under the enormous pressures of multiple collapsing asset bubbles. Even under minimal stress, ratings have not always been so accurate. As you may recall from Chapter 5, bonds from the global financial services firm Lehman Brothers had a very high rating from both Moody's and S&P until a few days before it went bankrupt in 2008.

Since insurance companies are so heavily dependent on bonds, what happens to bonds when inflation and interest rates rise (see Chapter 5) will happen to insurance and annuities, as well. Rising inflation will mean rising interest rates. Rising interest rates will mean falling bond values—and insurance and annuity companies, which are so heavily invested in bonds, will be in trouble.

In a rising interest rate environment, whole life insurance has a bit of a buffer. As their bond investments begin to fall, whole life insurance companies can still pay out for a while, dipping into the their large reserves. But as inflation and interest rates continue to rise, whole life policies will be worth less and less.

Annuities have less of an initial buffer than whole life insurance. They are basically just bond investments with some added bond insurance. At first, when interest rates start to go up and bond values falls. But it will only cover a small rise in interest rates, after which your annuity's value falls. As pointed out earlier, that bond insurance is itself mostly just bonds. So don't count on it holding up when interest rates rise and bonds fall. Also, many annuities have market adjustment clauses that adjust the cash value of an annuity if you take it out early.

Your Insurance Company Need Not Go Bankrupt for Your Policy to Be Worth Much Less in the Aftershock

Please understand that the value of an insurance company's assets do not have to fall to zero in order for the company to no longer be able to pay full value on your insurance policy or annuity. There is a fairly sensitive balance between inflow and outflow in these companies. If their bond investments fall, this balance will be undone and they won't have the resource to pay you as promised. Remember, they don't have a big pile of money stashed away somewhere; the money you have been paying them all these years is invested in bonds, stocks, and even real estate. A significant drop in those assets will have a big impact.

Please also don't make the mistake of thinking that your insurance or annuity company is "too big to fail" or has been around so long that it is "too safe to fail." *Whatever is the fate of bonds is the fate of insurance and annuity companies.* Please see Chapter 5 for details about the fate of bonds in the Aftershock. Rising interest rates will decimate bonds. Most insurance companies invest mostly in bonds.

And even if your company can somehow escape all of this and is fully functional and can continue to pay on your policy in full, you still have another very big problem: With rising inflation the value of that payout will be worth far less.

The bottom line: There will simply be no way to come out ahead on your whole life insurance or annuity policies when serious inflation and interest rates rise.

What About the State and Federal Governments— Won't They Protect Us?

For a while, yes they will. In the early stages, when only one or two insurance companies are in trouble, the state tax funds that we mentioned earlier will protect policyholders within that state. The problem will come when more companies need help or even go under. Quite quickly, state funds will get tapped out.

At that point, the federal government will surely step in to bail out insurance companies. But that will quickly become too large a task. Hence, as it becomes more difficult to bail out the entire insurance company, the government will focus on helping policy-holders. They won't have the money to pay insurance plans in full, but they will be able to make hardship payments that are means tested. If you have few assets or little income, you will likely qualify for some type of hardship payment from the government. The payments are low because at the same time that the insurance industry will need big backup by the government, many banks and other government-insured entities will clearly need backup, too.

And, even worse, just at the time when the government will be so badly needed for backup in so many financial industries, the government itself will be in financial trouble, as well. They will continue to print money for as long as they can (more borrowing at this point will be impossible), but eventually the money printing will have to end due to the rising inflation that it will cause. At first they can ignore rising inflation and will. But after a while people adjust wages and prices for inflation quickly, and the government finds less and less value in printing more money.

Eventually, with borrowing and money printing over, and income tax revenue declining, the federal government simply will not have the money necessary to cover your insurance or annuity policy. They will do all that they can, for as long as they can. But there will be a limit. Not every need will be fulfilled.

What's a Savvy Aftershock Investor to Do?

The first step, as always, is to face reality. No matter how much you may want to believe in the safety and comfort of these policies, how can you believe in them if you also believe that massive money printing will cause future inflation and that rising inflation will cause rising interest rates? If you believe our macroeconomic point of view—even if only partially—then how can you continue to trust that bonds will do well over the next several years? And if bonds don't do well, how can your policies be worth what you thought they would be worth? All insurance is an investment in bonds because that is what these insurance companies primarily own.

This isn't rocket science, as they say. It's just a matter of logic. So let's be logical and figure out what to do about your whole life insurance and annuities. Remember that the Aftershock is likely still a couple of years away, so there is no need to panic and nothing has to be done immediately.

Life Insurance

If you want to protect your financial dependents during your income-producing years, then term life insurance is preferable over whole life insurance. Whole life costs more, and when the Aftershock hits, your whole life policy will be worth a lot less than it's worth today.

If you have whole life insurance, now is a good time to explore your options for cashing out of it. Learning about exit options is a very important first step to protecting yourself.

Another option is to borrow against the cash value of the policy. Often, this money never has to be paid back and is simply subtracted from the death benefit. If you invest wisely, this is not much of a penalty. Borrowing might be difficult with certain policies, and it is valuable only if the proceeds are properly invested and not consumed.

If cashing out of or borrowing against your whole life insurance policy now seems a bit rash, there is no significant harm in waiting a while longer until you see more evidence that we are right. Keep an eye on interest rates, particularly mortgage rates. When you see mortgage rates climbing to 5 or 6 percent, that is a very good indication that interest rates are heading up and bonds are heading down.

For those looking to buy new life insurance policies, term life insurance is the way to go. Term life insurance makes sense for young and middle-aged people with dependents. Disaster could strike at any time, and it's important to make sure loved ones will be provided for.

Term life insurance will help replace your income should you happen to die while you are still a breadwinner, so the timing of the policy is important. If you get it for too short a term, the risk is that you may not be able to get it again because you may have developed a medical problem that will push up the cost of term insurance beyond your reach. Longer-term plans solve those problems. They are more affected by inflation, but the premiums you pay don't go up with inflation either, so you aren't losing money, just losing the value of your coverage. Hence, you may want to increase coverage over time as inflation is rising.

Annuities

To cash out of an annuity, there is usually a sliding scale of penalties that decreases over time. You should find out what these are.

Pulling out before you turn 59½ can also lead to penalties from the IRS. We hesitate to suggest taking penalties of any kind, but at a certain point it may be better to take a relatively smaller penalty than to lose most of your investment later.

If you have reached the age when you can make withdrawals without a penalty now, do so at the maximum amount. Regardless of your age, as we get closer to the Aftershock and you feel increasingly confident that we are right, you should move faster out of all bond-based insurances, such as annuities. The inflation and interest rate protections they offer will very quickly be overwhelmed by high inflation and high interest rates after the bubble economy fully pops. Again, no need to panic now, but exiting before that happens is wise.

Long-Term Care Insurance and Disability Insurance

Long-term care insurance will also not fare well as inflation and interest rates rise. Since long-term care insurance is generally bought while the policyholder is relatively young, these policies have an investment component (although less so than whole life insurance) that will not be reliable when asset values are falling. Even now, these policies can be challenging for some insurance companies. Many companies have already pulled out of the long-term care insurance business because they cannot make enough money on their bonds to keep up with rising costs of nursing homes and other health care expenses. In the Aftershock, this kind of insurance will all but disappear.

In many cases, long-term care insurance is not worth buying or keeping. However, if you already have long-term care insurance and you are in poor health now, or in your 70s or 80s and think you might need long-term health care in the next few years, then it makes sense to hold on to your policy.

But if you are in your 60s or younger, and in good health, the odds are that you will not need long-term health care for at least another 20 years, if ever. Most people will not need long-term care, even when they are older. For example, only one out of four people will go to a nursing home, and the average age of admission is 83, so it could be many decades before you would need this policy. And given the coming Aftershock, by that time you will not be able to count on it anyway.

Disability insurance is highly vulnerable to inflation. Although many policies do have some inflation adjustments, they often have limits on the amount of adjustment. If you are still in your working years and hold an individual disability policy, it makes sense to continue it for now. But when the bubbles pop and the Aftershock begins, these policies are going to become less reliable as the assets of insurance companies crash and state and federal governments are stretched very thin, trying to cover so many needs. So continue paying your premiums on the policy while all is still relatively well, but discontinue your payments as we near the Aftershock.

One important difference between long-term care insurance and disability insurance is that disability insurance is often provided as a benefit from an employer and is not bought individually, so even though the benefit will be worth less in a period of high inflation, at least you aren't paying for it.

Other Types of Insurance that Are Not Investment Dependent: Health, Auto, and Home Insurance

Not all types of insurance are dependent on the performance of investments. Health, auto, and home insurance, for example, are much more dependent on premiums and not very dependent on performance of the company's assets. If the values of bonds fall, your health, home, and auto insurance will be fine. Premiums may certainly continue to go up, but it won't be because of poor performance in the bond markets.

Because of this, we mostly agree with conventional wisdom on these insurances that are not investment dependent. These are good to have, and you should have them. But we do have a few suggestions that we think are worth noting.

First, when possible, choose the higher-deductible policies because they generally cost much less than the lower-deductible plans. Unless you are a frequent claimant of insurance, high deductibles usually make more sense in the long term and can pay for themselves in just a few years.

Second, on your homeowners insurance, make sure you are not overpaying because the land value shot up during the rising real estate bubble. You need to insure only the dwelling, not the land (it usually survives a fire and is hard to steal). You should check your insurance to make sure the dwelling value seems appropriate. If not, you should get the dwelling revaluated and/or get a second insurance company bid to confirm you have the right value.

Finally, if your employer provides your health insurance and you have some choices, take the best deal you can get. But if you must buy your own health insurance, shop around. There are a lot of choices and a wide range of costs. Choose a plan that best matches your best guess of your future health needs. Again, it usually makes sense to get a higher-deductible plan.

When to Exit Your Investment-Dependent Insurance Policies

In keeping with the three stages we described in the chapters on stocks and bonds, it is reasonable to expect insurance policies that are dependent on the performance of stocks and bonds to follow the same fate at each stage.

Stage 1: The Recent Past and Now

Just as bonds did okay during the global financial crisis of late 2008, so did most insurance companies.

Stage 2: The Short-Term Future

As long as interest rates remain low, all is well. In the short term (2012 and 2013), interest rates will not likely rise too dramatically. But remember, even just a small rise in interest rates will have an early negative impact on bonds. By this time you should have learned how to exit your bond-dependent insurance policies. It may be too early to exit, but you should be increasingly ready to pull the trigger.

Stage 3: Medium-Term Future

When bond markets start taking a big hit, you should have exited or should quickly exit bond-based insurance and annuities. High inflation and high interest rates are not going to occur overnight. It will happen over time. The more time that goes by, the greater the risk to bonds.

Bond-Dependent Insurance in the Aftershock

In the Aftershock, the government safety nets for insurance policies of all kinds will fail because the government will not have the money to cover all the demands on it. Some policyholders may continue to get some help, based on need, but that will be limited.

Getting out of your investment-dependent insurance policies *before* all this occurs is obviously a good idea. It is never too early to at least look into your various options for exiting, including finding out the face value of your policies, the options for borrowing against it, and the penalties (and tax consequences) for early withdrawal.

Your Best "Insurance" Is an Actively Managed Aftershock Portfolio

In deciding how to handle your whole life insurance, annuities, and other insurance policies, first, be aware of the risks; second, be ready to make a move; and third, build an actively managed Aftershock portfolio.

Money that you can rescue from these bond-based policies (that will be so badly impacted later by rising interest rates) can be better protected by investing in assets that can withstand and even profit from the economic changes ahead. You may choose to do this all at once and as soon as possible; or you can do it incrementally, perhaps making small regular purchases, just as you would if you were paying for an insurance policy.

The key to correct investing before and during the Aftershock is to diversify across a range of asset classes, not just within an asset class, and most importantly to *actively manage* those investments. That means not just setting it up once and walking away. Active management means making changes to your portfolio that are in step with the evolving economy. (More details about building an actively managed Aftershock portfolio are offered in Chapters 3 and 11.)

CHAPTER 8

Gold

THE ONCE AND FUTURE KING

Why do investors buy gold? Or should we ask why do so *few* investors want to buy gold now and why will so many more investors want to pile into gold later in the Aftershock?

Right now, the idea that gold is a good long-term investment is controversial and prickly. People generally don't like it. Gold may be favored by some unconventional investors, but by far, most Americans do not currently own gold and they have no interest in doing so. Their conventional wisdom (CW) portfolios are generally loaded with stocks, bonds, and perhaps real estate. The idea of adding a significant amount of gold to the mix seems unnecessary, even silly to them, just as it seems silly to many financial advisers and the famous investors they revere, like Warren Buffett and others.

This is what we meant earlier in the book when we said that Aftershock investing is so uncomfortable. It just doesn't *feel* right compared to the comfort of conventional investing, and you won't find strong mainstream support for it. It is hard—*very hard*—to go against Warren Buffett.

We released ourselves from that difficulty many years ago when we were writing *America's Bubble Economy* in 2005. With the correct macroeconomic view, it really was not that hard to see all the bubbles (stocks, real estate, etc.) rising and then beginning to fall. With this same macroeconomic view, it is also not that difficult to see that gold will eventually be the biggest, most profitable bubble of our lifetime. And there are multiple ways that you, or anyone at any level of wealth, can benefit immensely from that rising bubble in the coming Aftershock.

However, before we get to all that, we first need to tackle the reasons why gold is currently seen as such a long-term loser by CW investors like Warren Buffett and so many others. These are smart and successful people with stunning investment track records in the past. How could they be so far off track now when it comes to the future of gold? Are they right, or are we right? We invite you to review the basic macroeconomic evidence and decide for yourself.

Gold Was Golden for Centuries

Gold has been highly valued for a long, long time. We are talking millennia, not centuries. No one knows exactly when gold was first discovered and used by humans, but there is evidence that it may have occurred as early as 8,000 years ago. We do know that Egyptian pharaohs and priests used gold as an adornment beginning around 3000 BC, although at that point they still used barley, not gold, as a means of trade.

To the best of our current knowledge, gold was first used as money in about 700 BC. Since then, no other form of money has come close to gold's longevity or worldwide appeal. Regardless of the culture or the era, every form of gold—from gold nuggets to gold coins and gold bars, to gold jewelry and even gold teeth—have all commanded universal respect and buying power for more than 2,700 years.

In that time, people have found gold to be so beautiful, enduring, and scarce that it became more highly revered than merely money, and the elevated prestige of gold still continues today. Lovers seal their vows with gold rings. Kings and queens still wear gold crowns. Olympic winners still receive gold medals (although no longer solid gold). And a gold watch at retirement still symbolizes respect and accomplishment. Even our language continues to recognize the special status of gold with phrases like "our golden moment" and "his word is as good as gold."

Over the long haul of history, no other worldly substance has retained such a high and universal regard as gold. To say that this precious metal has staying power would be an understatement.

Paper Money Used to Be "Backed" by Gold

During the long evolution of money, beginning first with bartering and evolving to today's electronic money transfers, gold has played a prominent role. For centuries, gold, silver, and other metals were used for money, replacing the more perishable forms of currency, such as barley, seashells, and salt. After a while, as world trade expanded and economies grew, bags of metals-based money got too heavy to lug around (see the following sidebar) and paper money was created to make money more portable and easier to produce.

Heavy Metal

Did you know that gold is one of the heaviest metals around? With a specific gravity of 19.3, gold weighs 19.3 times more than an equal volume of water. That means just one cubic foot of gold (about the size of a basketball) weighs 1,206 pounds. That's more than half a ton! No wonder we eventually switched to paper money.

Of course, the ease of production of paper money naturally made people leery of its value. Gold and silver could be weighed and a trading value determined based on its physical size and purity, but not so with paper. This problem was addressed by certifying that the paper currency was "backed" by gold or silver, meaning there was a certain amount of precious metals set aside to back up the claim that the paper had any real value. Upon demand, this paper could be turned in for the amount of gold or silver it represented. Even when we went off of the gold standard in 1933, we still used gold to back our international transactions up until 1971.

Now the U.S. dollar is no longer backed by gold for either domestic or international transactions, and the Federal Reserve can print money whenever it wants. But even so, gold is still important today because people all around the world still think it is important. Gold continues to be considered a safe store of value by nearly every country. This includes the U.S. government, which currently owns more than 9,000 tons of gold with an approximate market value of more than $450 billion.

Current Conventional Wisdom on Gold as an Investment: Warren Buffett Says Stay Away!

Conventional wisdom on gold has evolved as the uses of gold have evolved. For a very long time, CW thought gold was wonderful and wanted to own as much of it as possible. Even in modern times, CW still valued gold to varying degrees for most of the twentieth century. But more recently—especially since the early 1980s stock market boom—CW's interest in gold as an investment has cooled off considerably.

Mainstream investors may have a small percentage of their conventional portfolios in gold, particularly since the financial crisis of 2008, but they generally say that gold is a bad long-term investment for the following reasons:

- Unlike bonds, gold earns no interest.
- Unlike stocks, gold earns no dividends.
- Unlike real estate, gold earns no rent.
- Gold is not a safe haven, like bonds have been.
- Gold has no "real" value, it is mostly all speculative.
- The price of gold is volatile, and investing in gold is unpredictable and unsafe.

In short, CW thinks of gold as just a volatile commodity—perhaps a bit attractive under the right short-term conditions, but too dangerous in the long run.

Instead, CW investors like Warren Buffett are constantly telling us to stick with stocks. Why? Well, for starters, gold has not done as well as stocks over the past four decades, as Mr. Buffett pointed out in his February 9, 2012, article in *Fortune* magazine. Mr. Buffett used the comparison in Figure 8.1 to show gold's relative performance. Gold still does well, especially compared to bonds, but not quite as well as stocks.

However, since 2000, after the stock market boom of the 1980s and 1990s, the S&P 500 has remained essentially flat. Meanwhile, during those same years, gold has climbed almost 500 percent (see Figure 8.2).

What does Mr. Buffett have to say about gold outperforming stocks in the past decade? He advises us to pay no attention to that. He says rising gold is nothing more than a bubble. Funny how he doesn't think stocks are a bubble, even though the Dow went up

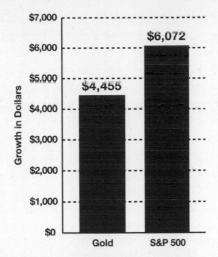

Figure 8.1   Gold versus Stocks from 1965 to 2000

What $100 invested in gold or stocks in 1965 would be in 2000. Stocks outperformed gold from 1965 to 2000.

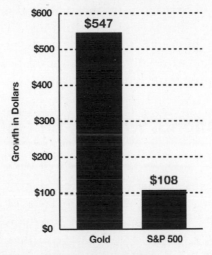

Figure 8.2   Gold versus Stocks since 2000

What $100 invested in gold or stocks in 2000 would be worth today. Since 2000, gold has far outperformed stocks.

over 1,000 percent between 1980 and 2000 while gross domestic product (GDP) went up only 260 percent. Mr. Buffett implores us to stick with stocks instead of gold because the main reason people buy gold now is in the hope that more people will buy gold later. He sees no fundamental economic reasons for gold to ever rise, so if it does ever rise, it has to be mostly because of speculation.

In the *Fortune* magazine article he wrote: "Gold has two significant shortcomings, being neither of much use nor procreative. True, gold has some industrial and decorative utility, but the demand for these purposes is both limited and incapable of soaking up new production. Meanwhile, if you own one ounce of gold for an eternity, you will still own one ounce at its end."

You see, according to current CW, since gold does not have utility value, it is not a worthwhile investment. Now Mr. Buffett would certainly agree that gold will have short-term increases, as will many investments, but it is not as good longer term as stocks are now.

Fundamentally, his concerns have a certain amount of merit. But gold has risen in the past, even for long periods of time, despite its not having a utility value. More important, the recent past of 1965 to 2000 is not necessarily a good indicator of what's going to happen in the next couple of decades. The fundamental economic conditions could be, and will be, very different. These conditions will work very poorly for stocks and very well for gold.

Although Mr. Buffett has a better analysis than most CW investors who dislike gold, the bottom line for most CW investors is that, whatever the price of gold is today, that is the price at which gold is about to "top out," while stocks, at whatever price they are today, are almost always poised for long-term growth.

Why Conventional Wisdom on Gold Is Wrong

As we said before, in the past CW loved gold. CW investors only stopped loving gold relatively recently, in favor of the stock market bubble, the real estate bubble, and the big run-up in bonds since 1980.

The irony here is that one of the reasons that CW does not like gold—because it is not driven by an income stream, such as interest, dividends, or rent (in particular interest)—will be the very reason that gold will do so well in the future, when high interest rates pop the other asset bubbles.

As discussed in detail in earlier chapters, rising interest rates (caused by massive money printing and the inflation it will create) will have a very negative impact on stocks, bonds, real estate, whole life insurance, annuities, and other interest-sensitive assets—some of which are already partially fallen bubbles. Rising inflation and rising interest rates will also pop our two remaining bubbles: the dollar and the government debt bubbles.

But there is one asset that rising inflation and rising interest rates will not be able to push down: GOLD. Therefore, by default, when most other assets are falling, gold is going to look increasingly attractive as people around the world begin to bail out of their sinking investments and pile into the gold lifeboat. Gold will be seen as a safe haven when the U.S. and world bubbles pop.

Greatly Limited Supply and Sharply Rising Demand Will Drive Huge Price Growth

A key reason that gold will do so well as the other bubbles fall is its very limited supply. Worldwide, only about 2,500 tons of gold are currently mined each year plus only about another 1,600 tons of gold per year are recycled, according to the World Gold Council.

Here is another way of looking at the relatively small size of total world gold. It would take less than three and a half Olympic-sized swimming pools to hold all of the gold ever mined—about 165,000 metric tons, most of which (about 85%) was mined in the twentieth century.

Despite the rise in gold prices in the past decade, the total output of gold mines, even with new mines coming on line, has actually declined or barely increased in recent years (see Figure 8.3).

Most Americans don't especially like to invest in gold right now, but keep in mind that the United States is only 10 percent of the world's gold market. China and India now make up more than half the world's gold market, and they clearly love gold. There are now gold vending machines on the streets of Beijing, and Chinese banks hand out lots of brightly colored brochures pushing gold to their customers. The Indian people like gold so much, they even have a gold-buying season when gold, mostly as jewelry, is traditionally purchased. High inflation in China and India has increased recent purchasing. Plus, in China, which has seen the highest growth in demand, interest paid by banks is very low, the stock market has done poorly, and real estate is very expensive for most people. So, the alternative investments to gold are not good.

So even if we don't generally like gold, the rest of the world is very pro-gold and they will not hesitate to rush into more gold in

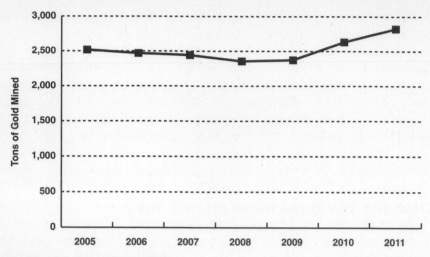

Figure 8.3 Gold Since 2005

Gold mining output has not increased greatly despite a massive increase in the price of gold.

Source: World Gold Council.

the future. That will make American investors highly interested, too, especially when our bubbles burst and they start looking for someplace to put what is left of their money.

Despite the CW assertion that there will not be enough demand to soak up future supply, just the opposite is true: Demand will far outpace supply, and that will rapidly push gold prices skyward. When the other bubbles pop, there will be a tremendous amount of money exiting stocks, bonds, and other investments. The tiny size of the gold market relative to stocks and bonds worldwide means that when people turn to gold, they will drive gold prices up fast and high.

Think of all the millions of investors around the world who will be trying to jump into those three and a half swimming pools. Explosive demand and tiny supply will create the biggest asset bubble we have ever seen. And as we will explain later in the chapter, after this bubble goes up, it is not going to come down anytime soon.

Why This Investment Is So Uncomfortable to Make Now: Gold Is the Anti-Stock

In general, gold does poorly when stocks do well, and gold does better when stocks do poorly. This is key to why CW doesn't like gold—they want their stock bubble back! Therefore, for CW, investing in gold is equivalent to shorting America's bubble economy. People don't like that because they want America's bubble economy to last forever.

It won't.

What's a Savvy Aftershock Investor to Do?

The first step, once again, is to logically face facts. Continuing to bet heavily on a CW portfolio as we approach the Aftershock is simply not rational. All the CW arguments against owning gold (it doesn't earn interest, it doesn't pay dividends, etc.) are all irrelevant if stocks and bonds are going to fall with rising inflation and rising interest rates. Those are the same conditions that will make gold soar. Do you really need to worry about not earning interest when your investment is rising 500 percent or more?

Remember three things: (1) the other bubbles will pop; (2) Apple's stock alone is worth more than all of the gold held by the U.S. government; and (3) the U.S. government bond market alone

Gold Is Not Just a Commodity

Gold holds an unusual position in the minds of many people around the world as a store of monetary value. Hence, it is not really a commodity in the same sense as wheat or zinc or oil.

For this reason, long term, it will act very differently from other commodities in terms of its price. Other commodities are driven by commercial demand. Gold will be driven by demand for it as a store of monetary value in times of great fear of other financial assets.

In the short run, before the bubbles pop, the price of gold may at times follow the rise and fall of other commodities. But as the world's bubbles continue to pop, gold's attraction as a traditional store of monetary value will set gold increasingly apart from commercial commodities. Yes, the demand for gold as jewelry will fall since jewelry is a discretionary good, but that loss of demand will be more than offset by a big increase in investment demand. Furthermore, a great deal of gold jewelry that is purchased in Asia and the Middle East is often for investment purposes since it can be easily resold when the money is needed.

is nearly 30 times larger than the value of all the gold that the government holds. Bottom line: Gold investments are very small relative to stock and bond investments.

What About Silver?

We have been focusing on gold in this chapter, but much of this discussion applies to silver as well.

Silver is different from gold in that it is a hybrid investment. It is both a precious metal investment and an industrial commodity. About half of silver's production each year is consumed for industrial purposes, heavily electronics. That means that it is also much more vulnerable to downturns in commodities prices caused by economic downturns. That bodes poorly for silver. However, it is also cheaper and easier for many people to buy and is very much considered a monetary asset. Even our coins were made of silver up until 1965.

So we expect that monetary value to keep silver following gold, but in a severe downturn silver will not track gold as well as it does now, given that industrial demand is still very high.

However, one offset to the downward pressure is that silver is heavily mined as a by-product from other metal mining, most notably copper. In fact, over 70 percent of silver production is as a by-product. So when demand for commodity metals such as copper falls, so will production of silver. This will help offset some of the downward pressure on silver.

The bottom line is that both gold and silver will do very, very well. There may be times when one outperforms the other, but at the height of the Aftershock, gold will be king and silver will be the prince. Regardless of which precious metal you personally prefer, the world thinks of gold as Number One and silver as Number Two (think of the Olympic first- and second-place medals).

Gold (and Silver) Will Rise in Three Stages

Unlike any of the other investments we describe in this book, only gold will do well in all three stages, despite its continued volatility. If you are in it for the longer term, there is really no bad time to buy gold. Buy now, buy later, or buy now *and* later. It is all good.

Any price we pay for gold before the Aftershock is going to look like a bargain to us in the Aftershock.

Stage 1: The Recent Past and Now

Gold is up almost 500 percent since 2001, and since the financial crisis of 2008, gold almost doubled, although it pulled back in late 2011. The price of gold has been quite volatile, which worries some investors, while others ignore the short-term action and see gold primarily as a good long-term investment.

Stage 2: Short-Term Future

Going forward, gold will generally continue to do well, but expect considerable volatility to continue. There also is some reason to think there may be a bit of manipulation of the gold price on occasion. Don't count on gold's rising more than about 10 percent per year during this time.

Stage 3: Medium-Term Future

As inflation and interest rates rise, expect to see stocks, bond, and real estate values begin or continue to fall. Because gold is not interest rate dependent, rising interest rates will not negatively affect gold. Quite the contrary, investors worldwide will be increasingly attracted to gold in a flight to safety as the interest rate–dependent assets fall. We call this rational fear, and it will push gold up significantly.

Gold Just Before and During the Aftershock: Rational Fear Becomes Rational Panic

To summarize what we already discussed, there are several good reasons why gold will shoot up just before and during the Aftershock:

1. The gold market is very, very small compared to the stock and bond markets. Even a small shift of capital out of these

larger markets and into gold will dramatically boost its price. And a large inflow of capital into gold will have a very huge, positive effect, indeed.

2. Gold is already viewed very positively as an investment in the Middle East and Asia, which are currently the biggest consumers of gold. When the U.S. dollar bubble pops, investors in those countries will move rapidly into gold when their economies tank even worse than the U.S. economy.

3. It is very difficult to quickly increase gold production. Gold mining will not be able to keep pace with demand.

4. Gold is often used as an illegal tax avoidance technique around the world. That is likely part of its attraction in China and India. We, of course, do not advocate illegal tax avoidance, but there's no denying that the world finds this appealing, further boosting the demand for gold.

5. Gold has traditionally been seen as an inflation hedge in the past, and in this case will be an extraordinarily good hedge against inflation in the future, so any significant rise in inflation in the United States or in other countries will drive the price of gold higher.

6. As the world's banking system comes under increasing stress, gold will have increasing appeal.

7. Dollar-based investors will get a double benefit by buying gold. If you buy gold with dollars, you are taking advantage not only of the price rise in gold, but also the fall of the dollar. As an example, if gold goes up four times, and the euro goes up two times against the dollar, your net increase is eight times.

The bottom line is that there won't be many investment options as good and easy as gold when the Aftershock hits. The rising gold bubble is your best bet for wealth protection and profits in the Aftershock.

How to Buy Gold

There are many ways to buy gold—some good, some not so good. We think the three best ways to buy gold are:

1. Buy Physical Gold from a Local Coin Dealer or a Reputable Online Dealer

Many people prefer to buy gold coins rather than larger gold bars. Coins are easier than bars to find a buyer for later when you want to sell. Some of the easiest coins to trade are the Canadian Maple Leaf, the American Eagle, and the South African Krugerrand. Coins are usually one ounce in weight, but often also come in smaller half-ounce and tenth-ounce sizes. You can buy these from local coin shops, but they will be a bit more expensive per ounce than buying online. However, there are no shipping and insurance charges at the coin shop. Some states may charge sales tax or, like Maryland, may require that you buy at least $1,000 worth of gold in order to be tax exempt. You can find local coin shops in the Yellow Pages or online. The U.S. Mint web site (www .usmint.gov) also has a searchable database of coin shops based on your location. Getting to know a local coin dealer now may help you later when you want to sell some coins.

Many people prefer to buy bullion online or by phone. Mail-order gold tends to be cheaper because the vendors have lower overhead than a physical store. You can simply type "gold bullion" into the search bar of your favorite Internet search engine and investigate your options, such as www.Kitco.com and others. Online outlets and retail stores require certified checks or cash to buy gold, or will ask you to wait until your check clears your bank before they ship or let you pick up your gold.

You can keep physical gold in a safe deposit box at a bank (even a small safe deposit box can hold quite a lot of gold), or in a lockable safe at home, which you can buy at any office supplies store. Eventually, as the various stages of the Aftershock occur, you may have to keep all physical gold at home for maximum safety.

2. Buy Gold Exchange-Traded Funds

Retail coin stores (online or in your neighborhood) often charge a much higher sales commission or "spread," often ranging from 3 to 6 percent per ounce. One way to avoid this is to buy gold exchange-traded funds (ETFs), which are traded like stocks on the New York Stock Exchange with the price roughly tracking one-tenth of the price of an ounce of gold, making them a very quick and convenient way to buy and sell gold.

First on the scene in the fall of 2005, gold ETFs now hold more than 1,000 tons of gold. The most popular ETF is GLD and is a product of State Street Global Advisors. Its competitor is IAU and is very similar. A different type of gold ETF is PHYS, which is actually a closed-end fund, rather than strictly an ETF. It holds physical gold in Canada. However, GLD and IAU also hold physical gold. GLD holds its gold in London. They actually list the serial numbers of the 400-ounce gold bars (London Good Delivery Bars) that they hold on their web site.

Gold ETFs have some tax disadvantages and expenses, but their trading convenience and small entry point make them quite popular with investors at every level. ETFs can also be bought on margin. Gold ETFs are safe for now, but could become less safe in the future, at which point owning only physical gold might be best.

3. Buy Gold Using a Gold Depository

An alternative to buying physical gold or gold ETFs is buying gold from a gold depository, such as Monex in Newport Beach, California. With a gold depository, you have ownership of the gold without necessarily taking physical possession, although you can at any time. As soon as you buy it, they sign legal ownership over to you and deposit it with a separate legal entity. If the depository were to go bankrupt, the gold would still be yours.

Gold depositories solve the problems of gold storage and safety, and also give you the opportunity to buy gold on margin (see the section on leveraging gold later in this chapter). As we mentioned earlier, at some point, you may do best to take physical possession of your gold, which is very easy with a depository and not really feasible for most investors with current gold ETFs.

For example, you may first buy gold ETFs because they are easy and convenient. Later, you might sell your gold ETFs and switch to a gold depository because of the ease of leveraging at a higher rate as the gold bubble rises, and because of ease of delivery when you want to take physical possession later. Finally, taking physical possession of your gold may make the most sense if and when the government begins to take adverse actions against gold, such as restrictions on the purchase or sale of gold or very high taxes on gold transactions. Some investors may eventually choose to buy their gold offshore, depending on their circumstances.

What About Gold Mining Stocks?

Gold mining stocks have the advantage of multiplying the profits that a gold mining company can derive from mining gold. Hence, they can rise faster than the price of gold itself because you receive a multiple of earnings made from selling gold. Revenues rise as the price of gold rises, but operating costs do not. Therefore, as gold prices go up, gold mining companies can do very well.

However, the downside of gold mining stocks is that they can be affected by three key issues that are outside of the price of gold. The first is the overall stock market, which, when it falls, will tend to take everyone down, at least for a while. The second issue is that each gold mining company faces the same company risks that any company can face. Remember, like Mark Twain said, "A gold mine is a hole in the ground owned by a liar." Third, many mining companies, particularly the larger ones, are not pure gold plays. They often get the majority of their revenues from other metals, such as iron and copper.

While many gold mining stocks will go down temporarily when the stock bubble fully pops, later on many gold mining stocks will do extremely well—in some cases even better than the price of gold itself.

So there is a lot of money to be made in gold mining stocks if you are aware of the risks we just mentioned. Long term, when the stock market falls and gold rises, there will be even better opportunities to buy gold mining stocks. You need sophisticated investment research or competent guidance before going into any gold mining stock. Another option is to purchase a diversified fund or ETF that holds a variety of gold mining stocks, such as the ETF GDX.

By the time the gold bubble is rising rapidly, the stock bubble will have been pretty well deflated so you will be buying gold mining company stock at low prices.

Gold mining stocks may be more attractive if your investment vehicle allows investments in gold mining stocks but not directly in gold. But remember, great care is needed to avoid the downward pressure of a collapsing stock market on gold mining stocks.

Leveraging Gold

One thing we've seen in recent years is that leveraging (borrowing money to fund part of the purchase of an investment) can light a fire under the growth of your assets. Hedge funds and private equity funds used leverage to create astounding returns for several years. But that fire can also burn you, as the hedge funds and private equity funds certainly found out.

The same goes for leveraging gold. There is no quicker way to make money on gold, and no quicker way to lose it. The greater the price volatility, the greater the risk, because even if you are right in the long term, you can be squeezed out by margin calls in the short term due to sharp short-term declines in the price. The price may jump back to its high very quickly, but you may have lost much of your money in the dip if you couldn't make the margin calls on your highly leveraged gold investment and had to sell your position at a low price.

Because we believe there will be greater volatility in the beginning of the gold bubble, we suggest you keep your leverage more limited in the early stages. However, as the gold bubble begins to take off with the dollar bubble pop, you could consider increasing your leverage.

If you decide to buy gold on margin, the amount of margin you can get is controlled by the government, like any brokerage account. But, depending on the volatility of gold, you can leverage three to five times. That means at a $3\times$ leverage you can get $30,000 worth of gold for $10,000 cash. There are also significant interest costs associated with leveraging.

Gold now and in the future will likely be highly volatile, so be careful. We can't tell you how much leverage to use since the amount of leverage you can take on is very much a factor of your wealth and willingness to take risks. All we can say for sure is that for most people leverage is like alcohol: Use it in moderation.

Owning Gold as Part of a Well-Diversified Actively Managed Aftershock Portfolio

As much as we like gold, we would never recommend that you put all your eggs in one basket. Without reviewing an individual's specific financial situation, it is hard to say what percentage they should hold in gold. Many people are comfortable and can handle the volatility of 20 percent in gold, but others may be more comfortable with less and some would be more comfortable with more. The rest of your portfolio requires ongoing active management, as described throughout the book and summarized in Chapter 11.

As we get closer to the coming Aftershock, moving to a higher percentage of gold will be prudent. For those who want to do that sooner rather than later, there is no long-term harm, as long as you are prepared for the significant short-term volatility in gold and you don't mind sitting out any additional short-term upside that may be left in the stock and bond markets.

The Biggest, Baddest Bubble of Them All

Gold might seem like the silliest of all investments. People spend tons of capital, time, and effort trying to haul a bunch of rock out of the ground at enormous expense and smelt out tiny bits of gold, melt them together, and then do absolutely nothing with it—just store it in some vault. How much sillier can it get?

But gold is not just metal in the ground; it is considered a universal store of value, and that will make "silly" gold a truly smart and spectacular Aftershock investment. Huge amounts of money will be made—*and lost*—in gold. Gold will be a rising bubble on its way to becoming one of the biggest asset bubbles of all time. Second only to the fall of the dollar bubble, the bursting of the gold bubble many years from now will be quite impressive, as well.

How High Will Gold Go?

Many people like to ask us this question and we hesitate to answer. What we can say is that gold is up by more than 500 percent since 2000, during a period of only moderate inflation and moderate investor anxiety—a very negative environment for gold. We have to assume that in the next several years, when inflation will be higher and returns on bonds and stocks will be low—a very positive environment for gold—that it could rise even more than the 500 percent it did in the past 10 years in a very negative environment.

Confiscation by Inflation

Will gold be confiscated or become illegal to hold individually, as it was during the Great Depression? Not likely.

Gold was much more important to the daily functioning of the economy during the Great Depression than it is now. It is almost an irrelevancy now; it wasn't then. Also, today, if the government needs money, they have a much more powerful tool for confiscating assets than confiscation of gold and that is: Confiscation by Inflation. When the government prints money, it is essentially confiscating certain assets, such as bonds, which will fall quickly as inflation and interest rates rise. Your stocks, real estate, pension, life insurance, and annuities will also decline as interest rates continue to climb.

Hence, you have little to fear from direct government confiscation of your assets, and much more to fear from indirect confiscation by inflation—unless you protect yourself. It's absolutely confiscation of people's assets, and it's a whole lot more powerful than confiscating gold. But the upside to confiscation by inflation is that, unlike government confiscation of the past, for those who are paying attention, this kind of confiscation will be easy to avoid.

But even if it doesn't do as well, and only increased 200 percent, how much better is that going to be than watching 50 percent (or more) of your CW portfolio eventually go to Money Heaven?

When Will the Future Gold Bubble Pop?

Not for a long time. That's because it will be a long time before investors feel confident in other assets. For that to happen, we will need to start seeing some real economic recovery, not the current money printing and government borrowing that is driving the fake recovery we have now, and certainly not the Aftershock economy we will have after the dollar bubble pops. We are going to need real economic growth driven by fundamental productivity improvements in order to get the U.S. economy fully back on its feet. When that happens, the gold bubble will come down.

However, the gold bubble will not exactly "pop" the way we will see many other bubbles crash. Instead, as the U.S. economy recovers, other economies will continue to struggle for a while longer.

Investors in those countries will not be eager to sell off their gold quite yet, not while they still have no or limited growth. So rather than quickly popping, the massive gold bubble will slowly decline over a period of many months, even years, giving us plenty of time to make our exits.

That means, like many big bubbles of the past, you will see this one rising and falling, and you will have time to buy in on the way up before the Aftershock and time to sell out on the way down before the full worldwide recovery. Of course, that's only if you know it will pop and are not covering your eyes to the signs of a pop, unlike most people.

What If I Cannot Afford to Buy Gold? Tapping the Power of Grandma's Envelope

If you don't have a lot of spare cash to put into gold, do not despair. Here is a time-tested way to get a piece of the action, even if only on a smaller scale. *Some gold is better than no gold.*

Get yourself an old-fashioned envelope like our great grandparents used to save up enough money to pay the rent or buy a new pair of shoes. Write the word GOLD on the outside and hide your envelope in some safe place. Every time you have a little spare cash—even if it is just 20 bucks—stick it in your gold envelope. Try to do it regularly, like daily or weekly.

If you never seem to have any cash to spare, cut back on something you really don't need and start feeding that golden envelope whatever you can. Even just a few dollars here and there will eventually add up.

As soon as you have enough to buy a gold coin, take your envelope out to your local coin shop and buy yourself a gold coin. As soon as you get home, hide your gold coin someplace safe and start feeding you gold envelope again. Even if you do this only once, you will have thousands of dollars more in the Aftershock than you do today.

PART
III

YOUR AFTERSHOCK
GAME PLAN

CHAPTER 9

Aftershock Jobs and Businesses

The economic cheerleaders want us to believe that if we will just be patient and wait a little longer, strong future job growth will soon return. It is true that the big job losses we saw right after the financial crisis of 2008 have stabilized, and some jobs have begun to return. Manufacturing jobs, for example, have made significant gains since the Fed began its first round of massive money printing (QE1) in March 2009. But more recently, the growth of manufacturing and other jobs has begun to slow again. And some jobs, such as construction, hardly came back at all.

As of this writing in June 2012, overall new job creation has been declining every month this year. If this is any kind of recovery, it is one without much job growth, and that kind of "recovery" is no recovery at all. Strong and sustained job growth is essential to any significant future economic growth—not only for the country but for most people's personal economies, as well. Slower job growth means less income for many Americans and less tax revenue for federal and state governments, which is a recipe for a deeper slowdown, not strong future growth.

That means finding and keeping a good job in this evolving economy of falling bubbles will become increasingly challenging as time goes on. Much of this you can do nothing about, but you do have some control over which jobs you try for and what you can do to keep your current job or prepare yourself to move to another potentially more secure job before the falling bubbles fully pop.

While the pressures on the slow-growing job market will continue and increase, all jobs and businesses are not created equal; clearly, some will fare better than others as the various bubbles continue to pop. The purpose of this chapter is to give you an overview of what is happening with jobs and businesses, and what to expect next.

The Rising Bubble Economy Created Huge Job Growth; Now the Falling Bubble Economy Means Fewer Jobs

As the conjoined real estate, stock, private debt, consumer spending, dollar, and government debt bubbles all rose in tandem from 1980 to 2000, the U.S. job market boomed, adding a whopping *40 million* new jobs during this time period. New employees were in such high demand in the late 1980s and 1990s that employment agencies and headhunters could hardly keep up.

But when the Internet bubble popped in 2000, much of that strong job growth began to unwind. The housing bubble pushed up job growth again, but nothing like the 1980s and 1990s, and so when it popped, jobs related to real estate, like construction and real estate sales, took an immediate and lasting hit. But our job problems didn't end at the edges of the real estate landscape; we had other falling bubbles, as well. Because the rising real estate bubble was so key in driving up the private debt bubble and the consumer spending bubble, when real estate began to pop, much of the hot air escaped from those other bubbles, too. With less home equity to tap into and rapidly tightening credit, consumers naturally spent less, which only made matters worse for businesses and jobs. So, along with the decline in housing-related jobs, big job layoffs were seen across the board, from the airline industry to shopping mall closures. And because the falling bubbles have not been reinflated, despite massive government stimulus to temporarily support them, many of those bubble-driven jobs have not come back either.

The bottom line is, even with the present massive government stimulus and the earlier rising housing bubble, we did not gain any net job growth from 2000 to 2010 (see Figure 9.1). While the number of jobs from 1980 to 2000 increased by 40 million, there was zero job growth from 2000 to 2010. In fact, we lost jobs—almost 200,000. Most of the nonfarm jobs created during the rise of the real estate bubble are now gone.

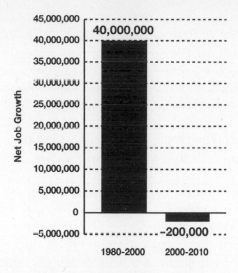

Figure 9.1   No Net Job Growth 2000–2010

From 1980 to 2000, 40 million new jobs were created. Then from 2000 to 2010, 200,000 jobs were lost.

Source: Bureau of Labor Statistics.

Conventional Wisdom about Future Jobs Is Based on Faith that the Future Will Be Like the Past

As with stocks, bonds, real estate, life insurance, and nearly everything else, conventional wisdom's faith in future job growth is derived from the assumption that what we had before (during the rising bubble economy) we will surely have again. CW loves to extrapolate trend lines—at least the trend lines they like. When things are going well, CW sees more great growth ahead; and when things are going not so well, CW says don't worry, the previous good trend line will naturally return very soon. For CW, good trend lines always continue, even if they happen to get temporarily sidetracked for a while.

For example, five years ago when the number of government jobs was growing significantly, CW said government job growth would always be strong. CW says all good job trends last forever. Not only that, CW also likes to believe that whatever is the current popular area of discussion—such as green jobs or nanotechnology jobs—will have strong job growth in the future. The CW winning formula for future jobs is the current trend line (or the recent past, if that looks better than today) plus whatever is in fashion at the moment.

One of the reasons that CW feels so confident about its views about the future is that extrapolating out the trend lines has worked pretty well for CW in the recent past. Naturally, in a rising multibubble economy, most positive trend lines have been remarkably reliable, and it has not been all that difficult for CW to be right on many near-term positive predictions in the recent past. This, along with the need to ignore unpleasant facts that threaten the status quo, has become the strong foundation on which CW now rests its firm faith that all good trends, including all good job growth trends, never end.

While this may sound like a bit of an exaggeration, if you look back at CW over the past three decades, you will see almost all the CW-oriented analysts and economic cheerleaders continuously telling us that everything is basically very good and will continue to be very good, even if we have a little down cycle occasionally. You never hear them say that a currently good trend is unsustainable because it is based on an unsustainable rising bubble economy. At this point, rising bubbles are considered both the norm and our American birthright. And, naturally, that will always include lots of good American jobs.

Even when CW acknowledges that many U.S. jobs have been moved overseas in recent years due to cheaper labor costs, there is no acknowledgment of how the rising U.S. bubbles created many jobs, nor how the falling bubbles have taken them away.

Why Conventional Wisdom on Jobs Is Wrong

Just as for stocks, bonds, real estate, life insurance, and nearly everything else, CW's views on future job growth are wrong for the same reasons that CW is wrong about all the rest: good past trend lines *cannot* be extrapolated into the future indefinitely. The future is not the past. Not even the present is the past. Good trends do not continue forever because *markets always evolve*, and this is certainly true for the jobs market as well.

The U.S. jobs market has always evolved over time, driven by real underlying fundamental economic drivers, not the latest fashionable interests. For example, more than a century ago, most Americans were actively involved in growing food, either for income or to feed themselves. However, farming jobs evolved and declined, as more manufacturing jobs were created in the rise of the Industrial Revolution.

There are countless other examples of how the job market has evolved over time, based on the evolution of the economy. In our current recession, unless the economy goes back fully to how it was before, the jobs are not going to come back fully to how they were before. Since economies never go backward, only forward, jobs evolve forward as well.

As discussed earlier in the book, the combination of the falling bubbles and the reality that there is no "natural growth rate," plus the coming future inflation (due to massive money printing by the Fed) is moving us forward to a new economic reality that we have not experienced before. It certainly will not move us back to the old rising multibubble economy, no matter how badly we may want our bubbles back. Once these jobs are lost, it is hard to bring them back without fundamental changes to the economy.

Does Government Stimulus Create Jobs?

The answer is most definitely yes! The stimulus of massive borrowing and massive money printing *does* lead to more jobs—as long as you keep pouring in more and more stimulus money to keep those new jobs going. But not long after the stimulus ends, so will the jobs. Why? Because big government stimulus does nothing to change the underlying reasons that jobs have declined in the first place; therefore, when the heat of the stimulus is withdrawn, the positive impacts of the stimulus will cool down quickly. That might not be the case in a normal, healthy economy going through a rough patch. In that case, a big temporary stimulus might help to get things back on track. But that won't work in a falling bubble economy. As soon as the stimulus is withdrawn, we are soon back where we were before or worse than before.

Remember what we said earlier in the book: Try as we might, a falling bubble cannot be turned into a rising bubble for very long, if at all. We may be able to keep the bubble from falling further temporarily, but not forever. Bubbles eventually pop.

In the short term, the current government stimulus programs (massive borrowing and massive money printing) are helping to slow the rate of job loss, and they may even create new jobs in some areas, but the stimulus alone will not be enough to permanently save us from the deteriorating jobs market. Even additional "incentive" programs, such as tax credits to encourage employers to hire more employees, are likely to have limited impact. Until demand returns because the fundamentals of the economy change, the jobs market will generally continue to experience slow or no growth.

What's a Savvy Aftershock Investor to Do?

As we said at the start of this chapter, *not all jobs are created equal*; some jobs will do better than others, depending on what sector they are in. So understanding how each job sector will fare in the future (explained below) is key to understanding which jobs will likely hold up best as the bubbles continue to fall.

Although job opportunities in the Aftershock will not be the same as in the recent past, there are similarities to what has happened since the financial crisis and what will happen as we get nearer to the Aftershock. Best job prospects are in the medical industry, while the capital goods industries, such as construction and manufacturing, will be hit very hard. Figure 9.2 shows what has already occurred.

While the bubbles are still partially inflated and the government is still pumping in stimulus to keep them afloat, now is a good time to start planning your next move, whether it is a move to a new job

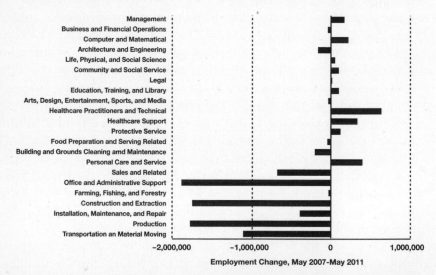

Figure 9.2   Gains and Losses by Types of Jobs, May 2007 to May 2011
Some job types have made gains, while many have sustained big losses.
Source: Bureau of Labor Statistics.

in a different sector or the same sector you are already in, or a new way to make yourself more valuable to your current employer or your customers.

But before we get to the details about each job sector, there are two important points to keep in mind, whether you are an employee or a business owner. First, keep your eyes open. Don't believe everything you see and hear from the economic cheerleaders about the so-called "recovery." We don't have one.

Second, please understand that this is not the recession of the late 1970s and early 1980s. What we have now is a falling multibubble economy, not just a typical economic slowdown. Don't expect big improvements to come quickly.

Some General Considerations for Employees and Job Seekers

- Understand that the overall economy and the job market are both evolving over time. A job that seems secure today may not be around in a few years. There is no need to panic, but now is the time to prepare for the changes ahead (see details about the job sectors below).
- Be willing to move from one job to another or from one job sector to another, but do not quit any job without having another one lined up.
- Consider your options for getting some extra job training, technical certificates, or academic degrees if they will help you move to a better-paying or more secure job, *but only if* this can be accomplished fairly quickly, such as in one to three years. Don't start a 10-year program and expect to be done with it before the Aftershock hits (for more details, see the section on college, later in this chapter).
- If you lose your job, consider taking a lower-paying job or doing temporary work, consulting, or even an internship (see the internship sidebar later in the chapter). Don't hold out for many months, waiting for the same job that you just lost to magically rematerialize. The further the bubbles fall, the less likely that will happen.

Some General Considerations for Business Owners

- Consider selling your business if it is in one of the more dangerous sectors of the economy (see details in the next section).

- If you were already planning to sell your business in the future, move up your time frame and sell it sooner, rather than later. It takes a fair amount of lead time to sell a business. Start now, before many of your potential buyers figure out what you already know about the future economy. The longer you wait to sell, the harder it will be to find a buyer and the lower the selling price, if you are able to sell it at all.
- Get as much cash as possible. If you must hold the note, make sure it is very short term. Try to keep it to less than five years—two to four years preferred. The more time that goes by, the less likely your buyer will be able to make your payments. Collect as much as you can up front.
- If you want to keep your business or start a new one, look for ways to cash in on or at least survive in the falling bubble environment (more details on this later in the chapter).

The Falling Bubbles Will Have Varying Impact on Three Broad Economic Sectors

In assessing the impact of the falling bubbles, we find it helps to think of the U.S. economy in terms of three broad sectors:

1. *Capital goods sector*—cars, construction, major industrial equipment, and so forth.
2. *Discretionary spending sector*—fine dining, entertainment, leisure travel, high fashion, jewelry, art, collectables, cosmetic surgery, and the like.
3. *Necessities sector*—basic food, shelter, basic clothing, energy, basic health care, basic education, and so on.

In a normal economic downturn, we would expect to see the capital goods sector slow significantly, the discretionary spending sector decline somewhat, and the necessities sector to be mostly spared. But this is not a normal economic downturn. The impact of the Aftershock will be felt by all sectors, even the necessities sector. This time, all three sectors will suffer significant job and business losses, with the capital goods and discretionary spending sectors performing worst, and the necessities sector faring better, but not entirely spared. All three sectors will have some safe jobs and profitable businesses, but competition for these will grow as time goes on.

Right now, there are still jobs available but not as many as needed. Even with the creation of some new jobs since the 2008 crash, jobs have not been coming back equally in all sectors, as shown in Figure 9.2.

The Capital Goods Sector (Autos, Construction, Major Industrial Equipment, Etc.)

In the Aftershock, high interest rates, coupled with a big economic slowdown, will be very bad news for the capital goods sector. Rising inflation and rising interest rates will make borrowing money very expensive for consumers and businesses. This will have a very negative effect on the capital goods sector, which depends on its customers having access to low-cost capital. High interest rates will also add to the reasons why full economic recovery will take far longer and be far more difficult than in previous recessions.

Jobs in the Capital Goods Sector

Jobs in capital goods industries will be the worst hit in the coming Aftershock. If you have one of these jobs now, there probably isn't a lot you can do to protect yourself other than to gear up to move on to a job in another sector. Your best bet may be to rethink your career now with an eye toward joining an industry that will do better when the bubbles burst. We certainly don't recommend quitting one job until you have another in hand, but we also don't recommend waiting too long to make a move, if you want to do so.

If a major career makeover is not your style, you may want to consider making a move to a more stable area within your current industry. For example, if you work in the construction industry—which has already taken a terrible hit and is not coming back any time soon—you may find that moving into repair-oriented work, rather than new construction, will keep you busy while others sit at home. Of course, many construction workers will also get this idea after the bubbles fully pop, so the sooner you begin your transition toward repair work, the better. Most types of maintenance and repair work, such as automobile repair, which will be in increasing demand, as people buy far fewer new cars and instead try to hang on to their older cars for as long as possible.

Most Businesses Will Fare Poorly in the Capital Goods Sector

We won't dress it up for you. The bottom line for business owners in the capital goods sector is not pretty. If you can sell now and get out, you probably should. No one can predict exactly when the Aftershock will hit, but even if it takes another two or three years, the marketplace for your business is unlikely to improve much during that time. The value of capital goods sector companies will not rise much under current conditions and will fall in value later, as unemployment continues to rise and the economy continues on its slow-growth or no-growth track. So if you have a business in the automotive, construction, industrial equipment, or any other capital goods industry, the longer you wait to get out, the more vulnerable you will be to significant losses.

As with selling homes and commercial real estate, your pool of potential buyers will get smaller and smaller as time goes by, so the sooner you go fishing in that pool for a possible buyer, the better. Selling any business takes time. Start now. Don't wait until the economy gets worse and most of your potential buyers have figured out that they should not own a business in the capital goods sector.

What will you do after you sell? Options include using your proceeds to invest in the kind of Aftershock portfolio discussed in this book. You can also be on the lookout for unexpected business opportunities in the Aftershock (discussed later in this chapter). If you decide to just hold it all in cash while you think about what to do next, be careful where you put it. Banks will be vulnerable leading up to and in the Aftershock and Federal Deposit Insurance Corporation (FDIC) will likely only cover up to $100,000 per bank account. Also, as inflation rises, the buying power of your cash is evaporating.

The Discretionary Spending Sector (Travel, Restaurants, Entertainment, etc.)

As the economy continues to fall, Americans are not going to run out to the mall every night after work (if they have work) and squander their very limited cash and even more limited credit on high-priced designer handbags or the latest CDs. Discretionary spending is, well, discretionary. Many items and activities that we may currently still enjoy will simply be left off our shopping lists after the bubbles continue to fall and eventually fully pop. Over time, this will slow many businesses to a crawl and force others completely out of the game, further driving up unemployment.

But discretionary spending will still hold up better than the capital goods sector of the economy because some people will still have money, and they will keep spending their money, but they will spend at a lower level than before. So, instead of discretionary spending disappearing altogether, the people who can still spend will simply buy lower-priced discretionary items. For example, instead of shopping for designer handbags at Saks Fifth Avenue, they may downgrade to Walmart or Target.

The restaurant business will face this trend as well. As the bubbles fall, fewer people and businesses will spend money on eating out. That will certainly affect all restaurants. But some people and businesses will have money to eat out and will be quite happy to go to restaurants, as long as they don't have to spend as much as they used to. So the restaurant industry will continue to be a huge industry in the United States, but business will begin a long-term shift toward the lower end. For example, Mexican and Chinese restaurants will continue to survive and will gain increased market share, while high-end seafood and steak houses will be much harder hit.

To a large extent, this same trend will happen throughout the discretionary spending sector. Instead of brand names, we'll want bargains. We will still want to buy some stuff that we don't absolutely need, but we will buy less of it and we will want it at lower prices.

Because consumer spending drives more than two-thirds of the U.S. economy, any decline in consumer spending has a big impact on the overall economy. This is a new situation for the United States. Back in the 1920s, when the nation was much less wealthy and was heading into the Great Depression, consumer spending represented a much smaller portion of our overall economy. So when the stock market bubble crashed in 1929, and the economy took a major downturn, the large dip in consumer spending back then had a much smaller impact on the overall economy because it just didn't make up that large a part of the economy. Other industries took a big hit, but people still had to eat basic food and buy basic clothing, so most of these industries just kept on going.

We are in a different situation today. So much of what we currently buy (and that keeps our economy going), we can easily do without. We may not like to skip the latest, high-priced fashions, but if we have to, we can easily shop at lower-end and discount stores. We can also survive quite nicely without $100,000 kitchen makeovers, complete with granite countertops and stainless steel appliances. As incomes and assets evaporate, Americans will learn to manage without these pricey pleasures.

While the discretionary spending sector will be hit less hard than the capital goods sector, the fact that discretionary spending has become such a big part of the current U.S. economy means a downturn in this sector will greatly accelerate the popping bubbles and make our postbubble recovery even harder.

Jobs in the Discretionary Spending Sector

We've already mentioned how the slowdown in the discretionary spending sector will harm many businesses in the restaurant, retail, and home improvement industries. The travel industry has already taken a big hit, and that will continue as the bubbles fall. Leisure travel will be especially stalled, while more Americans will travel to locations that are closer and cheaper—such as into their living rooms to watch TV. Major entertainment destinations, such as Orlando and Las Vegas, will hang on due to liquidation of assets and to foreign visitors coming to spend their more valuable currencies in our cheaper playgrounds. Once the dollar bubble fully falls and the Aftershock begins, leisure travel by Americans going overseas will face the double whammy of minimal discretionary spending and a dollar that has fallen dramatically against foreign currencies.

Business travel will suffer, as well. Domestic business travel will decrease as the bubbles continue to fall and companies become more interested in cutting costs. Overseas business travel will be hit by high costs and the low value of the dollar, so only the most important overseas trips will continue. Once the Aftershock hits, our imports will be way down and there won't be much need for business travel overseas at that point.

If you are currently employed in the discretionary spending sector and are in a position to retrain for another career, this would be a good time to look for a job elsewhere, such as the necessities sector.

Businesses in the Discretionary Spending Sector

Most businesses in this sector will experience some downturn as the bubbles continue to fall, and in the final pop and Aftershock, many will not survive. Businesses that have the best chances of survival during these increasingly leaner times will include low-end restaurants, low-end clothing stores, discount shops, used clothing and household furnishing stores, and businesses that cater to local or inexpensive travel.

If you own a business in the discretionary spending sector, you might want to give some thought to selling it. If you were already thinking of selling your business, you may want to move that time frame up and sell sooner rather than later. Waiting until many business owners start to realize that they need to sell will not be a good time to put your business on the market. Lots of sellers and not many buyers will mean prices will go way down.

In addition, you will be fighting against some demographics. Many businesses are owned by aging Baby Boomers, and as they get closer to retirement, they will become more risk-averse and more likely to want to cash out of their businesses. Having more businesses for sale when you want to sell your business will make it harder for you to find a buyer. If you wait too long, you may risk facing the coming price drops.

Some Limited Good News: The Necessities Sector (Health Care, Education, Food, Basic Clothing, Transportation, Government Services, and Utilities)

Here is where we actually agree (somewhat) with conventional wisdom. Jobs and businesses in health care, education, and the government will do relatively better than in the other sectors. But even jobs in the necessities sector will not be perfectly protected before and during the coming Aftershock.

Historically, many of the jobs in this sector don't pay very well, and they will pay a bit less after the bubbles pop, when there are more workers available than jobs. But if you have a job in this sector, at least you have a job, and it will be much more reliable than most other jobs as the bubbles fall and later in the Aftershock. Even at lower pay, necessities sector jobs will be a godsend for families with a spouse who used to make more money than his or her mate but is now unemployed. The lower-paid, still-employed spouse, working as a nurse, teacher, medical administrator, or other necessities sector employee, will likely retain his or her job and be able to carry the family through the worst of the downturn.

But please understand that even in this sector, not all jobs will be equally protected. Many necessities sector jobs will not survive in the Aftershock. Why? Because they may not be "necessary" enough. So even in this sector, you will need to plan ahead.

The necessities sector is composed primarily of health care, education, utilities, basic food, basic clothing, and government services, usually run by government or other nonprofit entities. The private companies that supply these government and nonprofit entities have the potential to survive, as well. Of course, as the bubbles fall and eventually pop fully, the necessities sector will also take a hit because it currently contains a larger portion of discretionary spending (spending on high-end items within the necessities category) that will eventually be cut. So even within this relatively good sector, some jobs will not stay.

Health Care Jobs and Businesses

Health care is currently a very strong element of the U.S. economy, and it will continue to be the best bet in the necessities sector as the bubbles fall and fully pop, but there will still be some negatives, especially as unemployment rises and health care revenues decline.

Health care capital goods, such as radiology machines and hospital construction, will not do very well. However, businesses providing services and supplies to the health care industry will continue to do okay, even though they too will experience some downturn. Health care services jobs that will do the best include:

- Nurses
- Primary care doctors
- Psychiatrists
- Nurse practitioners
- Physicians' assistants
- Medical technicians, support personnel, administrative staff, and others involved in primary care medicine (not specialties)

Specialists and their supporting staff and services will not do well, with surgeons taking the biggest hit due to falling demand. Elective procedures, such as cosmetic surgery, already had a downturn during the financial crisis. If you can, transitioning out of these kinds of nonessential medical jobs into more basic areas of health care would be ideal.

Health Care Could Become 20 Percent of the GDP When the Bubbles Pop

Health care will be one of the safest havens for business owners and workers in the Bubblequake and Aftershock. Currently, the huge health care industry accounts for about 16 percent of the nation's GDP. As other industries decline, especially in the discretionary spending and capital goods sectors, the more stable health care industry will naturally take up a larger percentage of our economy. We've seen this before on a smaller scale. For example, during the oil bust in the 1980s, the percentage of the Houston economy represented by non-oil industries grew dramatically.

Add to this an aging population with increasing demands for health care, and it is quite possible that health care could take over a staggering 20 percent of our economy after all six of the bubbles pop, even if we have what could be a 50 percent cut per person in medical care costs, primarily by limiting procedures and reimbursable rates.

That means that not only will the safest jobs and businesses be in health care in the Aftershock, but also that the nation's hopes for regaining significant productivity growth in the postbubble economy will lie with dramatic productivity advancements in the health care field.

Government Jobs and Businesses

After health care, the next best positions in the necessities sector will be government services jobs, such as police and firefighters. As in past recessions, government services will still be needed. However, unlike in past recessions, in the Aftershock, government services will have to take deep cuts when the government can no longer borrow money after the government debt bubble pops. Before the Aftershock, government service jobs will hold on and may seem protected, but they could be pulled out from under you later, when things get worse.

This will be particularly true for private companies that have contracts with the federal government or states. Businesses and individuals who supply capital goods or construction services to the government will be hit. Road construction and maintenance, and transportation in general, will do poorly as the money for these expenditures dries up. Businesses that can make the switch to repair work and repair-related services will fare far better.

Education Jobs and Businesses

Along with health care, the demand for public education will continue, so businesses that supply education or health care products or services to the government will benefit from strengthening their marketing and business ties to these areas and increasing their percentage of sales in these sectors.

Jobs in education will be more secure than in, say, the restaurant business (discretionary spending sector), but do not make the mistake of thinking that *all* education jobs will be fully protected as the bubbles fall. As tax revenues drastically drop at both the state and local levels, funding for education will fall. Long term, jobs at primary and secondary schools will hold up better than those in higher education. Some number of elementary, middle, and high school math and science teachers will still be in demand, but as class size expands, many math and science teachers will not find a job.

Music and art teachers will face more layoffs, along with extracurricular personnel. Once the bubbles are fully popped and the Aftershock begins, we may find that seniority and union membership won't matter much. Instead, if you want to get or keep a job in education, you will need to be very good at your job, be willing to teach more classes to more students, and be loyal to your school's administration.

The picture for higher education will be tougher. Strong departments in practical fields, like engineering and computer science, especially at top colleges and universities, will fare better than those in "soft" departments (sociology, English, etc.) at liberal arts schools. Don't count on tenure to save you if your department has to take big budget cuts. If you are lucky enough to be retained in a strong department, be prepared to teach more classes for less pay.

Broader Job Trends

One of the obvious job trends as we near the Aftershock will be growth in cash businesses and jobs. Expect that jobs in restaurants will increasingly be paid with cash and many people will be able to find temporary jobs or consulting jobs that pay cash and will be

Free Internships—Not Just for College Students Anymore

Free internships have been a good route for college students to potentially get a paid job by working for free. For the student, an internship provides an opportunity to get a foot in the door of an employer, as well as getting some on-the-job training. For the employer, the internship offers a chance to get to know the intern in the work environment before deciding to hire or fire, while also getting some work out of them for free, making the internship an effective win-win for both parties.

What is beginning to happen now, and will be more common in the future, is unpaid internships for adults who are not college students. In an increasingly tight job market, workers who are willing to work for free for a period of time will have a competitive advantage. Like college students, they will have the chance to get their foot in the door, while also gaining training and on-the-job experience. The value to the potential employer is obvious: free labor.

As the bubbles continue to fall, and even more so after they fully pop in the Aftershock, unpaid internships for non–college students will become increasingly common.

If there is a job you are going after now and they don't currently offer an unpaid internship, there is no harm in suggesting one. The company may not be set up to accept your offer, but you never know. Everyone likes a freebie.

willing to work at lower rates. The underground cash economy will likely grow substantially, as it has in other countries experiencing a major economic downturn. Jobs in repair, as we mentioned earlier, will be more resistant to the downturn and are the type of jobs that can be easily paid for in cash.

Also, another current trend that will continue into the Aftershock, and especially afterward, will be higher pay and growth in demand for highly skilled blue-collar jobs. Although highly skilled blue-collar workers will be hurt like most job seekers, this area will still offer reasonable pay and decent opportunities even during the Aftershock. This is especially true if these skilled jobs also involve difficult working conditions, such as being an electrical lineman who has to repair electrical lines in storms. Such jobs will continue to pay relatively well and there will be decent demand, mostly because many people with skills don't like those kinds of jobs. Even now, there are lots of vacancies for these types of jobs and significant turnover in many of them. Although conditions will tighten considerably in the future, this will still be an area for employment simply because of the skills required and many people's unwillingness to work under bad conditions.

Opportunities after the Bubbles Pop: Cashing In on Distressed Assets

In nearly every industry in all three sectors of the economy, there will be some opportunities to benefit from falling asset values. Just as high-priced office furniture from bankrupt dot-com companies ended up at auction sales for pennies on the dollar after the relatively small Internet bubble popped, there will be countless auctions of every description after our multibubble economy pops. Opportunities to make large profits by buying, selling, and servicing distressed businesses and other assets will actually become one of the good sectors in the postbubble economy.

As always, timing will be key. One of the biggest mistakes many people will make is buying distressed businesses or other assets too soon. In this very unusual economic downturn, involving the fall of multiple bubbles, we will face very high interest and inflation rates that will take a lot longer to come down than anyone might imagine. It will be easy to mistakenly think the worst has passed and the time is right to start buying up distressed businesses and assets, when actually the price of these bargain properties will likely fall *even lower*. For maximum profits, think years, not months. Many people in the real estate market are making this mistake right now. They think that because an asset has lost 25 to 50 percent of its peak value, it is a bargain. That is true only if it is not going to fall further.

That said, there can be some shorter-term opportunities to "flip" a distressed asset even before the Aftershock hits and assets fall even further, if you can find a willing buyer.

Once the Aftershock hits, the servicing of distressed assets and businesses will be an instant and long-term winner. People and companies who buy, restructure, manage, and resell distressed businesses and other assets will have the opportunity to make huge incomes and profits, including:

- Accountants and financial analysts involved with forensic accounting and distressed properties accounting.
- Consultants, bankers, managers, and others involved in the acquisition, restructuring, and management of distressed businesses and other assets.
- Bankruptcy attorneys.
- Liquidation companies and auction houses.

Should I Go to College?

For high school students or recent graduates, planning to go to college still makes sense. Even though the economy will be falling during that time and you will likely emerge from college in a difficult work environment with fewer jobs and business opportunities than before, it is still a good idea to get a college education if you can. The longer you wait, the less likely you are to go back to school, and a college degree will still mean something, even in the Aftershock. While a college degree is no guarantee of landing employment, it will definitely increase the odds of getting a job after you graduate and will also improve your chances of getting a higher-paying job. Obviously, you will do better picking a field in the more favorable job sectors mentioned earlier. If you already have a secure, full-time job, going back to college may not be worth it, unless you get your degree in a year or two.

Paying for College

Conventional wisdom's approach to saving for college (like CW advice on most investing) made sense during the rising bubble economy. However, in the falling bubble economy, traditional savings plans and college investment instruments, such as 529 plans, are not going to fare well as inflation rises and interest rates climb. Instead, put your college savings into a well-diversified Aftershock portfolio, as described throughout this book and especially in Chapter 11.

In terms of student loans, we suggest you get these while you still can if you need them to go to college. Right now, student loans cannot be discharged in bankruptcy, and student loan lenders, both private and government, go after student loan payments fairly aggressively. So do not borrow more than you can reasonably handle in monthly payments after you graduate.

However, just as the government has become more relaxed about the repayment of mortgages, we will probably see the government be much more relaxed about the repayment of student loans when the multibubble Aftershock hits—mostly because it will be very difficult to collect and politically more popular. Also, after our falling bubbles finally fully pop, there will likely be less money available for student loans.

10

Aftershock Retirement and Estate Planning

Retirement means different things to different people—tarpon fishing in Aruba, 18 holes every day before lunch, finally having the time to learn Spanish—but in financial terms there's only one real definition: no more upside income potential. As long as you're working, you have the power to increase your income, by getting a promotion or a raise, or changing companies or even careers. But on the day you leave the workforce, you're limited to whatever you've managed to save by that point, and a stream of essentially fixed income. (For the record, the numbers on retirement savings are pretty dismal. Among people ages 50 to 59, the median retirement savings is just $29,000. How long could you get by on that amount?)

That's why it's so crucial to plan for retirement, whether it's 5 years away or 35 years. For those who are nearing retirement or already retired, the information in previous chapters may seem daunting. But don't panic. You can still do plenty to protect yourself—and even come out more comfortable than you ever would have before—by adopting an Aftershock mentality to your financial situation during retirement.

We need to stress that *set it and forget it* will not work for retirement savings anymore. For a generation, people have been told to put their money in stocks and bonds and not worry about it. We've already seen some retirement accounts get hammered due to this strategy, but the future is going to be much, much worse for people who refuse to change with the times. The unfortunate truth is that the vast majority of retirement plans are still focused on stocks, bonds, and real estate. And just like with whole life insurance and annuities, as those major markets decline, so do those retirement plans.

Given that risk, *you have to actively manage your investments over time.* This is true if you're in your 30s or 40s, and even if you've put your retirement money into gold and Aftershock-safe investments. After all, those investments won't necessarily remain your best option 20 or 30 years down the road. Even if you're in your 60s, you want your investments to hold up into your 80s and 90s if necessary, don't you? And maybe even leave something to your loved ones, too? We say this often because it's so important: The investing world is a lot more complex than it used to be, and *active management is a must.*

Types of Retirement Plans

Generally, there are two types of investments in retirement plans: those you can control and those you can't. We're going to focus on what you can control.

Defined Benefit Pension Plans

A few decades ago, most retirement plans offered by an employer were defined benefit plans, also known as pensions. These are still around in some isolated cases, but they're increasingly rare. Under defined benefit plans, the company took care of everything—you just had to show up at work every morning, get your gold watch on your retirement day, and the pension checks would show up until your dying day, along with your spouse's (or you could opt for a lump sum payment). It was the company's responsibility to invest the pension plan and make sure it had enough money to cover the payments for their retirees. If the plan fell short, the company would have to dip into assets and earnings to cover the difference. Because this was a very bad thing, pension plan investments are usually very conservative—typically in bonds and more conservative stocks.

Defined Contribution Plans: 401(k), 403(b), 457

In the past 30 or 40 years, Congress has created a number of new retirement structures, and many employers have shifted responsibility for managing retirement plans to their employees. These generally work the same way, but they have different names— 401(k) accounts are for private companies, 403(b)s are for non-profits, and 457 accounts are generally for government workers and contractors. Regardless of the name, these accounts let employees choose their own investments, and their contributions grow tax free over time. In the decades since these accounts were created, they've been incredibly popular because they allow employees to take advantage of a booming stock market. Another advantage of these accounts is that many employers match their employees' contributions up to the legal limit of 5 percent of an employee's salary. This is a major incentive to contribute the maximum amount allowed—even if your company only matches 25 percent of your contributions, that effectively gives you an immediate 25 percent return.

A variation on the traditional 401(k) plan is the Roth 401(k), introduced in 2001. Contributions to a Roth 401(k) are not tax deferred—your contributions come out of your salary after taxes. But the advantage is that you don't have to pay any taxes when you make withdrawals. And as with a traditional 401(k), your investments can grow in a tax-free environment. This can be a big advantage over traditional 401(k) plans, especially for younger investors.

The biggest drawback of a 401(k), especially from an Aftershock perspective, is the limited number of investment options. Because your employer administers these programs, your employer also decides the mutual funds and stocks you can invest in. And in some cases, you may get stuck with only a handful of options. Even those with more expansive options tend to include only traditional investment strategies.

Individual Retirement Accounts (IRAs)

There's a lot to like about individual retirement accounts, especially from an Aftershock perspective. Contributions are still tax deductible and grow tax deferred—as with a 401(k)—but rather than being

The Nondeductible IRA

For individuals who don't qualify for a traditional or Roth IRA, or those who want to make more than the maximum allowable contribution, a third option is the nondeductible IRA. A nondeductible IRA works like a traditional IRA except that there is no tax deduction for contributions. This sounds like a raw deal. Why put money in a retirement account if you have to pay taxes on contributions *and* on gains when you withdraw? The answer is tax-deferred growth.

With a nondeductible IRA, your investments still get to grow in a tax-free environment, allowing you to put off taxes on earnings until you withdraw at a qualified age. This may sound trivial, but by having more principal in your account, any earnings on that principal are compounded. It can make a significant difference in the long run.

The trade-off, of course, is that nondeductible IRAs come with all the restrictions of other IRAs. You can't withdraw before age 59½ without paying a penalty, and minimum distributions are required by age 70½. But some people need an incentive to save for retirement, and if that's you, a nondeductible IRA is better than nothing.

run by your employer, IRAs are self-managed, giving you far more control over your retirement savings. You can open an IRA at just about any brokerage firm—full-service or discount—and you can invest them in just about any asset category out there: stocks, bonds, real estate, and even gold bullion. You can probably guess that this is our favorite retirement vehicle, as long as it's employed wisely.

Other Retirement Plans

There are a couple of other categories of retirement plans for workers in specific categories. For example, civil service employees have their own plan, called the Federal Employees Retirement System (FERS), which combines both a defined benefit plan and a defined contribution Thrift Savings Plan (TSP), as well as mandatory participation in Social Security. (Some long-tenured federal employees may still qualify for an older plan.) The investment options for TSP are extremely limited—just five funds: two for bonds and three for various stock indices.

Similarly, small businesses and self-employed people have their own types of plans: Keogh, Savings Incentive Match Plan for Employees (SIMPLE) IRAs, and Simplified Employee Pension (SEP) IRAs. These have various advantages and drawbacks, which are too complex to explain here. If you're in either of these categories, please understand the rules before opening any of these accounts, and remember—active management is a must.

The Conventional Wisdom on Retirement Plans

The conventional wisdom says that stocks, bonds, and real estate are all recovering or will recover. So the last thing most people are worried about is their retirement account. As long as people simply hold on to their diversified stock and bond mutual funds, this thinking goes, the markets will be fine and pensioners and 401(k) investors will be able to retire comfortably for years to come.

For pension funds, this conventional wisdom goes several steps further. Even amid concerns about underfunded corporate pensions, people tend to rest easy about them. After all, corporate pensions are overseen by managers with many years of experience, and they primarily invest in bonds, which are thought to be a more stable asset class, right? Ratings agencies like Standard & Poor's (S&P), Moody's, and Fitch provide objective analysis on corporate bonds, and many pension funds are restricted to bonds with the highest ratings.

Even if those bond holdings go bad, the company is still on the hook to cover the payments of their retirees. And if all else fails and the company goes bankrupt, there's a last line of defense: the U.S. government. Most pensions in this country are insured by the Pension Benefit Guaranty Corporation, or PBGC, which collects premiums in return for covering pensions in the event that they fail. (If the PBGC fails somehow, it's pretty much understood that the government will do what it has to do to guarantee pensioners get what was promised them, even if it has to resort to more borrowing and printing money to do so.)

This is a pretty exhaustive list of protections for pension plans. And the important thing to keep in mind is that *every single line of defense must fail* before pensions collapse. That has never happened before in history, so it's understandable that many people think it never will.

It's our job to help you understand why it will.

Why the Conventional Wisdom on Retirement Is Wrong

The truth is that retirement plans are in big trouble. Many pension plans throughout the United States have been notoriously underfunded and poorly managed. There are protection levels in place, but those were designed to handle individual failures, not widespread multiple pension plans going bad en masse. In fact, each level of protection has serious vulnerabilities.

Let's start with managers. While many pension managers are chosen for their qualifications and judgment, in practice these people rarely outperform market indexes. And if they haven't outperformed the market in the past—under stable conditions—why would they be able to keep their pension funds afloat in the case of a serious market crash?

Next are asset categories. Being invested primarily in bonds doesn't help much because we know that high inflation will be poison to the bond market. Ratings? The ratings agencies showed catastrophically poor judgment in the recent past, when they contributed to the 2008 financial crisis. They haven't changed much about how they operate, yet people still expect them to deliver good results. (What's that line about the definition of insanity?)

If and when bond issuers go bankrupt, bondholders will still have a high priority in liquidation proceedings, but if many companies go belly up at the same time, there will be a lot of sellers and very few buyers. Their assets will bring in only pennies on the dollar. Bad news for bondholders. Corporate backing for pensions is the same story—corporations will face failed pensions and collapsed earnings at the same time. Bankruptcy will be the only option.

Last is the federal government, which will certainly do its part—at least for a while—in making sure pensioners get what they need. But the PBGC is not well funded to begin with and will quickly be overwhelmed. The government can still step in and help for a few years, but eventually there are simply too many guarantees to cover—not just with pension plans but everywhere—and the Fed can't keep printing money forever. And down goes the last line of defense for pension plans.

Of course, long before a company goes bankrupt or the federal government has to step in, bonds can lose an enormous amount of their value when interest rates rise, as detailed in Chapter 5. Stocks and real estate are also very vulnerable, as described in Chapters 4 and 6. So, even if there were no corporate bankruptcies or no need for government bailouts, pensions can lose much of their asset value and, hence, their ability to pay those pensions.

Unfortunately, defined contribution plans like 401(k)s aren't in much better shape. Because most offer relatively few options based on traditional investing strategies, they make it very difficult for an individual to beat a total market failure while also protecting against inflation. When stocks, bonds, and real estate all fall, 401(k) plans will fall with them. In 2008, for example, 401(k) plans fell in value by 40 percent. This is just a taste of what's ahead.

What About Social Security?

If you've been in the workforce for a while, you probably qualify for Social Security benefits. Yet even if you work up until age 65, the benefits probably aren't much. In fact, Social Security was never meant to provide for all retirement needs (let alone comforts), but it has provided something of a safety net to millions of retirees for generations.

In recent years, the program's future has come into question, and for good reason. Social Security is an unfunded program, meaning that the Social Security taxes you pay today are being used directly to pay beneficiaries. In other words, it's a transfer payment, not a pension plan. In some ways, this was inevitable—for decades, Social Security was running surpluses and the government was borrowing those surplus funds to finance other parts of the budget. Now the surpluses are gone, and things aren't going to get any better in the Aftershock.

There's a good chance that many people reading this will never collect a nickel in Social Security benefits. The government will still offer some level of assistance, particularly for the elderly, but it will be means-tested. (That is, you won't get it if you don't really need it.) Even that level of support will depend on significant income tax hikes on the middle and upper class. Since the government will no longer be able to borrow money easily, and since printing money will become self-defeating, the government will have to strike a delicate balance: taxing enough to provide for those in need but not so much to discourage people from working, particularly if the alternative is to collect hardship payments. The bottom line? The days of universal Social Security benefits will soon be over.

What's a Savvy Aftershock Investor to Do?

With such an ugly outlook for pensions and other retirement plans, it's hard to know how to proceed. Unfortunately, the simple answer in most cases is to get out of your employer's plan, so you have more control and can put it into assets that will hold up in the Aftershock. However, *when* and *how* to get out are crucial questions. Because of the tax advantages in most retirement accounts, you often face steep penalties if you pull your retirement money early. In addition, as we write this, stocks and bonds are still doing okay—not great, but okay—and you need to strike a balance between maximizing your portfolio for the next few years and making sure your retirement savings will hold up in the Aftershock.

To determine your best option, we'll break down each category of retirement plan and the best way to protect yourself as much as possible.

Defined Benefit Pension Plans

Many defined benefit plans offer a lump sum at retirement as opposed to an annuity. This is great news for those approaching retirement in the next few years. Taking a lump sum and putting it into Aftershock-proof investments—which you actively manage, of course—is an easy way to minimize the risk of ever-shrinking payments down the road. Better yet, you can put the lump sum into an IRA account and enjoy the benefits of tax-deferred growth. (See the section on IRAs for more information on this approach.)

For those who don't have the option of a lump sum payment and are instead forced to take regular payments, the situation is more grim—especially for people near retirement or already retired. Remember, those are fixed payments, so when inflation kicks in, it will eat away much of their value. Market crashes, widespread bankruptcies, and an eventual government default will make the situation worse. The truth is that you can't depend on these pension payments to provide living expenses. When things get really bad, you can expect the federal government to step in and provide hardship payments, with pensioners among the first in line. Those payments will be limited—probably not much higher than $2,000 per month (in 2012 dollars)—since the government will have to rely on tax revenues to cover their cost. But they're better than nothing. People facing this scenario may need to plan on reducing living expenses as they approach their retirement years.

Younger readers with defined benefit plans may not be as concerned about retirement, but it's worth looking into your options now regardless of your age, so you know what your options are. Does your plan allow for early withdrawals? Paying a relatively small penalty now or in the next few years is almost certainly better than being wiped out later. What about early retirement? What are the costs and the benefits? If you're thinking about changing jobs, or if you lose your job, can you roll over your retirement benefits into a self-directed IRA?

No matter how close you are to retirement, if you're covered under a defined benefit plan, you need to know the choices your employer is making on behalf of your future. And if you work at a small company, you can always request changes to the plan. Even if your employers aren't sold on the Aftershock—and many employers are resistant to these ideas—they might be willing to offer options for employees who want to protect themselves. No matter what, it can't hurt to ask.

Defined Contribution Plans

As we said above, the biggest problem with 401(k)s and other defined contribution plans is that they limit your options. If you can only invest in traditional stock and bond funds, your retirement account is going to suffer when the stock and bond markets collapse. In most cases, employees with 401(k) plans have exactly zero Aftershock-proof options.

At some point, obviously, you'll need to get out. But not so fast. There are some mitigating factors that can make holding onto a 401(k) worthwhile, at least in the near term. First of all, you can always ask your employer for more diversity in investment options, including a gold or foreign currency fund that is more likely to hold its value in the Aftershock. If you work at a smaller company and several employees feel the same way, you might have enough sway to convince your employer to make a change.

Even if you are stuck with limited options, there are still legitimate reasons to continue making contributions to a 401(k) *in the meantime*, before the Aftershock. For one thing, if your employer offers matching contributions, that alone may be reason enough to keep making the maximum contribution for the next few years, while things are still relatively stable. After all, employer contributions are free money. Another factor to consider is whether you are close to being fully vested in your plan, or at least will be more vested than you are now. Employees in that situation should stay with their current plan, as the increased vesting could mean a substantial difference in potential income down the road.

If you're going to remain, what should you invest in? In the immediate future, cash-type investments, such as money market funds and short-term Treasury funds, will be the safest options. These funds still may lose value as inflation and interest rates rise, but the declines will be mild at first, and your employer's matching contributions should easily cover the difference. Better yet, investing in TIPS, or Treasury inflation-protected securities, will give you some protection against inflation.

Of course, sooner or later, if your 401(k) plan doesn't offer options that will hold up in the Aftershock, you will need to get out before things get too ugly. Borrowing from your 401(k) fund is one option, but it's not a particularly good one. Theoretically, you could invest the borrowed funds wisely and come out ahead, but this strategy can be very risky, given short-term fluctuations. If you leave your job *for any reason*, the repayment term for 401(k) loans shortens dramatically. That's a pretty big gamble, and it could leave you on the hook for ordinary income tax on the borrowed amount, plus a 10 percent penalty on any borrowed funds if things don't work out as you expected.

Hardship withdrawals are also available, but they also come at a steep price, and they are not available for those looking for other investment opportunities (except, in some cases, for buying a home).

For older workers, the choices are a little easier. If you're already older than 59½, or will be soon, some 401(k) plans will allow you to take an in-service withdrawal based on your age, even if you're not ready to retire. That way you can simply take a lump sum payment, preferably rolling it over into an IRA account, where you can invest as you wish.

Even if an age-based withdrawal is not allowed, early retirement may be the right option for you, depending on your financial situation and life plans. In fact, 401(k) plans even allow you to retire as early as 55 and begin withdrawals without penalty. (One caveat: If you roll these funds into an IRA, you'll still have to wait until you turn 59½ to begin taking withdrawals without a penalty.)

For younger employees, the answers aren't as simple, but you still have some solid options. First, some employers offer a partial rollover, allowing you to take out a portion of your 401(k) funds—usually not more than 50 percent—and put it into a qualifying IRA of your choosing. This may not solve all your problems, but it's a pretty good start.

Second, if you change jobs, you can roll over your 401(k) funds into an IRA. For some people who are on the fence about their current employer, this may be enough to help them make their decision. *Note:* You can also take this option if you're fired or laid off. While that's certainly not an ideal situation, the silver lining is that you can invest your retirement wisely and perhaps come out richer for it in the long run.

If none of these options is available, you can always simply withdraw your 401(k) funds early. You'll face a 10 percent penalty for the amount you take out, and the funds will be treated as ordinary income. If it's a significant amount, it could easily push you into a higher tax bracket for the year. But if the alternative is to lose nearly all of your retirement savings, this may be a price you're willing to pay. Like we said, you have a few more stable years between now and the Aftershock, giving you some time to preserve and even grow your portfolio. This is a big step, so it's worth looking into all the ramifications ahead of time so you're prepared to get out when the time comes. You can easily make up for the losses if you invest wisely.

We should also emphasize that for younger employees who haven't yet opened a 401(k)—assuming there is a significant employer matching contribution—it can still be worth doing so *even if you'll have to take the penalty to get out* in a few years. Remember, that matching contribution is essentially free money, and if you're sticking with cash-based investments like money markets and short-term Treasurys, even a 25 percent return (let alone a 50 or 100 percent return) is still a very impressive gain, especially in these slow economic times.

One note for readers in other employment categories: This advice also applies if you have a 403(b) plan, which carries the same rules and penalties for early withdrawals. If you have a 457 plan, you have an added advantage—you can still withdraw funds early without the added 10 percent penalty, though you'll still owe ordinary income tax on all withdrawals. Similarly, people with

A Note about Company Stock and Stock Options

Some companies encourage employees to invest their retirement money in company stock by offering it at a discount to the market price. But allocating a large amount of your retirement portfolio in your employer is a risky proposition under any circumstances. If your company hits a rough patch, you could lose both your job and your retirement savings at the same time. You might think this is unlikely, but it's happened all too frequently in recent years, and will only become more common in the future. You are already invested in your employer's success by working there. No need to double down.

Employee stock options are a different story. Options allow you to lock in the price at which you can buy company stock. The best part is that if you don't want to buy when the time comes, you don't have to. You usually have a long window of time before you need to make this decision. In the long term, there may be some upside to employee stock options, but there isn't any downside—they're risk free.

Keogh plans, SIMPLE IRAs, and SEP IRAs should follow the same advice—invest in Aftershock-safe assets. But the great advantage of self-employment is that you get to make the choices yourself.

IRA Rollovers

One of the great features of IRAs—both traditional and Roth—is the *rollover* function. If you have a 401(k)—or 403(b) or 457, for that matter—and are leaving your employer, whether it's due to a job change or involuntary termination, you can transfer your 401(k) funds into a self-directed IRA account without paying taxes or penalties. This gives you far more investment options than a typical retirement plan, letting you put the funds in Aftershock-proof holdings.

This is also a great option for those who are entering retirement. You can take your withdrawal in a single lump sum and roll it into an IRA, invest the funds as you wish, and continue to enjoy the tax advantages for the life of the account.

Here's another nice thing: The total contribution you can make into your IRA is capped each year, but there's no limit to the

It's the Investments, Not the Account

We routinely hear from concerned readers that one of their primary fears is that, no matter how well they invest, they could still lose everything if the financial institution holding their IRA, 401(k), or any other type of account goes bankrupt. We always tell these people the same thing—that's not likely to happen. At least for the foreseeable future, they should worry about their investments, not their accounts.

Yes, we will see plenty of financial institutions go under in the Aftershock. But at least in the immediate aftermath, all remaining assets will simply be transferred from one institution to another. (Former account holders with Wachovia or First Union have already been through this experience—it's not catastrophic.) In the very long term, especially as we get close to a government default, you'll want to eliminate all but the most liquid of funds (i.e., checking accounts). But that's a ways out, and things will have to have been very bad for a while before we get there.

number of IRA accounts you can have. You can put some funds into a gold IRA and another portion into a discount brokerage account, and still another portion into a full-service brokerage account (you just can't go over the maximum total for the year). The only potential drawback to this is that your broker may charge fees for transfers and for setting up new accounts. But if you have substantial retirement funds and you want to diversify, IRA accounts provide a great vehicle for that.

Federal Employee Retirement Plans

Because the federal government guarantees the retirement plans for its workers, those plans will hold their dollar value—though not necessarily an inflation-adjusted value—until the government defaults, which won't happen until we are well into the Aftershock. The downside is that retired federal workers could face serious problems before that. After all, once inflation kicks in, it will eat away much of the value of their monthly payments.

The biggest problem with the defined benefit plan for federal workers is that they don't allow you to take lump-sum payments. Instead, the government makes distributions on an annuitized basis, which means that you can't depend on these plans over the long term. Fortunately, as we discussed in the defined benefit section, if these plans run into problems, federal-service pensioners will be at the front of the line when the government makes hardship payments.

For federal employees who take part in the Thrift Savings Plan—which effectively functions like a 401(k)—you can take a lump-sum withdrawal when you retire, or a one-time, age-based withdrawal if you are older than 59½. That gives you some measure of control and lets you pick Aftershock-proof assets. But if you're younger than that and still working for the government, you're out of luck. The TSP doesn't allow early withdrawals for current employees. Even if you were willing to pay the 10 percent penalty, you can't do it. This puts younger federal employees in a bind—they may have to consider changing jobs over the next few years or risk a significant loss down the road in the retirement savings they've already accrued. (Again, for what it's worth, if you're involuntarily separated, this is the silver lining.)

Retirement Q&A

Question: Should I use a retirement calculator to see if I'm on the right track?

Answer: Retirement calculators can be valuable tools, but they won't be accurate unless they include Aftershock assumptions, and we don't know of any that currently do. In fact, while calculators are a way to gauge your progress, it's more important to get the fundamentals right and invest properly in an Aftershock-based portfolio.

Question: How much should I contribute to my 401(k) in the meantime?

Answer: As long as your employer matches your contributions, putting in the maximum amount gives you a guaranteed return—free money—which is a big advantage. However, if you normally contribute beyond the maximum matching amount, you're better offer putting that excess into an IRA or other account, so you don't have to worry about penalties for withdrawal later.

Question: When should I cash out my 401(k) and take the penalty?

Answer: This situation needs to be monitored very carefully, but we think you'll need to pull your money out in the next two to four years. As we've written earlier, the first sign will be inflation going above 5 percent and, as it rises further, global investors starting to move away from the dollar. It's important that you watch for these signs and be prepared to get out quickly. But remember: It's better to be out too early than too late.

Question: Should I take Social Security benefits early?

Answer: Yes. In the past, it was best to wait. But, as we've explained, Social Security will eventually be means-tested, so it's best to take what you can while you can. Even if you qualify for means-tested payments down the

road, you'll almost certainly get more money by taking
payments as soon as you can.

Question: What about my home equity? Won't that help me get
through retirement?

Answer: Historically, home equity has been a major part of
people's savings, especially in the United States. Some
middle-class American families have up to 90 percent
of their savings tied up in their homes, and many
people rely on home equity during retirement.

　　If you've read the chapter on real estate, you already
know the problem with this approach. Home equity is
not going to count for much when interest rates rise
and the real estate market crashes. Refinancing will
become virtually impossible, and the interest rates
will be staggering enough to scare away most homeowners—limiting their ability to pull money out of the
equity they've built up. Already, since 2008, American
homeowners have lost 55 percent of their home equity.
That doesn't mean their homes have lost 55 percent of
their value, but any time you owe money on a property,
a fall in the value of that property has a compounding
effect on your equity. Even those few who own their
homes outright, while they may be in a better position
than most, won't find much help from it in covering
retirement expenses. Clearly, home equity isn't going
to save many people.

Question: So then I shouldn't consider a reverse mortgage?

Answer: As explained in Chapter 6, a reverse mortgage is a losing proposition. It puts you on the line for significant
debt while still having a lien on a house that—very
likely, in most markets—has lost much of its value.

A Good Retirement

One of the myths about retirement is that you spend less money
than during working years. In fact, your spending often goes up.
First of all, retirees have much more leisure time, and it takes

money to fill up that time with travel and activities, things that many people consider necessary for a *good* retirement. Then there's the cost of inflation. This isn't an actual increase in expenditures, but for retirees who depend on a fixed income, it can be problematic. And it's not going to get any better when the dollar bubble bursts.

The good news is that if you're still working, you have time to save aggressively and invest intelligently. This means diversifying funds, and moving assets into Aftershock-safe investments in the next few years. But most of all it means *active management*. What works today may be poison tomorrow.

For those who are ready to retire soon and enjoy their pension, or perhaps are already on a pension, the Aftershock couldn't come at a worse time. But that doesn't mean you can't protect yourself now, while you still have some time. In fact, if you invest well, you can reorient your portfolio to limit your downside risks during the Aftershock and even come out ahead. The bottom line? Well-placed investments now can save you from a lot of difficulty down the road.

Estate Planning: Making the Most of Your Assets for Yourself and Your Heirs

For hundreds of years, estate planning was simple. You created a will that stipulated how your assets were to be distributed after you died. But things became much more complicated in the early twentieth century, when income taxes and estate taxes were first introduced. These extra costs motivated people to plan their estates in ways that helped them avoid taxes and the increasing cost of probate.

Probate

If you don't leave a will, your local estate court distributes your assets according to "intestacy" laws, which vary from country to country and state to state. Typically, this means equal distribution among heirs with no personal control over who gets what. For example, you might want one of your children in particular to inherit your wedding ring, or you might want to leave a certain amount to charity. Without a will, intestate distribution doesn't allow that.

Today, even if you have a will, your heirs still may have to go through probate to determine that it's legitimate and valid. Probate can be an ugly process—it often results in long delays before a will can be executed, along with legal fees that can eat away much of an estate. If a judge ends up appointing an executor and attorney for the will, some of those professionals will try to wring as much money out of the estate as possible. It's well worth your efforts to avoid a complicated probate situation.

If you have limited assets, you can accomplish much of this through a process known as "titling." In practice, titling simply means establishing control and ownership over something. For example, you can hold a bank account jointly with a spouse or another heir, stipulating a right of survivorship. That way, if you die, your spouse simply takes over the account outright, and it doesn't become part of the estate. Life insurance is another example—if you specify a beneficiary, that becomes a simple transaction when you die: The insurance company pays the beneficiary directly. If you're planning to distribute assets this way, it's critical to keep your records up to date. If you've remarried or had a new child, out-of-date documents could lead to problems.

Titling assets appropriately works well and removes the potential for disputes, but it has limited application. If you have complex inheritance situations, you can't handle them through titling alone. Another, more powerful method is to use a revocable living, or inter vivos, trust. You put the assets you want to distribute into a trust, and you control it during your life. Once you die, the trust is controlled by the trustee or by the successor of the trustee to continue to protect or to distribute the assets according to your instructions. It's an effective way to distribute assets and avoid probate. You can keep the entire inheritance process private. The process of creating a living trust usually requires an attorney, though some people do it themselves.

Estate Taxes

Estate taxes can be complex, but they're a lot less relevant today than they were in the past. As of 2011, the first $5 million of any estate is exempt from any taxes, and the remainder is subject to a flat 35 percent tax. That means that most people don't need to worry about this issue. Even some people who have estates above the $5 million limit will simply make a large donation to their favorite charity to get the overall estate below the cap. However, the rules are changing all the time, and it's difficult to predict how they might change even a few years from now.

A word of caution here: It's illegal to engage in *any* activity the IRS deems a deliberate attempt to avoid paying taxes. We don't condone tax evasion and are not recommending it under any circumstances. That said, there are some completely legal ways to pass assets to your heirs while minimizing taxes.

For example, people often minimize their potential tax liability by giving gifts to their heirs while the giver is still alive. The IRS sets a cap each year on the amount one person can give to another without a tax consequence (as of 2011, the cap was $13,000). That sounds small, but if you have multiple children and grandchildren, it can add up.

Another common practice is to put appreciating assets into a generation-skipping trust. This means that heirs are considered "life tenants" of the trust—they can benefit from the interest generated by the trust, but not the principal, which gets passed on to the next generation. In years past, the principal passed through tax free. However, Congress has since created a special "generation-skipping" tax to close this loophole, leaving descendants responsible for taxes on the trust's principal—but again, only for amounts over $5 million.

A more recent development in estate planning is the family limited partnership. This structure consists of general partners who retain control over the assets (typically the parents), and limited partners who have an ownership stake but no control (typically the children). A limited partnership offers several tax advantages. For example, it allows you to transfer ownership of assets to children over time through the standard annual gifts up to the IRS cap within the partnership, meaning you retain control of the assets. Above that amount, your family will have to pay gift tax only on the "fair market value" of any ownership transfers. And because the limited partners receiving the assets don't have control over them, this fair market value is often considerably less than the actual asset values. To use this approach, you need a qualified appraiser to assess the value of any gift in a family limited partnership to determine the appropriate taxable amount.

Estate Planning in the Aftershock

The biggest issue for estate planning in the Aftershock is that most traditional assets—stocks, bonds, real estate, whole life insurance, and annuities—will be worth only a fraction of their former value. For people who lose most of their wealth, estate planning will be moot because they won't have much left to give to their heirs. Of course, if you're reading this book, we're going to assume that you have protected yourself with safe investments and still have plenty of wealth to distribute.

When the government can no longer borrow or safely print money, its only recourse will be to dramatically raise taxes on those who are employed and have assets. That means the estate tax will become a much bigger issue and impact more people. We expect progressive estate tax rates in line with income tax rates, which will be higher than current levels. There will probably still be an exemption—maybe even as high as the current $5 million—but it won't necessarily be adequately indexed for inflation. And remember, $5 million in the Aftershock won't be what it is today.

Estate planning is rarely simple, but in an Aftershock environment it gets even more complex, especially for estates with various types of assets. If you have multiple assets you're trying to protect, you will likely need multiple strategies. For domestic assets, such as a house, car, or furniture, an inter vivos trust is usually the best approach. For assets like a family-owned business or real estate holdings, a family limited partnership is generally the best way to go. You can use joint titling with right of survivorship for assets like bank accounts that you want to be transferred quickly after death. Many of these assets won't be worth too much, but you will likely still want to transfer them appropriately for other reasons. Finally, you may still need a will for any residual assets.

Many readers of this book will no doubt hold a significant portion of precious metals. While exchange-traded funds are a fine way to invest in gold for now, for security reasons you may want to own gold bullion when the Aftershock hits. One of the advantages of physical assets like gold is that they're relatively easy to secure in a safe place that no one else knows about. The problem for estate planning is that if no one knows where you keep the assets, they can't be transferred after you die. And while your heirs may be trustworthy enough to know the location in advance, this is a risk you may not want to take—for these assets, physical possession essentially amounts to ownership.

Finally, you'll need to take capital losses into account. Capital losses are an almost negligible aspect of estate planning today, but they'll be critical in the Aftershock, as all kinds of assets will lose a great deal of their value. Realizing capital losses in your home and other assets could help offset any income from wages or gains and substantially reduce tax liability. In addition, you can also transfer some capital losses to your heirs in order to offset their income. There are some fairly restrictive rules on the books today about using capital losses to offset income, but in an Aftershock environment—with such widespread capital losses—these rules could be relaxed.

For many, an Aftershock portfolio will likely be heavily invested overseas in multiple tax-haven countries. Good estate planning in these circumstances generally would require the use of long term overseas trusts to protect the assets and ensure the proper transfer of these assets to heirs.

CHAPTER 11

Your Aftershock Investment Portfolio

As we said before, *The Aftershock Investor* is the guide to investing even if there is no Aftershock. Even if the bond market doesn't melt down, there are still big long-term problems to contend with. Even if the stock market doesn't melt down, there are still big long-term problems to contend with there, as well. The same is true for real estate. It won't take a big multbubble pop for these assets to fall in the future. So you needn't buy into our entire point of view to take heed of our warnings.

As we often say, you certainly don't need hyperinflation to cause major problems for stock, bond, and real estate markets. Even interest rates that were not atypical in the booming 1960s and absolutely benign compared to the incredibly high rates of the 1970s and early 1980s will cause real problems for all these markets at their very high prices today. You need to be prepared for them.

At the very least, you need to be prepared for lots of volatility. We think there will be an Aftershock at the end of this volatility, but even if there is not, you need to at least be prepared for the volatility in the near future and the likelihood of diminished returns from traditional investments.

So, to do that, let's summarize what we've discussed in this book about a diversified Aftershock portfolio. In particular, what is the overall portfolio strategy, what are its components, and what's the best way to implement that portfolio?

Aftershock Portfolio Strategy

The overall strategy of the Aftershock portfolio is:

1. Preservation of capital
2. Minimal volatility
3. Reasonable returns

Preservation of Capital

The term *preservation of capital* should be defined since it is used by many money managers. Most often what conventional wisdom (CW) money managers mean by preservation of capital is lots of safe long-term bonds, some safe blue-chip or high-dividend stocks, and maybe an annuity. We have discussed each of those in detail in the book, so you know by now that keeping those investments for a long period of time will not preserve your capital. It will do just the opposite.

So CW says safe bonds and safe stock are the way to go. We say those aren't safe for the long term anymore. What we mean by preservation of capital is protection against a long-term decline in the stock and bond markets and high inflation down the road. Those are the real threats to your hard-earned wealth.

The fact that stock and bonds are not good long term doesn't mean that they have peaked today. In fact, they probably haven't. Timing is always an issue in investing, and it's hard to time the market. We'll talk more about how to handle the timing issue later in this chapter.

Minimal Volatility

Minimal volatility isn't too hard to define, although exactly how little volatility you want depends on your financial tolerance for volatility. Also, there's no free lunch. To get higher returns you will have to accept somewhat higher volatility. But you can shoot for a happy medium that is less volatile than the stock market but still gives you returns that are comparable to a modestly rising stock market today.

Ideally, an Aftershock investor will have returns that look more like a nonvolatile upward movement as opposed to the highly volatile and very risky Standard & Poor's (S&P) index. It should be more of an arrow through a W. Even if you make the same returns as the S&P 500, do you really want all that volatility? And, of course, there is some risk (we think a very big risk) that at some point one of those downward movements on the stock market isn't going to fully rebound. Once we get to the point where the normal remedy for boosting the stock market (massive money printing and massive borrowing) that has worked so well in the past has increasingly less positive effect (and eventually has a negative effect) a big stock market drop could stay down and not rebound. This market isn't being kept up by economic fundamentals, it is being kept up by artificial means that the government has used effectively, in combination with stock cheerleaders, to maintain a bubble stock market valuation.

Reasonable Returns

Reasonable returns are hard to define. In the current market, 5% might be reasonable to many. For others it's quite low. The key is what level of risk you are taking to get what level of return. If you are getting a high return, you are likely taking a high level of risk. In conventional investing this is called the *risk-adjusted rate of return*, which is often expressed as the Sharpe ratio (the higher the Sharpe ratio of an investment, the better the rate of return you are getting relative to the risk you are taking).

Of course, we are seeing certain investments as risky long term that the market is currently not seeing as risky. So our risk-adjusted rate of return would be different from standard investing analysis. Nonetheless, the concept is correct, and we are advising a lower rate of risk taking now for most people and that will result in a lower rate of return. But it's better than losing your money. Also, you can also make very high returns as we near the Aftershock, but you will be taking more risk and will get higher volatility.

Key Components

So what are the key components of an Aftershock portfolio, and how do we weight them?

The primary components of an Aftershock portfolio today are given below. Remember, this will change over time, which we will discuss with each component.

1. Gold
2. High-dividend stocks
3. Shorter-term Treasurys
4. TIPS (Treasury inflation-protected securities)
5. Foreign currencies
6. Commodities
7. Short stock exchange-traded funds (ETFs)
8. Short bond ETFs

Gold

This is an important element of any Aftershock portfolio, and it will become increasingly important in the future. When we say gold, we mean physical gold and not gold mining stocks. As discussed in Chapter 8, this can be held via an ETF, such as GLD, IAU, or PHYS, which makes it easier to purchase. The big problem with a very large allocation to gold right now is the volatility. However, gold has been a very stable performer on a year-to-year basis, and the fundamentals of gold have never been better. As the Aftershock comes closer, and you are more convinced it is coming, you should be increasing your gold holdings accordingly. But buy some now even if you aren't very sure of the Aftershock. It could easily go down for a while after you buy it, but best to get your toes wet. You will need to be more comfortable buying gold eventually. Right now, many people don't buy gold because they missed it at a lower price earlier. Don't fall into that trap. Just start now by buying a smaller amount.

High-Dividend Stocks

Isn't this one of the assets we said the cheerleaders would suggest? Yes it is. The difference is that we are not recommending it as a long-term hold. It will work well in the current volatile and slow growth stock market. However, like all stocks, you will need to move out over time since high-dividend stocks do go down when the market goes way down. What they do is provide you with a buffer against the volatility of the current market and provide a decent dividend income as well. We particularly like electric utility stocks, but since they have done well in the past year, they likely won't do quite as well in the near future. However, they are still a better choice now than riskier stocks. One easy way to invest in a diversified group of electric utilities is through the ETF XLU.

Shorter-Term Treasurys

This is another temporary asset category. Like high-dividend stocks, which are more defensive in nature, shorter-term bonds are more defensive in nature than long-term bonds. They are not as vulnerable to changes in interest rates as are long-term bonds and they provide you with a buffer against any downward movements in bonds. Again, like high-dividend stocks, they will go down when the bond market goes down a lot, so you will need to move out eventually. But in the meantime it provides a good way to ride the bond bull until it finally turns for good. One easy way to invest in short-term Treasurys is through the ETF VGSH.

TIPS

TIPS are an investment you can keep for the longer term. Accordingly, it may also have a more difficult ride shorter term if inflation expectations decline for a while, as they could for the remainder of this year. Even though we think we will have higher inflation, it won't necessarily be proven for a while. Nonetheless, TIPS have done well in the past, including a 13% rise in 2011. So we like this asset because it will rise when inflation rises. Thus, you are fairly well protected. Shorter term, though, you could get lower returns. Risk-averse investors may even want to skip short-term Treasurys and just use TIPS instead.

Foreign Currencies

These are a trickier category because they are fairly volatile, especially now with the European debt crisis. It is a longer-term play. There is probably too much volatility now for most people to work with this asset category and not enough upside to make it worthwhile. However, longer term, when inflation rises and foreign investors become wary of the United States as a safe haven, the dollar will fall, and this will be a good buy. It's hard to invest in any given currency because it can be affected by country-specific issues. However, a good and relatively stable one for the future will likely be Canadian dollars. The ETF for those is FXC. Another option is to short the dollar index. The dollar index is a basket of foreign currencies measured against the dollar. As the dollar index falls, the short would go up. The symbol for that ETF is UDN.

Commodities

Commodities are a lot like currencies, and we would offer the same advice. It's a longer-term play. It's also a more specific play since we don't think most commodities will do well in the long term due to the worldwide downturn. However, the falling dollar will help agricultural commodities. DBA is an ETF that holds a basket of agricultural commodities. However, this is really only for more sophisticated investors, and the widow of greatest opportunity is a ways off since commodity prices will fall before they recover due to the falling dollar.

Short Stock ETFs

There are probably few instruments more difficult to work with than short ETFs or inverse ETFs. They are simple to buy, but they are difficult to profit from in the current market because it is highly volatile and has been on a modest upward trend in the last couple years. Inverse ETFs are also reconciled daily, so that's a technical issue that means they don't always follow the long-term trend exactly. Hence, they are best used when the trend is strongly in your favor, and that can be hard to predict. Clearly, at some point, there will be a time these can be used to make money, but it won't be until we start to see real weakness in the stock market. If you do use inverse ETFs in the next couple of years, don't be afraid to take profits. Markets can move against you quickly, and you can quickly lose whatever you have gained. One of the most popular inverse stock ETFs is SH, which shorts the S&P 500.

Also, you have to be especially careful about double short ETFs. These are leveraged, so you can make twice as much money, but you can also lose twice as much money. Plus, the daily reconciliation can have a greater effect in tracking long-term trends with leveraged ETFs than nonleveraged.

Short Bond ETFs

The same issues that apply to inverse stock ETFs apply to inverse bond ETFs. Bonds may turn earlier simply because interest rates have fallen so low that even a modest upward movement could damage bonds quite a bit and create nice gains for inverse bond ETFs. However, many investors have been hurt by thinking the bull in Treasury bonds has run its course, including the King of Bonds himself, Bill Gross. One of the most popular inverse bond ETFs is TBF, which shorts the 20-year Treasury bond.

Notice that we like ETFs? For one thing it is often the only way to invest in certain assets, like gold. They also tend to be relatively cheap since they are not managed like a mutual fund. They are very similar to an index fund in cost and structure.

Do It Yourself or Bring in Help?

It's not an easy decision. Either way, there are problems. It's hard to manage a portfolio yourself. Emotion gets in the way. Plus, it takes a certain amount of time and a *lot* of mental energy. It's not that it takes a lot of time, but it's hard not to focus on it a lot of the time. And all that focus energy can wear on you. So we tried to outline a plan in this book that will reduce your focus time by protecting you from a big decline in the stock or bond markets, but like we said, there is no set-it-and-forget-it option right now.

Bringing in help makes sense, but in today's market, that's almost always going to be a cheerleader of some sort. It's hard to find a sensible alternative. And you don't want a cheerleader who says they will invest the way you want. If they don't understand it, they can't really do it, even if you are telling them how. And if you are telling them how to do it, why are you hiring that person? So if you can find the right person, then great. Otherwise, you sort of have to do it yourself.

Timing—Better to Move Too Early than Too Late

You may kick yourself because of the money you "lost" if the market rises after you sell. Certainly, other people will kick you for sure!!! They don't like to see people selling out of the market. It's bad for business if you're a stock salesman, and it's bad for others who hold stocks, which is a lot of people. Don't expect their support, whether it turns out in the short term you were right or wrong. If you were right and stocks go down, it's like salt in the wound to others. If you're wrong and stocks go up, then that's more reason for others to feel good about owning stocks and proving to the poor fools who aren't as smart about stocks that they were wrong.

The last part of this chapter is devoted to the broader issues that will affect timing and how the market ultimately declines. Since we haven't had a long-term market decline since the Great Depression, the factors affecting this decline are different than ever before, even different from the Depression. Understanding how the market will decline and the forces driving it will help you better understand how to time your individual exit from stocks and bonds.

Government Intervention Is Making Any Portfolio Decision—and Timing—Very Difficult

The biggest change since the great stock collapse during the Depression is that government intervention in the stock, bond, and real estate markets now is enormous. Never before have we seen such massive intervention, both indirectly and directly, in those markets. And that intervention is being done worldwide, some-times, in a very coordinated fashion. The United States certainly doesn't have a monopoly on government intervention.

This government intervention makes timing even trickier, since it can be more difficult to predict the exact timing of intervention. It isn't difficult to predict that the government *will* intervene or *how* it will intervene, but it is difficult to predict the exact timing. Although government intervention sometimes responds quickly to market forces, it isn't driven by market forces in the same way a normal market would be. Hence, just following the financial news doesn't tell you *when* or *how much* the government will intervene at any given time.

It's much like a very unusual fire. You can predict that the fire department will try to put it out, but since it has never dealt with such an unusual fire before, it is difficult to predict exactly how it will react at any given time in its attempt to put it out.

Government Intervention, Not Market Forces, Will Have the Biggest Impact on Your Aftershock Portfolio for the Next Few Years

Because government intervention has been so massive, as discussed earlier in this book, it will be the most important factor impacting your Aftershock portfolio. It will be what fundamentally drives investor confidence, consumer confidence, economic recovery, housing, and even retail sales. Although there are other factors driving those aspects of the economy, the size of the government intervention in the economy and the markets is so large that most of those other factors are driven at least in part by the government intervention as well. Remember the chart in Chapter 3 that compared the amount of growth in our economy to the amount of increased government borrowing from 2007 to 2011? Increased government borrowing was far larger than the *entire* growth in the economy during that period. Government intervention is huge. It's of absolutely historic proportions.

And that has just an indirect impact on the stock and bond markets. Through its money-printing operations, it is also having a very direct impact on the stock, bond, and mortgage markets. So let's take a closer look at this all-important intervention—what's driving it and how it is likely to play out over time.

Most Economists and Analysts Don't Even Admit How Much Government Intervention and Market Interference There Has Been

But, first, it's important to point out that many people are loath to believe that the Federal Reserve and the U.S. banking system have taken such extraordinary and enormous measures to artificially prop up the stock, bond, and real estate markets in the past few years, especially considering how devastating the long-term consequences of this intervention are likely to be.

This resistance is understandable, not just because of the self-interest involved, but also because it flies in the face of how the banking system has operated for most of modern history. Going back to the nineteenth century, the powers that be in the U.S. banking system have generally operated with relatively high integrity, both financially and academically.

This integrity, in fact, was crucial in attracting and keeping depositors. In a "survival of the fittest" banking environment, banks that weren't honest and accountable couldn't expect to last very long. And when the Fed was established in 1913, ensuring the integrity of the entire banking system was a top priority. And for the most part, it did an excellent job.

Given this history, why should anyone accept that things changed 30 years ago? That the integrity of the Fed and other players in the financial community would act so irresponsibly, with such dire implications for the United States and the global economy as a whole? We'll go through the motives one by one, but first, let's remember a money manager named Bernie Madoff.

Madoff had been in business since 1960, had a terrific track record, and was beloved by many of his clients and colleagues in the financial community. He was one of the innovators behind the Nasdaq market and served as its chairman for many years. He was an upstanding leader in the investment community, and many considered it an honor to invest with his firm. No one could have believed that, as Madoff himself put it, "it was all one big lie."

If we don't want to end up like Bernie Madoff's clients, it's important that we don't make the same mistake they made. The fact that the players at the Fed and in the banking system may look the part and may have a good track record doesn't mean they can get us out of the mess they've created.

Why So Much Interference and Why Don't They Stop?

So what went wrong that made the government and the banks turn to market interference? And, more important, why can't they just stop doing it and let things return to normal?

We've already discussed how productivity growth slowed down in the 1970s. At this point, possibly facing an endlessly stagnating economy, a little artificial stimulus for the markets didn't seem like such a harmful idea, and it might not have been. But borrowing large amounts of money and not paying it back (both government and private borrowing) is like a drug: The more you use it, the more it takes to achieve the same results. And after a while, it becomes impossible to get off without serious, painful consequences. And the United States has been on this drug for several decades now.

So when we talk about the consequences of ending market interference, we're not talking about minor withdrawal symptoms but consequences that affect our very way of life. First, for many in the financial sector (and elsewhere), it's not just a matter of losing their jobs but their entire careers. Add to that the loss of most of their life savings, as well as potentially compromising their children's futures.

More broadly, letting go of the way things have been done for the past 30 years means, in a way, letting go of the American Dream—that is, the stability and upward mobility of the upper and upper-middle classes. Families that have been wealthy for generations will see much of that disappear. For such people, it's critically important to protect the status quo. They will take risks well beyond what would normally be acceptable, and they will welcome anything that keeps their lives undisturbed and relatively prosperous, altering their thinking to downplay any long-term consequences.

So now that we understand the why, let's look at the how. There are three techniques in particular that can be employed to manipulate the markets: misleading indices and statistics, market manipulation, and market holidays, which are discussed below.

Keeping the Market Interference Working for as Long as Possible: Misleading Indices and Statistics

Look at the financial news on any given day and there's a decent chance you'll read about the market moving according to an economic indicator that has recently been announced. Good news sends the markets up; bad news sends them down. Manipulating key statistics is an important tool to ease worries about the economy, and can provide a reliable short-term fix for struggling markets. Key areas for manipulating statistics include indices on growth, inflation, unemployment, and Federal Reserve open market activity.

Above all, authorities in the banking system want to avoid the appearance of a recession—that is, a decrease in economic production from quarter to quarter. So one of the favored tools used to disguise what might easily be called a recession is the "seasonal adjustment." It's a relatively simple matter to take a raw number, then "correct" for seasonal adjustment and make it look better than it is, or even make a negative number look positive. Later, it might be announced that the seasonal adjustment is being removed retroactively, but by then the objective has been achieved, and market panic has been avoided.

One of the easier indices to manipulate is the Consumer Price Index (CPI), which measures inflation. This figure is based on the prices of a wide variety of goods and services around the country, monitoring how they change over time. So all that has to be done to manipulate this figure is to alter the mix of goods and services in order to understate inflation, as well as using factors like "substitutability" and "quality adjustment" to massage the raw numbers. In fact, in the past couple of decades, the measurement of the CPI has changed so much that today's CPI registers inflation at about 7 percentage points lower than it would be under the old measurement!

Another misleading factor in measuring inflation is shrinking asset prices—such as real estate or commodities—that may be due to falling demand and have little to do with the value of the currency. But because these assets represent large portions of the inflation measurement, their decreasing prices can cover up any real inflation in the measurement.

We've talked a lot in this book about how the Federal Reserve increases the money supply through buying bonds. Of course, everyone knows that increasing the money supply leads to inflation—though they may pretend not to in some cases—so it can be in the Fed's best interest to understate these numbers when they might otherwise cause concern in the markets. We won't go so far as to make accusations here, but it's certainly possible that the Fed has done or will do what many banks and private companies (Enron, anyone?) have done in recent history: off-balance-sheet accounting. By not reporting every bond purchase openly and accurately, the real increase in the money supply can be obscured, maintaining confidence in the dollar.

And then there's a more crude way for governments to mislead the public and stave off worries: just lie. We can be fairly certain, for example, that the government of China does this regularly, with statistics created by government employees under orders from their superiors. These lies can be spotted pretty easily by those with access to reliable information, though. For example, we can monitor the use of electricity in China—if electricity use is going down, it's a sign that the economy is contracting, regardless of what the government says. It is likely there is some manipulation of electricity statistics but likely not as great as gross domestic product (GDP) or inflation numbers. Perhaps an even more reliable way is to look at exports to China from other countries. If exports to China are slowing, that's a bad sign for the country's economy. (In fact, this is exactly what has happened recently, indicating that China's economy may be slowing even faster than the government is willing to admit.)

Granted, in most of the developed world, outright lying like this is somewhat unlikely, and would likely be ineffective. But attempts to mislead like this are not inconceivable, and it's important that we be rigorous in finding reliable, accurate information at all times.

So if this is the case, why don't journalists, analysts, and academics catch it and report on it? Remember what we said earlier about the motivations for continuing on the path of manipulation. The truth is that there is very little reward out there for professionals who call the government and the financial community out on its misleading or outright wrong figures. Aside from often wanting to believe the cheerleaders themselves, those who speak out are often labeled "doom-and-gloom" pessimists and ridiculed throughout the financial community and in public, possibly even blaming such people for falls in the markets. We have some small experience with this, as do some of the people we've profiled in our ABE Awards throughout our books.

When All Else Fails . . .

Misleading numbers and market manipulation can go on for quite some time, but sooner or later they aren't enough to keep things afloat. Eventually, losses become too large to hide with a little mathematical creativity. Even if the government outright lies, indicators elsewhere will eventually be too strong to ignore—just like we're beginning to see now in China.

Direct manipulation can't prop up the markets forever either. Once people lose confidence in the markets, it's very difficult to restore it. Even buying stocks to prop up their price might create a short-term upswing, but the losses that follow make this tactic unsustainable in the long run. The amount of capital that would be needed to sustain prices would be astronomical, which brings us to the next failure: quantitative easing.

Expanding the money supply is always going to be a recipe for inflation. Governments do it because it's a short-term fix, but eventually it catches up with them, and it can snowball very quickly. In the early going, investors may cheer quantitative easing and respond by buying up assets. But once inflation really takes off and panic sets in, there comes a point when quantitative easing becomes counterproductive. The inflationary response to any increase in the money supply becomes almost immediate, as the flight to safety becomes even more frantic. We're left with no stimulus, just a devalued currency.

Inflation is really the key here. Our guess is that people will be relatively content to stick with traditional assets as long as inflation is low and the dollar remains stable. Only when inflation becomes a major concern do we expect most people to get spooked and cause the stock, bond, and real estate bubbles to pop, and pop very rapidly. With U.S. markets collapsing, expect foreign investors to pull out en masse. This is the Aftershock. And it will necessitate more dire measures than what we've discussed so far.

The Last Resort: The Stock Market Holiday (the Ultimate Reason Why You Need to Move Early Rather than Later)

Right now, we have an oscillating market. It goes up a little, then down a little, then up more, then down more. But what we're not seeing is significant sustained gains over time. Instead, we have a market that, left to its own devices (without continuous money printing or the hope of money printing), will trend downward. Eventually, that oscillating market will turn into a consistent down market, with losses for the Dow potentially approaching 500 points a day or more.

At this point, the government will need fast action. The old way of doing things—massaging numbers, manipulating prices, and flooding the market with capital—will not be nearly enough to stop the plunge. As it happens, there are already systems in place to shut down the stock market in this situation—often referred to as "circuit breakers." The idea is to shut down the market for only a few hours and address whatever issue is causing the plunge in prices. In this case, we might see this initial shutdown last up to a day or two before reopening.

Of course, the problem in this case is a bubble economy. That's not something that can be fixed overnight. So when the market does eventually reopen, the plunge continues, and the government will need another shutdown, one that will last more than a day or two.

In 1933, Franklin D. Roosevelt declared a national bank holiday in order to shore up the problems that had been leading to runs on banks throughout the country. During that time, the Emergency Banking Act was passed, and when the banks reopened the following week, depositors came rushing back with renewed confidence. Likewise, when the stock market has to be shut down, the government will be frantically looking for whatever reform it can implement to send investors rushing back to stocks.

But without being able to assuage fundamental investor fears about the economy and the markets, the name of the game here will be finding ways to encourage purchases and discourage sales. Brokerage firms will have no qualms about playing along, and what we might see for some time is that clients who want to sell their stocks have a difficult time getting past their broker's secretary or voicemail, while those who want to buy will get top priority. Whatever happens, the government and the financial industry will surely go to great lengths to prevent anyone from selling stocks when the market reopens.

What we will *not* hear from the Fed, or from most of the financial industry, is that stocks and other assets have been in a bubble all this time, that the implosion was inevitable and irreversible. Instead, we'll hear all kinds of excuses, perhaps blaming the crash on culprits such as high-speed trading, which may have irresponsibly flooded the market with sellers (since they do more than half of the trading on the market and they do it quickly, they will clearly be involved in any crash). Another likely target will be the short sellers, among the favorite scapegoats from 2008.

In addition, we'll almost certainly hear that it's a temporary irrational panic, and that everything will be fine once people come to their senses and bet on the U.S. markets again. Anything to convince the public—and themselves—that it's just a temporary crash and not a bubble economy popping, will be discussed and praised at length.

This might sound unimaginable in 2012, not to mention horrifying, that the stock market could just close down for an extended period. But what we'll probably find, when the market can't stay open without huge losses, is that the public will be surprisingly content with this action—or rather, with *any* action that might stop this downward spiral.

Meanwhile, bonds and real estate will have their own shutdowns. But that won't happen because of government action. With soaring interest rates that the Fed can no longer control, lending will dry up, and the bond market will effectively shut down on its own. When the bond market shuts down, there's no mortgage money available, and thus essentially no real estate market left to speak of.

The one oddity will be the gold market, which will behave in exactly the opposite way. With assets tanking across the board, people will rush to what they consider the intrinsic value of gold and precious metals. This is the last thing the Fed wants, and so measures will have to be taken to discourage gold purchases. A prohibition is possible, but more likely we might see a punitive tax on proceeds from gold sales. The Fed might even prohibit the redemption of paper gold, such as through gold ETFs, into physical gold. The idea is to prevent investors from leaving traditional assets and rushing to gold instead. But again, once investor confidence is lost, it's very difficult to gain it back. And the reason why discouraging gold purchases won't be successful is the same reason shutting down the stock market won't be successful: The United States is not the only country in the world.

The U.S. government can pass all kinds of regulations and restrictions on market activity, but it can't do much to prevent those same transactions in overseas markets. Gold, of course, will be easy to buy and trade elsewhere in the world regardless of what the U.S. government does—in fact, restrictions in the United States would just send the price of gold up even more.

Even if U.S. stock markets are shut down, U.S. stocks will still be readily traded overseas as well. And this is why it will be clear to anyone who's paying attention that U.S. stock prices are plummeting even while the market in the United States is on a holiday. Remember what we said about the limitations of lying.

The Aftermath: So Then What?

We can't say exactly how long the stock market will be closed, but it could be months, not days. It can't last forever because at some point many of the people who got caught holding on to their stocks when the market closed will need to sell their stocks. They may need to cover unexpected expenses, a lack of cash flow, or any of the other problems that come up that force people to sell their assets no matter how low the price may already be.

When the market does finally reopen, it will look dramatically different than it does today. It's not just a matter of losing all the bubble value that's been building up for 30 years. Investor confidence will have been devastated.

Will the financial industry—or what's left of it, anyway—admit at this point what the problem really was? We're not optimistic. The problem will continue to be things like irrational fear, political mistakes, and other nefarious forces. It's the earlier prices that were the correct ones, if only everyone would realize it. Expect that drumbeat to continue for a long time.

But, sooner or later, people will understand what happened: We had a bubble economy and it's not coming back. And the road to recovery will be a long and difficult one. It won't be fueled by low interest rates and overextended debt, but by slow and steady growth driven by real productivity gains—the same way we built the U.S. economy into the most powerful in the world.

The Moral

In case we haven't made this clear yet, let's say it one more time: The key is to *get out early*. You may often hear about opportunity costs and kick yourself when a stock rises after you've sold it. But it should be clear by now that any potential short-term gains are nothing compared to the cost of staying in the markets too long. The fall is likely to be sudden and unpredictable, and it's easy to get trapped. Those who wait until things have already started to collapse will find themselves surrounded by a massive sell-off, and everyone cannot fit through the exit door at the same time.

For those who do get out early, though, life can be prosperous for years to come—much more so even than before the Aftershock. Think of all the people who put their assets into gold during the 2008 crisis when it was below $800/oz. They're pretty ecstatic right now, and gold will only go up faster when times get truly tough for other investments.

You're Not Alone—People Are Already Moving Out in Big Numbers

If you think you are alone in being nervous about the stock market, you are not. Enormous numbers of individual investors are leaving the market. Remember the chart on the massive continuous outflows from stock mutual funds over the past few years despite the big rebound in the market? Many people say this is stupid money leaving the market. As we said earlier, this is not stupid money leaving the market, as stock cheerleaders would have you believe. It is people who aren't investing OPM (other people's money) so they really need to protect their capital and be careful—not just keep their high-paying money management jobs by investing in a stock market that is not performing and has increasing risks of a long-term downturn.

The Fact that the Alternatives Aren't Very Good Doesn't Mean You Should Do Nothing

A lot of investors are concerned about the economy and agree with much of what we say. However, since the alternatives like gold are uncomfortable, and other alternatives like TIPS or cash don't earn much money, they decide it is best to do nothing and just stay in the market. Unfortunately, this is a big mistake long term. As we just explained, you can get caught in a market downdraft and not be able to get out quickly. Also, the fact that there are no good alternatives doesn't mean you should stay in and lose a lot of your money. There's a popular myth that there is a bull market somewhere all the time. This simply isn't true and hasn't ever been true.

When Charlie Merrill (co-founder of Merrill Lynch) told his colleagues in 1928 that it was time to get out of the market it wasn't because he had spotted a bull market elsewhere. He didn't tell his colleagues to move out of stocks and put the money in another investment. He told them to get out—period. Yes, there weren't many good alternatives other than cash. Even gold was a bad alternative. And, yes, he was early. Many who took his advice probably kicked themselves for missing out on the big gains in stocks that their friends were getting after they sold too early. But, he was still right. Long term, his colleagues that simply got out of the market were much better off than those who stayed in. Having a good alternative to stocks was quickly shown to be irrelevant. The key was to get out before you lost your money.

The Cartoon that Sums It All Up

We end this book with our best and most important cartoon. Everybody loves a bubble and *no one* wants to lose it. That's perfectly reasonable. But when the bubbles burst, it's time to move on and recognize that a new era of investing has begun. Unfortunately, what many people want is to think that the bubble will somehow come back. This is fantasy (a great fantasy, but a fantasy nonetheless). Even worse, it makes you blind to other bubbles. So we use the cartoon below as a fun way to tell an important message.

Leave this book with a laugh. Humor has been and always will be a valuable commodity. You'll need even more of that in the future and, unlike other commodities, it won't fall in value, even with a greater supply. There will always be strong demand for good humor.

"I want my bubble back."

Staying Afloat in a Sinking Economy

It's one thing to read about the changing macro economy; it's another to actually *do* something about it. Most people will take no new actions until it's too late. For those who want to prepare for, not just react to the coming Aftershock, we offer the following services:

You are welcome to visit our website www.aftershockpublishing. com for more information as we approach the Aftershock. While you are there, you may sign up for a two-month free trial of our popular Aftershock Investor's Resource Package (IRP), which includes our monthly newsletter, live conference calls, and more. Or you may reach us at **703-787-0139** or info@aftershockpublishing.com.

We also offer **Private Consulting** for individuals, businesses, and groups. Please contact coauthor Cindy Spitzer at **443-980-7367** for more information.

Through our investment management firm, **Absolute Investment Management**, we provide hands-on, Aftershock-focused asset management services on an individually managed account basis. For details, please call **703-774-3520** or e-mail absolute@aftershockpublishing.com.

Epilogue

If, after reading this book or any of our books, you think America has made mistakes, you're right. If you think America has somehow lost its ability to change and improve itself, you're wrong. In fact, the United States is still, and will likely be for decades to come, the most resilient, flexible, and dynamic economy in the world. That's due in part to one of the world's most flexible, dynamic, and strongest political systems.

While the short term may be filled with many seemingly insoluble problems, don't be fooled. The long term is very bright indeed. More than any other country, the United States has been able to forge a path toward greater productivity and higher standards of living. Many countries have benefitted from the groundbreaking work of the United States. China didn't grow so fast because it was able to innovate on its own. It grew so fast because it adopted the methods of free markets and efficient industrial production, many of which were pioneered or perfected by the United States.

Other countries around the world have grown and benefitted as well by simply watching the United States and learning how it's done. Not only can they learn directly from our universities, but they can visit our country, see our government, form joint ventures with our corporations, and receive our investment and the business acumen that often comes with it—everything you need to move any developing economy forward.

No, we're not the only country who has pioneered better methods for greater productivity. But no nation has pioneered in more ways than the United States. From our revolution for democracy, which has inspired and changed the world, to our economic system that has led to the most rapid increase in productivity in human history, we have led the world in many of its most important and beneficial changes.

That we have been distracted by our economic bubbles and away from our relentless focus on productivity in the pursuit of easy money is understandable. It's a regrettable and costly mistake. But it's a mistake we will learn from.

By focusing again on improving productivity, the economy will rebound to a much, much higher standard of living than today. The United States has shown time and again it can lead itself, and the world, forward in improving both productivity and quality of life. The two are by no means mutually exclusive. In fact, they are mutually dependent.

But, like all our changes in the past, the ones in the future will be no different. They will not be bestowed on us. We will have to make them. They will be difficult and controversial. That's nothing new for the United States. We have done it before, and we will do it again.

What's new for the United States is that in this bubble economy, we have lost that willingness to change and to be controversial. To throw out a king and establish a democracy in 1776 was about as controversial as any country had ever been. Now, we have become more like other countries. It's not that all other countries have done poorly, but they surely haven't done as well as the United States. Our ability to change quickly, effectively, and beneficially has been far beyond what any other country has shown in the past two centuries.

That ability is still there but will need to be rekindled. After this bubble economy falls, the rekindled spirit of America will rise again.

Appendix: Additional Background on Stocks and Bonds

In Chapter 4 (on stocks) and Chapter 5 (on bonds), we purposely left out some of the more technical details in order to not interrupt the flow of the chapters. Not everyone wants so much information, and we wanted to focus primarily on the evolving macroeconomic story that will lead us to the coming Aftershock. After all, it is pretty easy these days to look up definitions online or in conventional investment books, but harder to find information about what is really going on, from our non–conventional point of view. We saw no point in giving you yet one more mainstream investment guide.

So here are some of those more technical details we left out of the chapters. This is hardly an exhaustive guide, but it will give you a bit more background on stocks and bonds if you have an interest. For more information than the brief explanations here, we recommend you visit some educational web sites, such as www.investopedia.com and others.

Stocks

Basically, when you buy a stock, you are making a bet that the future earnings of a company will grow. The company initially sells stock certificates in order to raise capital, and the stockholders then own a part of the company. After the initial offering, company stocks can then be sold and bought on the stock market in a giant trading game, where those who want to bet on more future growth are buyers and those who are done with their bet (at least for the moment) are sellers. Like any investment, traders naturally want to sell for more than whatever they paid to buy—that is the only way to make a profit on your stock investment. Once you sell and realize a profit on your investment, you generally have to pay taxes on that capital gain.

Of course, there is much more to the story. Here are the stock topics we will discuss in this appendix:

- Understanding the public offering
- Knowing the difference between common stock and preferred stock
- Options for buying stocks
- Making sense of stock and company data
- Using a registered investment adviser
- Securities Investor Protection Corporation (SIPC) protection
- Knowing your options for "short" selling, including put options and long-term equity anticipation securities (LEAPS)

Understanding the Public Offering

The goal of any well-run company is to keep growing. In order to do this, a business requires capital. In the early stages, a business might rely on earnings, private equity, bank loans, or bonds. But, eventually, many businesses turn to the public offering, allowing common investors to buy shares in the business in exchange for the opportunity to profit from the company's growth. These investors may also get a voice in determining the company's direction, but with only a percentage of the company's value up for grabs, and shares going in various portions to numerous investors, the voice is a small one.

To begin an initial public offering, or IPO, a company generally goes through an investment bank, which assesses the value of the company and underwrites the sale. That is, the investment bank purchases the portion of the company that's being sold—assuming all risk for the company's value—then divides up the shares and sells them to the general public, the "primary market." The bank then collects a small fee while passing on the proceeds to the company. By "small fee" we mean percentage-wise. If you were an investment bank selling $16 billion worth of Facebook shares, for example, a 7 percent fee would amount to more than $1 billion. Not a bad payday.

Once the initial shares have been purchased, they are tradable on the open market, or "secondary market." All the major stock markets you've heard of—the New York Stock Exchange, the

Nasdaq, the London Stock Exchange, for example—are secondary markets.

Knowing the Difference between Common and Preferred Stock

Common stock is generally what we mean when we discuss the stock market. A common stock represents an ownership share in a company, which, in addition to investing the shareholder in the future of that company, often grants the shareholder certain voting rights, such as in electing the company's board of directors.

Note that we said that common stock invests the shareholder in the future of that company. That's important because, generally speaking, the company doesn't owe common stockholders anything other than due diligence in managing the company's affairs. If the company grows and the value goes up, the shareholders are happy. If it falters and the price goes down, they may be unhappy and they may complain, but there isn't much they can do about it, other than sell their shares at a cheaper price and take their money elsewhere. This is why common stock is among the most volatile investments: plenty of room for growth, but plenty of room for losses, too.

Common stocks are traded on stock exchanges all over the world. The oldest exchange in the United States is the Philadelphia Stock Exchange, established in 1790. The largest exchange in the country, and in the world, is the New York Stock Exchange (NYSE), located on Wall Street, along with the American Stock Exchange, or the "Amex." Other major exchanges in the United States are located in Boston, Chicago, Cincinnati, and San Francisco. You've probably also heard of the Nasdaq, the world's first electronic stock exchange. A primary exchange for high-tech business, the Nasdaq has among the highest trading volume of any market in the world.

Many common stocks pay dividends on a quarterly basis, dividing up their profits among shareholders. Some pay more than others. High-dividend-paying stocks can be a strong incentive for investors, but keep in mind that dividends are optional, and if a company starts to struggle, common stock dividends are often the first thing to go.

Preferred stock, in addition to representing a share in the company, also represents a debt obligation from the company to the shareholder. Before any dividends are paid to holders of common stock, the company must pay a fixed dividend to preferred shareholders. And in the event of liquidation and any monetary distributions that might come from it, preferred shareholders are in line ahead of common shareholders, who usually won't receive any compensation at all (although preferred shareholders are still behind bondholders).

Of course, the preferred shareholders don't always get their dividends either. This is what makes preferred stock a useful tool for companies that need to raise capital. Because preferred stock is a hybrid investment—not quite a stock, not quite a bond—companies have some flexibility in choosing to defer dividend payments when capital is running low. Preferred stocks are rated just like bonds, but they naturally come with lower ratings to begin with, and a company's credit won't be affected too significantly by holding off on dividend payments to preferred stockholders. (Doing the same thing to bondholders would be a default and carries major consequences.)

So preferred stockholders don't have all the rights that bondholders have, and they also don't have all the rights that common stockholders have. Most notably, preferred shareholders have no voting rights in the company, except in certain special circumstances. Also, preferred shares usually come with a call feature, which allows the company to repurchase the shares at its discretion.

Options for Buying Stocks

If you want to buy a stock, you don't walk down to Wall Street, hop on the trading floor and make your bid. You have to have a broker execute the trade for you. Traditionally, a broker offered an array of services for clients, getting to know their portfolios and providing research and investment advice, and charging heavy commission fees in return.

These full-service brokers are still in abundance, but a popular alternative that has developed in recent years is the *discount broker*. These brokers are for investors who don't need or want the handholding of a full-service broker, and instead just need a way to execute trades based on their own research and analysis. Discount brokers often charge a very low, flat fee for trades, and often have very low minimum account balances, so they are a popular way to get involved in stock trading for people who aren't ready for (or don't want) a traditional broker. But they also pin all responsibility on the investor.

Another advantage of discount brokers is that, unlike many full-service brokerage firms, discount brokers don't risk their own money in the market. This is important because accounts at a discount brokerage may be in less jeopardy in the event of a major market downturn. Plus, discount brokers sidestep the temptation to unload their own bad positions on their clients, a temptation that has gotten many full-service brokerage firms in trouble.

Whether to go with a full-service or discount broker is a personal decision, but if you're going to go with a full-service broker, first, be sure they really know what they're doing and have your best interests at heart. Furthermore, even though someone else is doing much of the work for you, you still have a responsibility to be an informed investor and to not let yourself be pressured into positions you know aren't good for you. Before deciding on a full-service broker, it is important to check with the Central Registration Depository (CRD), which will provide you with information about an individual broker's history, including employment history and any complaints filed by former clients, as well as any relevant information about brokerage firms.

Making Sense of Stock and Company Data

If you decide to go with a discount broker and make your own trades (or even if you have a traditional broker and want to be better informed), you have a wealth of real-time information available to you thanks to the Internet. Looking at the data for a particular stock may be daunting, but the numbers aren't really so complicated. You'll see things such as the bid price (the last price a buyer was willing to pay for it) and the ask price (the last price a seller was willing to sell it for). You'll probably also see the range of prices the stock has sold for over the last year, the average daily trading volume, and the price-to-earnings, or P/E, ratio. Most financial web sites have a key for you to look up the more difficult-to-understand numbers and how they've been calculated.

Using a Registered Investment Adviser

For those looking for a little more help with their investments, a registered investment adviser, or RIA, may be the answer. RIAs are basically money managers and will make decisions about your investments based on your goals and their own investment philosophy. RIAs often require large minimum investments, typically at least $100,000 and possibly going as high as several million dollars.

An RIA will manage your investments through your brokerage account, with authorization to buy and sell assets on your behalf. This sounds like a set-it-and-forget-it strategy, and indeed RIAs can make trades without notifying the client every time, but this doesn't mean investors should forgo all responsibility for their investments. It's important to find an RIA who not only understands your financial goals but also shares your macroeconomic view of the near and longer-term future. And it is also important to stay up on what's happening with your money and continually confirming that it's in good hands.

RIAs collect their fees based on the total amount of funds under management, generally never more than 3 percent (usually around 1.5 percent). This gives an RIA a strong incentive to make money for clients because, unlike with a broker who collects fees based on commissions, the success of an RIA's investments directly impact the RIA's fees. If your assets shrink, so does the RIA's takeaway.

Be careful that your RIA does not overly crowd your portfolio with mutual funds. Aside from the problems with mutual funds, which we'll get to later, remember that a mutual fund is a managed fund, which is what you are already paying your RIA for. If your RIA heavily uses mutual funds, you are essentially being charged twice for management, paying double the fees.

SIPC Protection

In order to protect investors when their brokerage firms go bankrupt, Congress set up the Securities Investor Protection Corporation, or SIPC, in 1970. The SIPC is a nonprofit organization that collects insurance fees from member brokerage firms in return for insuring customer accounts up to $500,000 each. Any brokerage firm that is part of the National Association of Securities Dealers (NASD) is a member of the SIPC.

This provides some peace of mind for investors, and many brokers carry their own insurance on accounts in addition to the SIPC insurance. But the problem is that these insurance policies, like everything else, are designed with the rare occurrence in mind. They aren't designed for a system-wide failure in the markets. This is a big reason why we prefer brokers that don't risk their own money in the markets—they are more likely to survive the future Aftershock.

Understanding Short Selling, Put Options, and LEAPS

Short selling is what some investors do when they think the price will go down. Short selling is effectively three transactions rolled into one. The first transaction is the sale of a stock at the current market price, or close to it. The second transaction is borrowing that stock—generally from the broker executing the trade—in order to give it to the buyer. Finally, the third transaction is buying the stock later when the loan period is over to repay the broker and hopefully make a profit (assuming the buying price is lower than the earlier selling price).

During the period between selling the borrowed stock and buying the stock to repay the loan, the investor has a "short" position in the stock or commodity. (In contrast, if the investor owned shares of the asset, that would be considered a "long" position.) If the asset price goes down during that period, the investor makes money by buying it for less than he or she sold it for. On the flip side, if the asset price unexpectedly goes up, the losses are potentially unlimited, since the short seller is obligated to buy the stock to pay back the original loan (plus any fees that might be associated with the loan).

Put options are an alternative to short selling. An investor can purchase a put option on a security, which gives him or her the option to sell that security at a specified price (the *strike price*) to the seller of the option during a specified time period. If the price of the stock goes down during that time, the buyer of the put option can simply buy the stock and sell it to the other party at the agreed-upon price, pocketing the difference. If the price doesn't go down and the buyer doesn't exercise the option, the loss is limited to the price of the put option. A put option is the opposite of a call option, which gives the buyer the right to buy a security at a specified price.

Put options (and call options, for buying instead of selling) are generally limited to terms of a year at most.

LEAPS are like put options for a longer period of time. LEAPS, which is short for long-term equity anticipation securities, can have terms extending more than two years. One quirk is that equity LEAPS always expire in January, so the term is determined by the expiration year of the option. The further out the expiration date is, the more expensive the option will be.

Bonds

A bond is essentially a loan made to the bond issuer in exchange for future repayment of the principal of the loan plus interest. Various factors affect the interest rate offered on the loan, which were discussed in Chapter 5. Once a bond is issued, it may be sold and bought on the bond market, which adds layers of complexity for a number of reasons. Primary among these is the fact that current interest rates change, making previously issued bonds either more valuable or less valuable, depending on the details of the bond. In addition, other things change as well. For example, the creditworthiness of the bond issuers may change over time, which impacts the value of the bond on the bond market. Also, changes in the inflation rate matter, too, because if inflation goes up, it subtracts from the value of the bond.

Chapter 5 provides a basic explanation of bonds and the bond market. For this discussion, we will now focus on:

- The call
- U.S. Treasurys
- Zero-coupon bonds and Separate Trading of Registered Interest and Principal Securities (STRIPS)
- Treasury inflation-protected securities (TIPS)
- Savings bonds
- Mortgage-backed securities
- Municipal bonds
- Corporate bonds
- Certificates of deposit
- Money market funds
- Bond sensitivity to changes in interest rates and inflation

The Call

Even if an investor does not sell a bond for a gain when prevailing interest rates go down, having a relatively high interest rate locked in is a pretty nice perk. This perk is eliminated if the bond has a *call* feature. Some indentures give the bond issuer the option of paying off the principal before the maturity date, thus ending the debt obligation and any future interest payments to the bondholder. In many cases, this option may be triggered a certain length of time into the bond's life span.

Why would a bond issuer want to do this? Just like if you wanted to pay off a mortgage early and refinance at a lower rate, the bond issuer would be at a great advantage by refinancing if interest rates go down. It's easy to see that this feature benefits the bond issuer, and only the bond issuer. If interest rates go down, the issuer has every incentive to execute the call feature, refinance, and leave you to find another suitable investment. If interest rates go up, however, when you would *want* the call feature to be executed, the issuer has no motivation to refinance. The bond issuer can keep paying you at a lower interest rate until the maturity date. Many indentures may specify a premium to be paid in the event of a call, but it is sure to be paltry compared to the interest that would be earned over the remaining life span of the bond.

U.S. Treasurys

As the name suggests, U.S. Treasurys are bonds issued by the Treasury Department of the United States. When people talk about public debt in the United States, they are talking about outstanding U.S. Treasurys. Treasury securities are owned in huge amounts by big government agencies and corporations, such as the governments of China and Japan, as well as our own Federal Reserve, but these securities can be purchased by individual or institutional investors.

Backed by the full faith and credit of the U.S. government, U.S. Treasurys have traditionally enjoyed the highest investment grade awardable. As a result, they tend to offer among the lowest yields of any bonds, but this is acceptable to many investors, who view our Treasurys as risk free. This view took a small hit in the summer of 2011 when Standard & Poor's downgraded the Treasurys credit rating to AA+, after 70 years at AAA, but U.S. Treasurys are still considered a rock-solid investment, especially given the current turmoil and potential risks in Europe.

Another reason why Treasury securities can afford to offer low yields is that the interest paid on them is not subject to state and local taxes. This makes Treasurys especially attractive to investors in states with high income tax rates, but less so to those in states like Texas or Washington with no individual income tax. Treasury interest is, however, subject to federal income tax.

Standard-issue Treasurys are divided into three categories based on their lengths of maturity. *Treasury bills*, or *T-bills*, usually range from 90 days to 12 months, *Treasury notes* from 2 to 10 years, and *Treasury bonds* up to 30 years. Keeping this terminology straight can be difficult, and you might hear some people use the terms interchangeably if they don't know the difference. If you have trouble remembering which is which, the blanket term *Treasurys* works just fine (as long as you know when the maturity date is, of course).

Most Treasury securities make payments just like any other bond. T-bills, however, don't make interest payments due to their short maturity. Instead, you buy the bill at a discount, and receive the full face value at the maturity date. The difference between the price you pay and the amount you receive is the interest.

Zero-Coupon Bonds and STRIPS

A zero-coupon bond is just what it sounds like: a bond with no coupons. Interest is accrued and reinvested in the bond to be paid back in one sum at maturity. In many cases, this means taxes must be paid on the interest before the investor receives it. This drawback can be eliminated by purchasing zero-coupon bonds through an individual retirement account (IRA).

STRIPS are another kind of zero-coupon bond. Back when bonds were issued on paper, they would literally have their coupons "stripped" by brokers before sale. An example of this type of bond is U.S. Treasury STRIPS, which are not sold by the Treasury itself but through private brokers. The bond is separated from its coupon payments and sold by itself at a discount. As a result, taxes on reinvested interest are not an issue with these bonds. The difference between the amount paid on the market and received at maturity represents a capital gain.

The market value of zero-coupon bonds tends to be subject to more volatility than that of regular bonds. Be careful about purchasing zero-coupon bonds if you're not planning on holding them until maturity.

TIPS

TIPS are designed to keep the bondholder's investment current based on inflation. TIPS come with fixed-interest payments just like other Treasurys, but the principal amount is adjusted twice a year, according to the current Consumer Price Index (CPI). For example, if you invested $10,000 in TIPS at a rate of 0.5 percent, you would continue to receive that 0.5 percent annual interest until maturity, but you might be earning 0.5 percent interest on $10,500 or $11,000 at some point, depending on current inflation.

The fixed rate of TIPS tends to be relatively low, and in fact we have even seen it effectively drop below zero recently. When fear of inflation is up, many investors are willing to take a small hit now in order to protect themselves from inflation later. (This doesn't mean that bondholders will get a bill when the coupon payments are due. What happened is that bidders agreed to pay a small premium for these bonds at auction, and the premium effectively canceled out the even smaller coupon payments at the current rate and then some.) If inflation rises significantly, the par value of these bonds goes up and a bondholder can come out ahead. We will discuss inflation and its effect on bonds a little later.

Savings Bonds

Unlike other Treasury securities, U.S. savings bonds are not exchanged on the open market. They are tied to the bondholder's Social Security number (or tax identification number), which means no one but the bondholder can redeem them. Savings bonds can be purchased in many different denominations ($25 and up), which, along with the fact that they can be owned by minors, has made them a favorite investment tool for parents and grandparents to give to children, often to save for education.

Savings bonds are zero-coupon bonds, so both principal and interest are paid in one sum when the bond is redeemed. Interest is accrued regularly, and the current value of any given savings bond can be calculated at www.treasurydirect.gov, though there is a small penalty if you redeem before five years have passed since issue. Current savings bonds offered are the Series EE (formerly Series E) and Series I bonds.

Series EE bonds have a maturity of 20 years, but continue to earn interest for another 10 years after maturity. Formerly, the interest rate on Series EE bonds was adjusted based on current rates, but bonds issued after April 2005 earn a fixed rate. Patriot bonds are a paper version of the Series EE bond. As of January 2012, these bonds (along with all paper Treasurys) are no longer available.

Series I bonds are savings bonds that are linked to inflation, much like TIPS. Series I bonds come with two different interest rates: a fixed rate that doesn't change over the course of the bond's term, and a variable rate that is adjusted twice a year based on the CPI. The adjustable rate might be negative during times of deflation, but the combined rate of the bond cannot fall below zero percent.

Mortgage-Backed Securities

Mortgage-backed securities include those issued by government-sponsored agencies Ginnie Mae (Government National Mortgage Association), Fannie Mae (Federal National Mortgage Association), and Freddie Mac (Federal Home Loan Mortgage Corporation), as well as some securities issued by private corporations. Ginnie Maes are unique among the group in being backed by the full faith and credit of the federal government, just like Treasury securities.

Mortgage-backed securities are issued using a pool of home mortgages as collateral. Because most mortgages are paid monthly, most of these securities pay interest monthly as well. Because mortgage loan principal is prepaid in various ways and at various times (such as extra payments or paying it off all at once), the time to maturity varies widely.

Municipal Bonds

Municipal bonds, or *munis*, are issued by state and local governments to finance new projects or to improve infrastructure. Munis have the advantage that interest paid is exempt from federal taxes, and in some cases from income taxes in the state in which the bonds are issued.

There are two principal types of municipal bonds. *General obligation* bonds are backed by the full faith and credit of the issuing government, based on its ability to raise revenue through taxes.

Revenue bonds are backed by revenue to be raised from the specific project the bonds are funding—for example, if the bonds are being used to finance the building of a toll road or an airport.

The tax advantage is generally the key attraction for these bonds. The higher taxes you normally pay, the more attractive munis become. The way to assess the value of a tax-exempt interest rate is to calculate its *taxable-equivalent yield.* The formula is to take the yield of the tax-exempt bond and divide by 1 minus your tax bracket percentage. For a bond exempt from state taxes, you would combine federal and state tax percentages in the calculation.

Corporate Bonds

Private corporations also issue bonds in order to finance and/or expand their business operations. Many companies that issue corporate bonds also have shares traded in public stock markets. But owning a corporate bond is very different than owning a share of a company.

When you buy stock in a company, you are buying ownership in the company, and the value of the share will rise or fall in accordance with the company's market value. You might receive dividends from company earnings, but this is not at all guaranteed (especially if the company has no earnings), and dividend payments can be very low compared to the stock price. But when you purchase a corporate bond, you are making a loan to the company, which has an obligation to return your principal and make interest payments. If the company's fortunes rise, you will still get only the amount that was agreed to in advance. You might lose your investment if the company goes bankrupt, but as a creditor you will be ahead of shareholders (even preferred shareholders) in line to receive money in a bankruptcy settlement. So while purchasing bonds has a speculative element to it, it is not nearly as speculative as purchasing stock.

Most corporate bonds are *unsecured,* meaning the debt is not tied to any collateral, and the bondholder is relying on the general credit and continued solvency of business. Secured bonds may be backed by claims on specific assets of the company, possibly including new equipment that the bonds were used to purchase. Other bonds may be backed with stocks and other securities, or can even be guaranteed by a company other than the bond issuer. Owners of secured bonds will take priority over owners of unsecured bonds in the event of bankruptcy.

Corporate bonds are available on the New York Stock Exchange or over the counter (directly from the issuing companies). The advantage of corporate bonds is that the coupons tend to be higher than government-issued bonds. But, of course, these higher yields come with higher credit risk. Some investors will take the higher risks along with the higher payments, even going after junk bonds issued by companies with poor credit ratings. But if capital preservation is your goal, corporate bonds are generally not your best bet unless you stick with rock-solid companies with great track records, and only if you get out well before the Aftershock hits.

Certificates of Deposit

Certificates of deposit (CDs) behave similarly to zero-coupon bonds, in that you deposit money for a certain amount of time, and receive principal and interest back at maturity. The differences are that CDs are offered specifically by financial institutions to their customers and that they are usually insured by the federal government. CDs fall under the category of *time deposits*, meaning you lock up your money for the specified period, and they cannot be sold on the open market or called by the issuing bank before maturity.

CDs tend to offer lower rates than comparable bonds, but interest rates can vary depending on a number of factors, including the size of the principal, the length to maturity, and the size and reputation of the financial institution, among other factors. On the plus side, interest is usually compounded monthly, which can be an advantage for deposits of longer time periods—as long as interest rates don't rise. Unfortunately, both inflation and interest rates will rise, and CDs will not fare so well. Because they are guaranteed by the government, CDs have a reputation for being virtually risk free. That is not a reputation that will survive the coming Aftershock.

Money Market Funds

If you've ever had an account at a brokerage firm, you have probably had cash in a money market fund. Money market funds invest in a highly diversified pool of securities, with maturities usually no more than two or three months. These include government bonds, CDs, and commercial paper (short-term, unsecured debt obligations issued by corporations with rock-solid credit). The aim for a money market fund is to keep a constant share price of $1, with yields paid as dividends that can be reinvested.

The short terms of the investments and the solid credit ratings of the issuers make money markets very low risk, relatively speaking. If investments do fail and the share price of the fund falls below $1, it is referred to as *breaking the buck*, something that is never supposed to happen. It was an especially rare event before September 2008, when Lehman Brothers' bankruptcy and the ensuing panic led to the Treasury Department's setting up an insurance program for many money market funds.

Bonds Vary in Their Sensitivity to Rising Interest Rates

Changes in interest rates impact some bonds more than others. Long-term bonds are much more reactive to interest changes than are short-term bonds. Long-term bonds can punish or reward the bondholder long after interest rates have changed. So it does not take much of an increase in interest rates to push the value of long-term bonds down significantly.

Changes in interest rates also have a greater impact on the value of bonds issued by less reputable companies than on high-grade bonds issued by solid corporations and agencies because of the combined concerns about both rising interest rate risk and credit risk. Bonds rated from AAA to BBB are considered investment grade. Anything below BBB– or Baa is considered to be speculative. Traditionally, most experts would advise sticking only with bonds among the A to AAA categories because they are considered the safest bets to get your money back, even if they don't come with the highest interest rates. However, in this economic environment, it's sometimes necessary to look past a good rating. Even very good ratings can drop very quickly and unexpectedly, as we'll see later on.

To limit the risk of rising interest rates, many investors turn to inflation-protected or floating-rate bonds, such as TIPS. These are less sensitive to interest rate changes than fixed-interest-rate bonds because they adjust with prevailing rates. Therefore, rising interest rates are not expected to lower the value of inflation-protected or floating-rate bonds as much as they will lower the value of fixed-rate bonds. But do not be fooled into thinking that these floating-rate bonds will be risk free. As interest rates go up, credit risk will also go up significantly. Remember: It doesn't matter how good your interest rate is if your bond issuer is unable to pay.

Under normal economic circumstances, bankruptcies are relatively rare, especially among larger corporations and banks, not to mention governments. And even when bankruptcies happen, even debtors holding unsecured bonds still usually end up getting back at least a portion of their principal from the settlement. So it is understandable that bonds, especially those issued by governments and blue-chip companies, have traditionally been viewed as safe from credit risk. But there is one circumstance that is always bad for bonds: *inflation*.

Inflation, Interest Rates, and the Aftershock

The conventional wisdom is somewhat divided when it comes to the impact of inflation on stocks. (Some say stock prices will rise with inflation, which is true to some extent, but it doesn't account for the rising interest rates that can kill earnings and hurt stocks in the long term.) But pretty much everyone knows that inflation is poison to bonds. If money is losing value quickly, then tying it up for a considerable length of time at a fixed interest rate is a losing proposition. With inflation at 2 percent, a bond with a 3 percent coupon has a *real* interest rate of only 1 percent. But if inflation rises to 5 percent, suddenly your real rate of return is minus 2 percent. You may have more dollars in the end, but you are losing buying power; you are losing wealth. And the picture looks even worse if you spent your coupon payments along the way. The principal you get back when the bond matures will not be worth nearly as much as it was when you invested it. Now imagine inflation goes to 10 percent annually, or 20 percent, or higher, and you see how destructive inflation can be.

But it is even worse than that. Rising inflation, as we have said repeatedly in earlier chapters, eventually causes interest rates to rise. Rising interest rates only hurts the value of existing bonds even more. Now you have the double whammy of both falling value of your money due to inflation and falling value of your bonds due to rising interest rates.

And, unfortunately, the bad news doesn't stop there. Not only is inflation making your money worth less and not only are rising interest rates making your bonds worth less, you also now have to face another rising menace: *increasing credit risk.* You see, the entities that issued your bonds may very well go out of business under these difficult conditions, or at least be unable to repay you. We saw in the last chapter what rising inflation and higher interest rates can do to company earnings. Unable to refinance their debt without paying high interest rates, and caught in a spiral of laying off workers to stay afloat, how will companies generate the new revenues to pay off their existing debt obligations? It is going to become harder and harder to do so.

And the problem will not stop with just corporate bonds from companies that can no longer pay their debts. It will also extend to governments that can no longer pay their debts, whether it is state munis or U.S. Treasurys. Even CDs and money markets will be in trouble.

As we've already said, there are factors delaying the onset of inflation. But once it gets going, it can snowball very quickly. When inflation passes 5 percent, as measured by the CPI, and then approaches 10 percent, it will become impossible to ignore. Interest rates will rise regardless of what the Fed wants, as lenders become cautious to tie up their cash and get it back at a lower value.

We already know that inflation eats away at a bond's value, and the rising interest rates that follow hurt bonds in the secondary market. For example, with 10-year Treasury rates hovering around 2.2 percent as of March 2012, imagine how much the value of these bonds would fall if inflation hit double digits less than halfway into their lives. But this is only the beginning of the problem. In a bubble economy overextended with debt and artificially propped-up markets, inflation is the first big trigger to send it all toppling down.

The first casualty will be the housing market. New home purchases will be out of reach for most at higher interest rates. And homeowners who are already in precarious debt situations will not be able to make payments on adjustable-rate mortgages. When real estate prices fall accordingly, even homeowners who were once in relatively stable positions will find themselves underwater, and new debt defaults will spike upward.

Banks will be forced to write off huge amounts of loans. Mortgage-backed securities will fail. Insurance and derivatives meant to protect against failure will turn out to have little value when everyone is overextended. Failures lead to government bailouts. Bailouts mean more money printing. More money printing means more inflation. And the vicious cycle continues.

Clearly, inflation cannot go up significantly without also raising interest rates. Who in the world will lend anyone any money if they cannot at the very least be compensated for what they will lose to inflation? That means if inflation is 10 percent, interest rates will have to be at least 11 percent for lenders to make even 1 percent on their money. Interest rates will have to exceed inflation.

When interest climbs, in addition to harming businesses, real estate, stocks, and corporate bond values, we will have one other devastating problem: State governments and the federal government will have to make interest payments on their debt with newly borrowed money at the higher and higher interest rate, adding exponentially more and more to the total public debt as time goes on. Eventually, they will not be able to borrow more at any interest rate level because investors will have no confidence in their ability to repay. At that point, the public debt bubble will pop and the borrowing will end. Without newly borrowed money and without the ability to print more money (due to high inflation caused by earlier money printing), state and U.S. governments will not be able to pay on their debt and will be in default—just like overextended homeowners, businesses, consumers, and investors.

Index